DEATH IN THE DESERT

Geronimo, the great leader of the hostile Apaches in the Eighties. This photograph was taken when he was an old man, after his Florida captivity.

DEATH IN THE
DESERT

The Fifty Years' War
for the Great Southwest

BY

PAUL I. WELLMAN

University of Nebraska Press
Lincoln and London

First Bison Book printing: 1987
Most recent printing indicated by the first digit below:
    2   3   4   5   6   7   8   9   10

Library of Congress Cataloging in Publication Data
Wellman, Paul Iselin, 1898–1966.
  Death in the desert.

  Reprint. Originally published: New York: Macmillan,
1935.
  Bibliography: p.
  Includes index.
  1. Apache Indians—Wars. 2. Indians of North America
—Southwest, New—Wars. 3. Modoc Indians—Wars, 1873.
4. Indians of North America—California—Wars. I. Title.
E99.A6W38 1987   979′.02   87-10978
ISBN 0-8032-4748-6
ISBN 0-8032-9722-X (pbk.)

Reprinted by arrangement with Paul I. Wellman, Jr.

To

CYRIL KAY-SCOTT

sapientior illis

ACKNOWLEDGEMENTS

AN AUTHOR owes much to his friends—for their forbearance as much as for their help. In the first regard mine have been uniformly tolerant. In the latter respect many have rendered valuable assistance in the research, organization and final preparation of this volume. Particularly do I acknowledge my indebtedness to the following:

Mrs. Hortense Balderston Campbell, reference librarian at the City Library of Wichita, Kansas, for sustained interest, voluminous correspondence in search of material and other invaluable aid contributed to this book.

Hon. W. A. Ayres, former member of Congress, for many courtesies extended.

The United States Department of War and the Bureau of American Ethnology, for valuable pictures furnished and records consulted.

The state historical societies of Arizona, New Mexico and Kansas for material assistance in many ways.

The Wichita City Library, the Library of the University of Texas, the Library of Congress and the Library of the University of Arizona for their unfailing generosity in tracing and lending material without which this volume could never have been completed.

PAUL I. WELLMAN

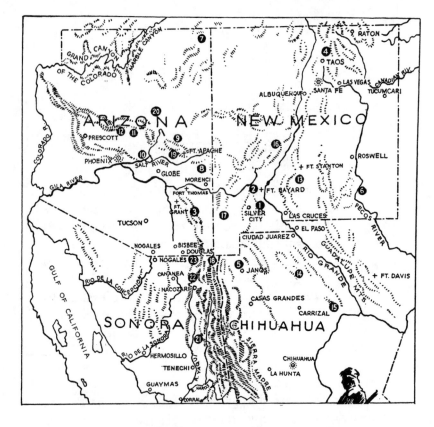

SKETCH MAP OF THE APACHE COUNTRY

1. Santa Rita del Cobre, scene of Johnson's massacre.
2. Piños Altos, where Mangus Colorado was flogged.
3. Apache Pass, where two battles were fought.
4. The Pueblo de Taos.
5. Where Governor Carasco massacred the Mimbrenos in 1858.
6. The Bosque Redondo Reservation.
7. Canyon de Chelly, the Navajo stronghold.
8. The San Carlos Reservation.
9. The Tonto Basin, scene of Crook's campaign of 1872–73.
10. The Salt River Canyon battle.
11. Turret Butte.
12. The Camp Verde Reservation.
13. The Mescalero Reservation.
14. The Candelaria Mountains, where Victorio's double massacre occurred.
15. The Tres Castillos Mountains, where Victorio made his last stand.
16. Nana's camp in the San Andreas Mountains.
17. Horse Shoe Canyon fight.
18. Where Colonel Garcia ambushed Loco's band.
19. Hentig's fight on Cibicu Creek.
20. The Cevelon Fork battle.
21. Where the Mexicans shot Captain Crawford.
22. Country where Lieutenant Gatewood found Geronimo.
23. Canyon des Embudos where Crook was double crossed by Geronimo.

FOREWORD

CENTURIES ago, out of the bleak wastes of the arctic snow-lands, a people began its southward march. It was a poor people, schooled by rigid adversity, used to the pang of hunger, the bite of the elements, the constant struggle for existence. Though lacking every form of material wealth, it was rich in courage and pride, a pride which found expression in its name for itself—*Tinde, Tinneh, Dine* or *N'de* in various dialects—which has always the same meaning wherever it is found today, *The People*.

Filtering slowly southward, the People debouched at last upon the great plains. Here for the first time they found plenty and some surcease from the pitiless fight for life. Bison, in limitless herds, were ready at hand for meat and shelter. There was other game in plenty, and the killing frost, far behind them, was forgotten. Gradually, through the years, the People moved farther and farther southward. And when the first precursors of the white race reached the plains they found the former children of the tundras living in a far-flung territory, ranging from the Black Hills almost to the Sierra Madre. These first white explorers called the Tinde by various names, *Vaqueros, Escanjacques, Faraons* and *Padoucas*,[1] among others.

Then new forces began to be felt. The Sioux, impelled by pressure from the east where the Paleface was forcing

[1] George E. Hyde is authority for the statement that Padouca was an early French name for Apache, instead of for Comanche as some writers have claimed. He cites Margry, a French writer of the early 18th Century who "speaks of the tribe who are called by the Spaniards Apaches but are known to the French as Padoucas." ("Rangers and Regulars," p. 40.)

the Chippewas westward, emerging with teeming numbers into the flat country. From the west came another people, a hungry people, the Shoshoni race, out of the barren desert lands in the high reaches of the Rocky Mountain plateaus.

The impact of these two vast migrations occurred in the regions at that time north of the habitat of the People, but its repercussions were soon felt. Invincible in war, the Sioux smashed the Shoshoni back to their mountains— all but one branch, a numerous, wily, lethal division which history was to call the Comanches.

These last moved southward to make room for the Siouan hordes, and where they went they drove the Tinde out. An epic story might be written on the wars of that slow invasion, but no chronicler was present. We only know that some time, within the last three hundred years, this race which once called the arctic tundras its home, found itself forced farther and farther into the equally barren, though this time torrid deserts of our Southwest.

And now a strange thing happened. In some manner, from the very ferocity of their surroundings, the People attained a ferocity of their own. The enervation of the sun which subdued the Pueblos, the Pimas and the Diggers, failed to tame the Tinde. Their warriors became lean, sun-baked, imbued with shocking cruelty and vitality, endowed with deadliness and malice beyond all other tribes of American Indians. So it was that, after centuries of wandering, they were named from their one outstanding trait, *Apache—Enemy*.

The white man found the Apache after the Mexican War, when the surging migrations across the continent reached the Southwest. And there, backed up at last in the least desirable of all the corners of the continent, the Apache made his final stand. Other desert tribes fought also. But the Apache was ever the great opponent.

CONTENTS

V.

THE WAR IN THE LAVA BEDS
1871–1873

VI.

NAN-TAN LUPAN
1871–1876

VII.

THE HUNTING OF VICTORIO
1877–1880

VIII.

WARRIORS WITHOUT LEADERS
1880–1883

IX.

THE GERONIMO WAR
1883–1886

ILLUSTRATIONS

I.

THE PURGING OF SANTA RITA DEL COBRE
1822-1840

Chapter I

AT THE COPPER MINES

THE WEAKNESS OF JUAN JOSÉ

To the Apaches, the Copper Mines of Santa Rita del Cobre had been for years an abomination and a menace. The mines were situated in the southwestern corner of what is now New Mexico, the very heart of the Apache country; and that Mexican miners should be permitted to live and work there, without harm or hindrance, ate like a canker into the heart of every warrior.[1] Moreover, the miners were driving their shafts into what had been for generations the council rocks of the tribe.

It was a supreme tribute to the power of Juan José, chief of the Mimbreno Apaches,[2] that the settlement of squalid adobe houses and the tiny *presidio*, had not long before this been pulled to pieces. To ask the lean, harsh desert destroyers to withhold their hands from the sleek Mexicans, was to ask the lobo wolves to refrain from worrying a flock of stupid, woolly sheep. Yet such was the prestige of Juan José that Santa Rita, its three-cornered fort with the squat, turret-shaped towers looking over the jumble of

---

[1] "The Mexican government . . . held that the Indians had no rights, as original possessors of the land, which it was in any manner bound to respect, and to this policy is due the unceasing war which has been waged by this brave people (the Apaches) against the Mexicans."—Vincent Colyer's Report to the Board of Indian Commissioners, 1871 (p. 5).

[2] The Mimbreno Apaches at this period ranged from the east side of the Rio Grande in New Mexico, to the Verde River in Arizona. Prior to the Santa Rita massacre they were one of the most numerous branches of the Apache people.

casas scattered without plan about the wide, dusty *plaza,* existed for years with never a thought of death to disturb it.

Little pot-bellied Mexican children played in the dirt. Broad-hipped *casadas* shrilled to each other from house to house. In the evenings men slouched across the *plaza* or lounged in lighted doorways. With night came the tinkle of guitar strings as youths serenaded their *señoritas* in the dusk.

Strange sights, strange sounds, strange odors for Apacheria. Yet Juan José, the fat and lazy, kept his people in leash when their every instinct maddened them with the desire to kill.

The chief's own degeneration was to blame for his complaisance. In his youth he had been an Apache of Apaches. None had been allowed to surpass him in the long, dangerous raids down into Sonora and Chihuahua, as the Indians waged their bitter, unending war with the Mexicans. But age and much booty had taken away the rancour of his nature, so that he grew broad of back and loved no longer the feel of a straining pony beneath him, nor the hunger of the war path and its hot triumph.

In 1822 there came to Juan José the envoys of that wealthy Spanish grandee, Don Francisco Manuel Elguea of Chihuahua, with proposals for a treaty of permission to work the copper mountain which Don Elguea had purchased from its discoverer, Colonel Carrisco. The latter had found the great lode in 1804, but it was worthless to him since the Apaches would not permit him to remove the ore. Don Elguea was a different man. He well knew how to appeal to one like Juan José. The offers of cloth, of weapons and horses, were clinched by a present of strangely shaped casks of ardent spirits. Juan José, drunk by that time, gave permission to establish a settlement and work the mines.

There were, to be sure, some restrictions. The Mexicans were not to leave the settlement without permission. Even then they must agree to follow only two specified trails back to Mexico in their activities, one toward Chihuahua and the other toward Sonora. Yet, although they meticulously observed these restrictions, anyone could see that the Mexicans grew daily in numbers at Santa Rita del Cobre. Women came, among them the young *señoritas*, who swung their hips along in a peculiar, insinuating walk, causing the eyes of the Mimbreno warriors to glow as they watched them.

Still Juan José forbade hostility. And his word was yet law to the Mimbrenos. Even though he no longer rode, they remembered that he owned the strange magic of reading the thick-writing. A *padre*, hoping to win him to the priesthood and thus obtain a foothold in the wild tribe, had trained him in his youth. But Juan José was too truly an Apache to linger long with the gentle teachings of the Cross. He returned to his people and used his learning to intercept messengers and read dispatches, thus forestalling by lightning escape or well-planned ambush, the military movements against him.

So long had he been successful as a leader in war, that now, although his warriors' hands itched for the bow and spear as they watched the great *conductas* with their pack mules wind their way periodically south, they remained quiet. While Juan José was chief, Santa Rita was safe.

It is not to be supposed that all of the Mimbrenos submitted tamely to such a condition. Perhaps more than half of them broke away and established their camp at Ojo Caliente (Warm Springs), about eighteen miles east of the Copper Mines. This division came to be known as the Warm Springs Indians, as distinguished from the Copper Mines Indians who remained with Juan José.

While Juan José, on the heights above Santa Rita, looked down on the miners at work, the Warm Springs Apaches maintained the old ways of the tribe. Under the bitter leadership of Cuchillo Negro (Black Knife) they continued the great, killing raids deep into old Mexico, bringing back ponies and plunder and captives. The Warm Springs Indians kept the lean Apache look. The Copper Mines Indians were grown fat with their chief. They learned to go among the adobe houses of Santa Rita village, to beg for food or *mescal*, occasionally to sell furs, and to acquire habits and manners which were looked upon askance by the elders of the tribe. Many now spoke Spanish. The younger squaws began to swing their hips like the *señoritas*. And the youths adopted the insolent Mexican swagger.

It was high time for a change. The Copper Mines had now run fifteen years—this was in 1837. Many of the warriors were beginning to look beyond Juan José at another figure—Mangus Colorado, who was of Cuchillo Negro's mind, but of Juan José's camp.

MANGUS COLORADO

In many ways Mangus Colorado had focussed the eyes of the people upon himself. He was that anomaly among the Apaches, a giant. Six feet, six or seven inches tall he stood in his moccasins.[3] Yet his legs, vastly bowed, were scarcely longer than those of an ordinary man. All of the great difference was made up by his tremendous torso. His head was great in proportion, huge enough to fill a cask,

---

[3] There is dispute as to his exact height. John C. Cremony ("Life Among the Apaches," p. 48) says "about six feet." Lieutenant Cave C. Couts ("Diary of a March to California") says six feet, two inches. Other authorities say, however, that he was taller than either of these estimates. Charles F. Lummis ("Land of Poco Tiempo," p. 161) gives his height as six feet, six inches.

the eyes deep sunk and very bright, lips wide and thin as a knife slash, and a vulture's beak of a nose curving down to meet the rocky up-jut of his chin. Among a people who averaged below the usual height and size, his mightiness had no parallel.

His strength was that of two or three men. Two Apache squaws were already in his lodge, but he captured a beautiful Mexican girl and added her to his household. This was contrary to custom, under which he should either have killed her or turned her over to his wives as a slave. But Mangus Colorado made his own customs. In the face of tribal disapproval he established the foreigner as an equal with his other women. It was, to them, a slap in the face. Apache law gave both his wives the right to appeal to their relatives. Mangus Colorado was challenged by a brother of each to the terrible Apache duel—naked, with knives as weapons and death to the vanquished. He accepted. And before all the people the great Apache bull slew both his challengers. After that nobody, least of all his wives, dared question his right to bring anybody he desired to his lodge.[4]

Mangus Colorado signifies (in defective Spanish) "Red Sleeves." One story is that he won his name by leading the band of Apaches which followed for weeks the Sylvester Pattie party of American trappers as they worked down the San Pedro River in the spring of 1825, finally running off their horses. The white men concealed their furs and went to the Copper Mines for help. Then the Apaches robbed them of their entire catch. In the loot, so the story goes, was a red flannel shirt which Mangus donned and thus obtained his name. Whether or not this be true, it is certain that in 1837, when he was about forty

[4] This incident is vouched for by Cremony ("Life Among the Apaches," pp. 47-48).

years old, he was the most talked about of all the Copper Mines Indians.

He was a friend of Cuchillo Negro, the Warm Springs leader, a sullen, vicious Apache, much esteemed among his people for his craft and for the burning hate in his being. The two of them saw eye to eye in the matter of Santa Rita del Cobre. Either would gladly have led an attack on the place. But had not the government of Chihuahua taken a hand, the opportunity to slake their Apache hatred for the Mexicans would possibly never have come.

Rendered desperate by Apache incursions which never left them in peace and which their soldiers seemed powerless to stop, the *junta* of Chihuahua promulgated, in 1837, the *"Proyecto de Guerra,"* or project for war. It was a barbarous law, a law conceived by men who despaired of ever meeting the Apache menace by any civilized means. It was a last-ditch law, dictated by the fear which death from the north had engendered in every Mexican heart. The state agreed to pay a sum equivalent to one hundred dollars for the scalp of every Apache warrior brought to the capital; fifty dollars for the scalp of each squaw; and twenty-five dollars for the scalp of each child. Sonora already had such a law.[5]

Here was a peerless opportunity for the unscrupulous. And it carried in it the seeds of bitter hatred which the Apaches were eventually to bear for every member of the white race. Up to this time the Apache hostility had been directed at the Mexicans with whom they had a feud for generations. There were only a few white men in the country, trappers or traders, and toward these the Indians had a more or less friendly attitude. Beyond occasional

[5] As late as 1866, Grant County, Arizona, offered a bounty of two hundred and fifty dollars each for Apache scalps.

petty thievery along the trap lines, or, as in the case of the Pattie party, the stealing of horses, there was remarkably little hostility shown toward the whites. Among the trappers in the country at the time was one James Johnson. Not much is known of this man, save that he was driven by an all-encompassing greed for gold. There is some dispute as to whether he was an American or an Englishman.[6] No matter; he was of the *Pinda Lick-o-yi*, the White Eyes,[7] and generations were to suffer because of him.

With a mind less scrupulous even than the Mexicans, Johnson plotted a wholesale slaughter which should put scalp-collecting into the realm of big business. With his partner, a man named Gleason, he enlisted to his project a party of Missouri trappers, led by one Eames. The whole band went to Santa Rita, where an additional bounty was offered by the owners of the mines, an inducement for Johnson to commit his crime there.

Letters of introduction from Chihuahua authorities and from the company officials obtained full cooperation for Johnson at the mines. The plan was simplicity itself. A great feast was held to which the Apaches were invited. Such an invitation was an immediate lode-stone to the glutton Juan José. At his eager acceptance, the Copper Mines Indians agreed to come almost en masse. Numbers of squaws and children from the more remote Warm Springs village also rode over to attend.

The Mexicans lived up to their promises of hospitality. Roast steers, *soccoro* mush, and *mescal* were served in

---

[6] Cremony calls Johnson an Englishman. Wilson says he was an American.

[7] The word "Paleface" was unknown among the Apaches. Their generic name for members of the white race was *Pinda Lick-o-yi*, "White Eyes," and seems to have referred to their blue or light gray eyes which looked white in comparison to the Apaches' own black orbs.

abundance. The Indians gorged themselves, with the huge-paunched Juan José showing his people the way.

In the middle of the feast, laborers carried out bags of *soccoro* meal—corn grist—and heaped them in the *plaza*. To one side was a screening of branches and sacking. Here lounged Johnson and most of his men.

Best proof that the Apaches were thoroughly drunk is contained in the fact that none of them investigated the screen. That was not Apache. Had anyone taken the trouble to look, he would have seen something which would have sent him screaming an alarm to his people.

Behind the branches squatted the ugly bulk of a howitzer, loaded to the muzzle with bullets, nails, pieces of chain, slugs and stones. It was trained directly upon the pile of *soccoro*.[8]

THE MASSACRE

And now the *alcalde* came forward with an oily invitation to the Apaches to help themselves to the *soccoro* as a free gift from the people of Santa Rita. Not dreaming of treachery, the squaws and children gathered around the pile in a laughing, chattering mob. Now was Johnson's time. When the crowd was thickest about the bags, he touched his lighted *cigarro* to the vent hole of the gun.

The screen of branches and sacking was burst asunder by the shattering blast of the howitzer. Right into the thick of the unsuspecting Indians hurtled a devil's collection of missiles. It mowed a swath as clean as if a giant scythe had slashed through the heart of the crowd.

At the roar of the gun, the trappers, led by Johnson,

[8] Accounts differ as to the type of gun used. Cremony says it was a six pounder, Wilson a blunderbuss, Dunn a howitzer. Whatever it was, all agree on the results which followed.

and the Mexican soldiers from the *presidio*, leaped forward to finish the slaughter. Muskets thudded and knives and sabres flashed and sank home. In wildest panic, bewildered, terror-stricken, the Apaches fled in every direction. Only the swiftest-footed escaped. The ground was heaped with corpses, foul with blood.[9]

As the surviving Indians stampeded into their own village, they began to count their losses. Juan José did not appear. He was dead. How naturally the tribe now turned to Mangus Colorado. He had escaped death by some miracle and they looked to him for leadership in the crisis. The Apache giant was ready for the responsibility.

Mangus Colorado was forty and he had spent his manhood preparing himself for this moment. He had studied the Mimbreno warriors. On the heels of the greatest disaster his people had ever known, or soon thereafter, he named a group of warriors to positions of responsibility under him, who were afterward to be known as the most redoubtable in the history of the Apache nation. Delgadito (The Slender), Poncé, El Chico, Pedro Azul, Coletto Amarillo (Yellow Tail), Cuchillo Negro, and last, but not least, the warrior who was to go down in history as Victorio, were selected to serve as sub-chiefs under Mangus Colorado.

It was to be a holy war of vengeance. For the first time in fifteen years the Mimbrenos were together. The Red Sleeves abandoned the old Copper Mines camp and took his people to their kindred at the Warm Springs. Thenceforth all were known as Warm Springs Indians.

Meantime, like ripples of a pool into which a pebble is

---

[9] According to Cremony ("Life Among the Apaches," p. 31) four hundred Apaches lost their lives in this massacre.

thrown, the lines of Apache fighters moved swiftly outward. There were several parties of American trappers in the country. The Indians knew where to find every one. Santa Rita was the main objective, but meanwhile the Apaches could whet the edge of their appetite for blood atonement upon these white men outside the village.

Two trapping parties were on the Gila River. One, composed of twenty-two men led by Charles Kemp, was forty miles down-stream from the mines. Another, of only three trappers, headed by Benjamin D. Wilson, was even closer to the Mimbreno headquarters.

In the gray of a dawn the Apaches opened fire on the Kemp party. Surprised, caught in a deep ravine with high walls all around and commanding it, the white men died like sheep under the Mimbreno arrows. Not one survived. Particularly careful to take every rifle and all ammunition, the Apaches looted the camp. Then they passed on and the buzzards dropped down into the gorge.

Forty miles up the river, Benjamin Wilson and his two companions camped. Silent shadows slipped around their tent and the Americans found themselves suddenly caught and bound. It was Mangus Colorado again. Wilson's story of what followed is extant in the form of a manuscript.[10]

Mangus Colorado tried to preserve their lives. But his people demanded the trappers. At last the chief brought about a compromise; two of the Americans should die; the other be released.[11] To the teepee where the three prisoners were confined, he went. Wilson was the lucky

[10] Quoted by Frank C. Lockwood in his "Pioneer Days in Arizona," pp. 155-157.
[11] This is Wilson's story and it is certain that he did survive while his companions were killed. But the writer is at a loss to explain why Mangus Colorado had this sudden softness of heart. There is something behind his sparing Wilson's life. Perhaps even this early Mangus Colorado was beginning his long effort to conciliate the white man.

man who was given his freedom.[12] His companions died horribly, hanging head down over a slow fire.

Mangus Colorado had struck two blows. It was now time to consider Santa Rita itself. Like wolves the Apaches turned toward the Copper Mines.

[12] Wilson, in the final stages of exhaustion, eventually reached Santa Fé. He recovered his health and lived to become noted as a rancher, merchant, Indian agent, state senator in California and later the first mayor of Los Angeles.

Chapter II

APACHE RETRIBUTION

THE FEAR OF SILENCE

Sun-baked and hot the village of Santa Rita del Cobre lay athwart the landscape as if a giant hand had cast a fistful of adobe blocks haphazardly. Above loomed the summit of the Needle [1] from which the Mexicans were wont to watch for the *conductas* bringing pack trains loaded with provisions and mail from Sonora or Chihuahua. Within the town, huddled close to the walls of the ugly little *presidio*, the usual activities went forward. Miners, shop-keepers, a few *ricos* and perhaps a *padre* or two, strolled in the narrow, crooked streets. The throng of children still tumbled underfoot and kept up an indescribable babel of sound, while their mothers looked on proudly from their various occupations.

Yet there was definable about the place an air of uneasy expectancy—a feeling which a close observer might have identified as dread. Now and again, wandering toward the *plaza*, the eye of a citizen might have gazed askance at a long, low ridge of fresh earth beyond the limits of the village. It was not strange if he crossed himself as he gazed.

It was a place of ill omen, that ridge of new-turned earth. Beneath lay the bodies of many Apaches, mostly

[1] Now called the Kneeling Nun.

women and children, massacred in the *plaza*, victims of
the gold lust of the American trappers, Johnson, Gleason,
Eames and their followers. The scalps had been torn
from the heads of the murdered Indians, to be taken to
Chihuahua for the bounty there offered.

Not a single Indian now squatted in the sun of the
plaza. None lounged in the shade of the adobe shops.
Yet the people of Santa Rita del Cobre derived small
comfort from the circumstance. Had they known the
Apaches as the Apaches knew them, they would have
sweated with something even more poignant than the sick
dread of the silence which now oppressed them. At this
very moment the village was under the surveillance of
Apache eyes—beady, glittering eyes—focussed telescopi-
cally upon the place, observing every movement in it.
The watch had been maintained unceasingly by the Mimbrenos since the hour of the massacre. Not a man left his
home, not a movement was made, which was not seen.
And yet no glimpse of an Indian was ever caught by any
inhabitant of the town.

Forty or fifty miles away in the Gila valley, lay the
hacked and mutilated bodies of twenty-two American trappers. Thirty miles further up-stream, the corpses of two
more still hung, head down from the trees, their skulls
burst open over the black ashes of fires now dead.

This, so far, was Apache vengeance. But bigger game
was afoot. The great, hulking shadow of Mangus Colorado visited the Apache observation posts at night. Nothing less than the destruction of the settlement of Santa
Rita itself would satisfy the chief.

Far to the south the Apaches met a *conducta* in a mountain pass. The soldiers guarding it knew little of Apaches.
They entered the valley trustingly . . . like little children . . .

At the counting of the loot that night the Mimbreno chiefs enumerated many rifles and great store of powder and ball; much cloth, *soccoro* and horses and mules to gladden the heart. It had been a rich *conducta* carrying supplies for the Copper Mines. None remained alive of the pack train and its guards. The Apaches had finished them all—some of them quickly, in the heat of the fight; others slowly, with ingenious devices to prolong life and bring out the finality of agony in dying, while voices made their plaint from the dark valley in which little groups of Indians squatted about prostrate figures.

Later another, smaller *conducta*, on its way north from Janos, was similarly cut off by the Mimbrenos. Nothing of this was known at Santa Rita. But as the days lengthened, the people began to realize that the time for the coming of the *conductas* was long past and their supplies were so low that, if it was much longer delayed, starvation faced them. In the fifteen years during which the mines had been operated, the *conductas* had come with such regularity that the miners grew to count upon them absolutely. Long ago the practice of keeping stores for possible emergencies had been given up. Santa Rita lived very much from hand to mouth.

Still time passed. Work at the mines ceased altogether. The miners wandered uneasily about the village. Children wailed with hunger in the adobe *casas*. The Santa Ritans began the habit of toiling up the steep slope of the Needle, to gaze anxiously south from palm-shaded eyes, for signs of the dust cloud which would herald the coming of help. But the horizon remained bleakly bare.

Johnson, Eames and the rest of the Americans grew tired of the monotony and struck out from the village toward the Chiricahua Mountains on the west. These men the Apaches attacked and almost exterminated. Johnson,

A pair of young Tonto Apache warriors, showing the typical war and hunting costume of these Indians. The red cloth turban, the buckskin breech-clout and the high-top moccasins of the Indian on the right are typical, although the left-hand Indian has a pair of woollen army socks on his feet instead of moccasins.

A *ranchería* of "broncho" (hostile) Apaches in the days when the desert country was a place of peril to every white man. Note warrior at left, with rifle. Also *jacales* made by throwing blankets over bushes to form shelters.

Rose Collection

A hostile Apache camp photographed while negotiations were under way for the surrender of the Indians.

the arch-plotter, was one of the few who escaped. Even of this attack Santa Rita knew nothing.

All this activity and tragedy around them had occurred with no intimation to the people. There was nothing tangible for them to lay their hands or minds to. It was clearly apparent, however, that things had reached a stage where it was no longer possible to remain at Santa Rita. The *alcalde* and the commandant of the few soldiers of the *presidio* sat long at night, with their heads together.

One day they called the people into the *plaza* and announced to them that, as a last resort, a heavily armed force of men, strong enough to hold its own in case of an Indian attack, would ride south to find the missing *conductas*. At once protests arose. It was urged that such a force would take practically all the armed men in the settlement; that those who stayed behind would be defenseless. There was only one alternative. The whole population of some three or four hundred men, women and children, was ordered to prepare to travel.

THE DEATH FLIGHT

And so the desert witnessed a pitiful hegira. Out of Santa Rita del Cobre filed the long, motley caravan. Every kind of a vehicle obtainable was there, loaded with belongings of the people. Few of them understood what actually awaited them on a march such as the one upon which they were embarking. They tried to take along their most precious possessions, sacrificing speed with useless treasures, adding weight to the burdens. Even wheelbarrows from the mines were requisitioned. Mules and burros staggered under towering packs. And many of the men and even women and children walked with their shoulders bent beneath heavy bundles.

Leaving their little homes, which would presently become the abode of pack-rats and coyotes, they commenced the long trek southward. It is not likely that the women wept much at the departure from Santa Rita. Apprehension sat too heavily upon all of them.

One day—two days—they travelled. Their path presently became a tragic *via dolorosa*, strewn with bundles, broken vehicles, dead animals—and, with growing frequency, graves, particularly little graves, with tiny crosses stuck hastily into the heaped-up sand.

So far they were not molested by the Apaches. The crags on either side of the trail appeared deserted. Not a sign of life could be seen in the yellow-gray waste. But although they knew it not, every foot of their way was paced by unseen human wolves whose eyes did not miss a movement the fleeing Santa Ritans made.

It is not known just when or how fate overtook them. Probably it was upon the third or fourth day. The reader can picture for himself what happened: Without warning, without preliminary, from the sides of a narrow pass, arrows and bullets whizzed. Men died and with them women and little children. Those who escaped the missiles struggled desperately forward out of the gorge. The wounded were abandoned where they fell. Presently the surviving Mexicans heard behind them the outcries of these deserted ones, under the expert hands of Apache torturers.

Ahead was another narrow canyon and the Santa Ritans knew too well what awaited them between its jaws. Yet the gantlet must be run. Men clenched their teeth and gripped their muskets; women wailed and clung to their children as the train plunged into the gorge. Again the blighting sleet of death from the walls above: stricken people and animals in the canyon. No time to stop and help them now. The soldiers tried to fight back, but how can one fight when he cannot see his enemy? The remnants at last escaped from the gulch. Behind was repeated again the dolorous sound of Apache death being brought to the wounded.

All this is only a conception of what took place. There is no detailed account. But this we know: Harried, pursued, never permitted to rest, the three or four hundred souls who left Santa Rita were almost wiped out. Scarcely half a dozen ever reached Janos, the first settlement to the south. The bleaching skeletons of all the rest sprawled on the road between.

Thus Mangus Colorado took payment for the treachery of Johnson and his *soccoro* bags.

.   .   .   .

Once more the Mimbrenos pitched their camp on the high ridge overlooking the valley of the Copper Mines. They were one people now, with Mangus Colorado their recognized chief. Under him served at least two of the authentic blood of chiefs—Poncé, nephew of Juan José, and Cuchillo Negro—yet both were content and proud to be his lieutenants.

War was the accustomed state of the Apaches and the whole people breathed more freely, more cleanly, now that they were in their element again. Mangus Colorado did not propose to lose the white heat of this new spirit. He began again the raids into Mexico. And he spent his brief leisure between forays in numerous acts of policy, designed to knit the surrounding tribes to him. Born to him by the Mexican girl for whom he had fought the double duel, were three comely daughters. These he presented to Cochise, chief of the Chiricahuas; to Hash-kai-la, of the Coyoteros; and to Ku-tu-hala, of the White Mountains, thus drawing the three groups to him.

It was a time of fulfillment for the Mimbrenos. In the years which followed the purging of Santa Rita del Cobre, no Mexican dared enter the borders of Apacheria. The Indians, on the other hand, raided often and far into Mexican territory, and Sonora, Chihuahua and Durango were loud with wailings because of the *ranchos* burned, men slain, and women and children carried way.

Beside their Warm Springs, or near the Council Rocks, the Mimbrenos feasted after raiding, and planned new exploits. All men looked to Mangus Colorado for leadership. Those were good times for the Apaches.

But a change was coming, and that soon.

II.

BLOOD IN THE PUEBLO
1846

CHAPTER III

THE MASSACRE AT TAOS

PEOPLE OF THE PUEBLO

ROSE-BROWN in the glory of the New Mexican sunlight, Taos Pueblo crouched in its surrounding amphitheater of mountains—crouched like a beast gathering for its spring. Within eye-shot of whoever stood upon its higher *azoteas* was the town of San Fernando de Taos, the village of white men and Mexicans which lay a short ride to the westward.

Tomasito, the war chief of the Pueblos, could remember when San Fernando de Taos had been a sleepy Spanish town with never an *Americano* in it. Those were the days before the trappers began to filter down from the high Rockies; before the Bents and Ceran St. Vrain established their residences in Taos; before Broken Hand Fitzpatrick and Kit Carson, with their train of strenuous, hard-bitten mountain men, had converted the picturesque village into a white man's outpost.

The Pueblos had never grown used to the white men and their high-handed ways. The half-humorous contempt, with which the *Americanos* treated them, was resented. And now, in the dying months of the year 1846, conditions had changed even more for Taos Pueblo.

The annexation of Texas by the lusty new republic of the United States in December, 1845, together with many other causes in which the people of the Pueblos were not in the remotest way interested or concerned, brought about war between the power of the north and Mexico, which was formally declared in May, 1846. By April an army was moving across the plains, and down through the mountains toward New Mexico. Don Manuel Armijo, the showy governor of New Mexico, issued a bombastic proclamation, and gathered an army, but when he met General Stephen W. Kearny, and his Missourians and Tennesseeans, "half hoss, half alligator," the Mexican soldiers melted away and the glittering governor himself led the flight out of the territory. Thus it came about that on August 19th, 1846, Kearny occupied Santa Fe, the capital of New Mexico, raised the flag of the United States over the governor's palace, and proclaimed the country a possession of his government by right of conquest.

It did not seem to occur to the American commander or any of his officers that the Taos Indians might be a factor to be considered in governing the new-won territory. For centuries they had been known to be peaceful. When the Spaniard first crossed the deserts, he found the Pueblos there, already civilized, hard-working and prosperous. At that time they occupied seventy-six towns[1] which were scattered over an area hundreds of miles in extent. The largest of these, and the most notable for its location, with the single exception of cliff-perched Acoma, was Taos, which was also the most northerly of all the Indian cities.

The Spanish were struck with wonder at the progress which the Pueblo Indians had made up the ladder of civilization. Five-story Taos Pueblo, for example, was

[1] Now reduced in number to thirty-six.

three stories higher than the houses to which the Dons were accustomed in their own lands. And the Pueblo irrigation systems showed skill even superior, in their way, to the buildings. Some of these great aqueducts have been traced for as much as fifty miles, and their design is so perfect that modern engineers have been unable to gain an inch a mile in fall over these masterpieces of antiquity.[2]

Every Pueblo Indian was a combined farmer and trader. He was a hunter and warrior last of all. In the latter respect, the Pueblo was America's first pacifist. He believed, however, in preparedness—for defensive warfare. His communal houses were primarily fortifications and his very life depended upon their impregnability. For hungry killers came out of the desert and sat slavering outside the walls as they sensed the richness of the Pueblo possessions. Ordinarily these killers—Apaches, Utes, Comanches, or Navajos—when they had traded their meat and furs for blankets and grain, returned to their wilds. But sometimes they made a savage effort to carry the place and thus possess its wealth without having to barter.

None of the pueblos was superior to Taos as a fortress city. Built of native adobe, and tinted the gorgeous titian shade which, once seen, is never forgotten, its two large community buildings had long laughed at any threat from the neighboring tribes. Their first stories had no doors or windows looking outward. Their roofs could be reached only by ladder over the outer wall. Upper stories receded

[2] Several of these old canal beds have been used to advantage by modern irrigation ditch builders. In one case, the Mormon settlement of Mesa, Arizona, saved thousands of dollars by employing an ancient aqueduct which curved around a volcanic knoll for three miles, at one point being chiseled twenty to thirty feet deep into the solid rock for several hundred feet. Through this remarkable system of irrigation the Pueblos were able always to keep the spectre of starvation away; even to acquire a surplus of food for barter. (See F. W. Hodge, "Handbook of American Indians," p. 621.)

in succeeding terraces, giving pyramidal shape to the whole.[3]

At nightfall, or whenever danger threatened, the ladders were drawn up. Sentries patrolled the walls. If attacked, the whole man-power of the pueblo, and the women also, swarmed to the defense. Small wonder that the Comanches and the Navajos, when they prowled through the mountains, gave Taos Pueblo wide berth.

THE CONSPIRACY

The yoke of Spain had been accepted by Taos with comparative meekness. Even in the furious outbreaks in which their brethren of the south once or twice indulged, bringing death to hundreds of Spanish settlers, the Taos people figured slightly, if at all.[4]

But this was a different day. After Kearny swept the Mexican army out of northern New Mexico, he consolidated the territory, then moved on toward Chihuahua and California. Everything in his wake seemed peaceful. The Mexican residents of the country apparently had accepted the inevitable. The Pueblo Indians showed small concern in the change of overlords.

Troops occupied all the more important cities, including Taos village, and Charles Bent, a resident of Taos, was appointed the first governor of the new territory. Bent was one of the famous brothers who built Bent's

[3] The present day Taos Pueblo is but little changed from the structure of 1846. Tourists who have seen it can gain a clear picture of the scenes here described. In one respect the pueblo is different. Modern day Taos has windows and doors in its first story, since the need for safety from savage tribes has passed.

[4] The Pueblo revolt of 1680 was one of the bloodiest which ever occurred on the North American continent. On August 10th of that year, the Indians, goaded to desperation, broke out, killed a score or more Catholic priests who had served them devotedly as missionaries, and slaughtered more than four hundred Spanish colonists. The revolt was put down by Diego de Vargas, in 1692, when he reconquered New Mexico, twelve years after the Spaniards were driven out. Taos was isolated and took a minor part in the revolt.

Fort on the Arkansas River, and with St. Vrain controlled the fur traffic of the southern plains. He had a Mexican wife. His neighbors at Taos included men like the famous Kit Carson, Judge Beaubien, St. Vrain and others. He was liked and respected by everybody.

But a sinister influence was working in Taos Pueblo. While all moved so smoothly on the surface, an internal volcano seethed in New Mexico, and the smouldering flames had reached the *kivas* of the Indians. There had been secret councils at Taos Pueblo. Tomasito had presided at conclaves where others than Indians spoke.

The truth was that the Mexicans hated their conquerors. And with Kearny barely started on his march south, a plot was already hatching to overthrow the government of the *Americanos*. Colonel Diego Archuleta and Tomas Ortiz, the arch-conspirators, knew well the fury of the Indians when aroused, and one of their first steps was to enlist the support of those at Taos. In this they received the help of the mission priests, "black robes" whom the red people trusted and believed. With the *entrée* gained for them by these priests, the conspirators laid optimistic plans and promises before the Taos Indians.

As had been said, the Pueblos had accepted the change in rule over New Mexico with much indifference. But Ortiz and Archuleta told them that the *Americanos* were pitifully weak, unable to defend themselves; and that, if revolt was successful, the plunder would be rich. The council agreed to take part in the insurrection.

And so, in the waning days of 1846, Taos Pueblo lay, instinct with menace, crouching for the signal to unleash its fury.

The Mexican leaders of the revolt showed their usual incompetence. Plans miscarried; delay followed delay. The outbreak was first set for December 19th. The church bells were to ring, and, at the signal, the conspirators were to go to the *plaza* of Taos, seize the artillery parked there, and kill every American in the village. But the irresolute leaders changed their minds. They postponed the date until Christmas Eve, to take advantage of the celebrations all over the city which they felt would make the time more propitious for their coup. This time the plot was exposed. A mulatto girl, who had married one of the disbanded soldiers of Armijo, the former New Mexican governor, heard of the plan and hurried with it to Colonel Sterling Price at Santa Fe, three days before the time set. At Price's orders several of the ring-leaders were arrested. Ortiz and Archuleta fled to Mexico. Early in January Governor Bent proclaimed the suppression of the revolt and enjoined the people to be loyal to the government. It was hoped the trouble was over.

But the Pueblo Indians were less vacillating in their temper than their Mexican friends. The conspirators were gone but the organization they had built was still present, awaiting only something to put it into action. That something occurred January 19th, 1847.

Three Taos Indians had been arrested for stealing and were locked up in the Taos jail. On the morning of the 19th a rabble of men from the pueblo marched into the town, crowded in an ugly, restless mob in front of the prison, and demanded the release of their tribesmen. Stephen Lee, an American, was sheriff. One look at the scowling faces around him, and he moved to comply. But before he could do so, the *prefect*, a Mexican named Cornelio Vigil, appeared. Vigil was both tactless and pompous. He loudly forbade Lee to obey the Indians. Then he began to insult and abuse them.

It was as if a taut cord snapped. Like snarling dogs the Pueblos leaped at Vigil, hurled him to the ground, liter-

ally cut him to pieces. All in an instant they were mad with
the fury of killing. The *prefect's* voice was heard, momentarily, calling upon all the saints for succor, then was
stilled as a Taos knife slipped through his throat and the
choking blood stopped further sound.

Stephen Lee fled. But the Indians were after him as
soon as they released the prisoners in the jail. They
"treed" him on his own house-top and shot him down as
if he were a catamount in a pine.

James W. Leal, the circuit attorney, blundered into
the mob. Him they scalped alive, then dragged him shriek-
ing through the streets, pricking him with their lances
until at last he died. Narcissé, the young son of Judge
Beaubien, and his companion, Pablo Harvimean, were
found in an outhouse and ruthlessly killed. Judge Beaubien himself would have shared their fate had he not,
the day before, gone to Santa Fe on business. All through
the village groups of Indians hunted Americans out of
their hiding places and mercilessly slew them.

And now came the climax. With their blood at fever
heat, the Indians gathered around the house of Governor
Bent, who was home from Santa Fe for a brief visit with
his family. He was still in bed when the mob gathered.
His terrified wife called to him, telling him of the gathering danger outside. Then, frantic with fear, she rushed
in with his pistol, imploring him to fight, to make his assailants pay, even if he must die in the end. He could
easily have killed several of them, but he refused.

"I will not kill any of them—for your sake," he said.
"At present, my death is all these people want." [5]

He meant that if he allowed himself to be killed without resistance, the mob might be satisfied, but if he fought
they would massacre everybody in the house.

[5] Dunn, "Massacre of the Mountains," p. 62.

By this time the Indians, aided by Mexicans, had chopped and broken a hole through the roof. They poured into the room. Governor Bent made the appeal to them which he knew would be futile, calling to their minds the many favors he had done for them in the past. They laughed in his face.

An arrow flashed into his body—another—another. As the governor tottered, a bullet tore through him. He fell, and Tomasito stepped forward with a pistol and blew his brains out.

Mrs. Bent and the family were spared, but the Indians scalped Charles Bent as he lay twitching in his death struggles on his own bedroom floor. The scalp was nailed to a board with brass-headed tacks and, shouting and dancing, the whole wild mob roared down the street, carrying the ghastly trophy at its head, like a bloody banner of insurrection.

CHAPTER IV

TURLEY'S MILL

A FRONTIER BARONY

SIMEON TURLEY was a character unique even in a land and time of unique characters. An ex-trapper, he had found his way into New Mexico by way of the fur trade, met there a bright-eyed *señorita*, married her and settled down.

On the banks of the Arroyo Hondo he built a grist mill and a distillery, where he produced more than his share of the famous "Taos Lightning," a fiery whiskey made from the native wheat, much in demand among trappers, traders and wild Indians because of its potency.

The years passed and prosperity came to Turley. His *rancho* in 1847 included numerous substantial buildings such as granaries, stables and offices, as well as the mill, distillery and his home, all arranged in a hollow square with a large front gate and a small postern gate, leading to the corral enclosed within. Here Turley lived in feudal happiness. His door was always open to the wayfarer; his table groaned with the luxuries of the country and guests were ever welcome to it. He was never known to refuse a request for financial or other assistance. Well did he merit the esteem in which his neighbors held him.

The morning of January 19th, 1847, Simeon Turley, at peace with the world and entertaining a half-dozen or more of his friends who had "dropped in" for a meal or two and copious draughts of the fiery Taos Lightning, received ominous information. A rider sped by, halting just long enough to drop word that the Taos Indians had broken out, had raged through the streets of Taos Village killing every American they met, and had murdered and scalped the governor of New Mexico himself—Charles Bent.

Turley's face was grave as he heard this news, but so friendly were his relations with the natives that it did not occur to him that he might himself be in danger. But there were with him eight men who never took anything for granted. Not for nothing had those trappers fought Indians and grizzlies through the Rockies and shared a thousand adventures.

"Better bar them gates," was their laconic recommendation. To please his guests, Turley did so. The trappers lounged about, loose-jointed and deliberate. One took his hickory cleaning rod and ran an oiled rag down the polished barrel of his rifle. Another whetted his hunting knife to razor keenness on the sole of his moccasin. They did not appear apprehensive but they seemed watchful, as men who expect momentous events.

Loud yells down the valley sent the men to the windows. Armed with guns, bows and lances, a mob of Pueblo Indians and Mexicans could be seen coming toward the mill. It was the same crowd which had murdered Bent and other Americans at Taos that morning.

A white flag broke out at the head of the on-marching Indians. Shortly a small group came forward to negotiate with Turley.

"Have you anybody in there beside yourself?" they demanded.

"Yes," said Turley. "There are eight *Americanos* here."

"Señor Turley, you are a friend of the Indians and of the *Nuevo Mejicanos*," was the next remark. "We do not wish to shed your blood. But every other American in the valley must die. Surrender these men with you and you will be spared."

That was a hard choice which Turley faced. If he surrendered the trappers, he and his family and property would be safe. He did not hesitate.

"I will never surrender my house or my men," he growled. "If you want them, you'll have to come and get them." [1]

Events moved rapidly after that. At Turley's refusal, the Indians, with wild yells, scattered and took to cover in the cedar and piñon brush, and the rocks which covered the hills on each side of the narrow valley. White smoke wreaths began to curl up from the shrubbery. Like a rattle of hail the first volley of bullets thudded into the sides and roofs of the buildings. From that moment to the end of the bloody episode there was scarcely a second when the leaden balls were not smacking into the house, seeking every cranny and crack and loophole, a constant danger to the men inside.

The defenders knew exactly what they were about. No green-horns these. Every man had been through many a "scrimmage." Shifting their quids in their jaws, they

[1] Perhaps his refusal was due in part to his distrust of the offers made. On that very day two American trappers, Markhead and William Harwood, were treacherously murdered after they trusted to peaceful offers of a similar nature. Not dreaming of danger, they permitted the Indians and Mexicans to disarm them, under assurance of safe conduct to Taos. As soon as they started a Mexican rode up behind Harwood and shot him. "I'm finished, Markhead," the trapper cried as he fell. Markhead, one of the most famous mountain men, the hero of a hundred hair's-breadth escapes, saw that his time had come. He made no attempt to resist or escape, but sat his horse until he was shot several times in the back and killed. Both were scalped and horribly mutilated. This occurred on the Rio Colorado. The same day eight other Americans were ambushed, captured and murdered near Mora. These included L. L. Waldo, Benjamin Prewitt, Romulus Culver, Louis Cabana, one Noyes and three others.

moved deliberately to points of vantage. The windows were blocked with sacks of grain and chunks of wood, leaving only narrow apertures through which the trappers aimed their long rifles. Whenever a gun spoke from Turley's mill, it generally carried death to an enemy.

TO THE FINISH

Through the whole day the fight continued—tumultuous, noisy and harmless on one side; slow and deadly on the other. Now and then a besieging Indian or Mexican fell bleeding among his bushes or rocks. By night several had been killed or wounded, while Turley's men had not yet suffered a scratch. The trappers knew they were scoring by the sight of the Mexicans down the valley carrying away the wounded.[2]

Darkness came and with it a new peril—the enemy might attack under the cover of night. Sentinels watched but the veteran mountain men wasted no lead in the gloom. Inside Turley's house they discussed the chances of escape, ran bullets, cut patches. With Turley were Albert Tarbush, William Hatfield, Louis Tolque, Peter Roberts, Joseph Marshall, John Albert, Austin and one other whose name is not recorded. All knew their chances of escape were almost nonexistent. But there was no sign of fear as they prepared in the morning to resume the fight.

During the night the attacking party, which had originally numbered about five hundred, had grown greatly. They spent the dark hours shooting at the Turley house.

[2] The exact loss of the attackers in this fight was never ascertained. Benjamin M. Reed ("Illustrated History of New Mexico," p. 447) says five Indians were killed. He does not attempt to state how many Mexicans lost their lives and makes no mention of the number of wounded. The losses must, however, have been very heavy.

Some time that night a few of them sneaked through the gloom and reached the stables in the square. One of these adjoined the main building in which Turley and his men were barricaded. Here the Indians tried their best to break through the wall. Of adobe reinforced by logs, however, it resisted them so well that they gave up the effort.

All at once it seemed very desirable to the Indians in the shed that they get back to their friends. To do so they had to cross a wide stretch of open ground in order to reach the far side of the enclosure. Several had already dashed to safety when the trappers noticed them. The very next man who made the attempt was a Taos chief. A rifle rang from one of the loopholes and the chief, "drilled plumb center," dropped dead in almost the exact middle of the area.

It was an instinct with most Indian tribes to try to rescue the bodies of the fallen. As the chief dropped, one of his braves ran out and tried to drag the corpse to shelter. Again the rifle spoke. The second Pueblo crumpled, inert, across the body of the first. Surely the fate of these two should have warned the others. But with heroic, though futile resolution, the Pueblos tried and tried to get that body. A second rescuer, followed by a third, added their bleeding forms to the gory heap in the corral. And now three Indians, with courage worthy of the highest admiration, rushed out together. One took the chief's legs, another his head and the third his body. Lifting together, they had started toward safety when three puffs of blue smoke sprang out from Turley's house, and all three collapsed in a pile.

As the bloody wreck fell, a single, concerted yell of rage rose from the attackers. An instant later the heaviest volley they had so far discharged, blazed at the house. For the first time two of the trappers were hit. One, shot through the loins, suffered excruciating agony. He was carried to the still house and laid on the grain in one of the bins, the softest bed which could be found for him. Both wounded men died soon.

The shooting lulled. Only seven defenders were left and their ammunition was running low. The Indians and Mexicans had lost heavily. Both sides rested.

Shortly after noon the attack began again. The Americans, unruffled and calm, watched with keen eyes for any exposure of their enemies and made every shot tell. In spite of this the besiegers succeeded in setting fire to the mill. It blazed up in a shower of sparks and smoke. This new danger was met only by the greatest effort on the part of Turley and his men, but they succeeded in quenching the flames before they spread to the rest of the structure.

While the trappers were busy with the blaze, the Indians occupied all the out buildings on the other side of the corral. There they vented their anger in typical Indian fashion by slaughtering Turley's hogs and sheep. Fires kept breaking out in different parts of the defenses.[3] It was increasingly apparent that the place could not be held another twelve hours.

Turley called a second council of war. The trappers voted to wait until night. Then each was to make his escape as he could. Darkness fell at last. Suddenly the wild trapper yell rang out. Together they charged forth, long rifles cracking. John Albert and a companion rushed through the little postern gate, firing their guns right into the faces of the enemy, then leaped forward with clubbed rifles. As his comrade was beaten down, Albert threw himself under the fence. There he lay in the dark-

[3] The Pueblos were probably using fire arrows, although the chronicle does not say so.

ness, listening to the other trapper's screams as they clubbed and stabbed him to death. The Indians thought Albert had escaped and made no search for him. Later he found a chance to get clear away, reached the mountains and eventually a rendezvous of his friends near the present site of Pueblo, Colorado.[4] Two others also escaped and got to Santa Fe.

The crowning tragedy befell Simeon Turley himself. Having risked and lost for his friends, he broke through the cordon. He reached the mountains and was hiding when he saw approaching a Mexican he had known for years. Turley stepped out from his hiding place and asked for help. He offered his valuable watch for the use of the Mexican's horse, although the animal was not worth half as much. The Mexican refused, pretended pity, and rode away, promising to bring help. As fast as his horse could carry him he galloped to the mill and told the Indians where Turley hid. A little later they found him and mercilessly killed him.

[4] It is to this circumstance that we owe the preservation of the story of the defense of Turley's Mill. George Frederick Ruxton was at the rendezvous when Albert reached it. He heard the story from Albert's own lips and later included it in his book, "Wild Life in the Rocky Mountains," pp. 135-145.

Chapter V

THE STORMING OF TAOS PUEBLO

PRICE MARCHES

It must have been a "morning after" feeling with which the Taos Indians surveyed the results of their orgy of bloodshed and looting. A few days of retrospection showed them that the outbreak would have most dire consequences. In the first place, although they were gorgeously successful at Taos, things grew more difficult for them every hour after that. Turley's Mill was a bitter lesson. Considering their losses they may well have felt the results hardly justified.

Then they learned, with disquieting suddenness, that their Mexican allies were already regretting their part in the revolt. Word of the massacre at Taos reached Price at Santa Fe on the 20th, brought by Charles Towne, one of two Americans who escaped from the slaughter. Sterling Price was a man of prompt action. Within three days he had concentrated his troops at Santa Fe and was on the march northward. A second expedition under Captain Isaac R. Hendley started from Las Vegas at about the same time, but was driven back from Mora, in a sharp fight in which Hendley was killed. Captain Morin revenged him on February 1st, when he returned to the town, attacked it, and destroyed everything in it.

While this was going on, Price's force marched rapidly toward Taos. The American army included a battery of four 12-pound howitzers, three hundred and fifty-three infantry and—in many respects the most formidable of all—a company of "cavalry," sixty-five mounted men led by the redoubtable Ceran St. Vrain. These cavalrymen doubtless had a motley look. But they were more to be dreaded, man-for-man, than any other body of fighters in the whole American force. They called themselves "the Avengers." They were led by a mountain man whose dearest friend was the murdered Governor Bent. And in their muster roll were many other mountain men, long, lean, buckskin clad, whose fine instinct for killing had been whetted by the death of some comrade or friend at Taos, Mora, the Rio Colorado or Turley's Mill.

With growing dread the Taos Indians heard of Price's approach. He met the Mexicans at La Cañada on January 24th, 1847. They outnumbered him three to one, but he routed them with a brief cannonade and a sharp charge. Four days later he was joined, at Luceros, by Captain Burgwin and his company of United States dragoons.

Next day after receiving this accession to his forces, Price reached a canyon leading to the village of Embudo, where he found six hundred and fifty of the enemy posted along both sides of the gorge. But Burgwin's dragoons took one side and St. Vrain's "Avengers" the other, and the Mexicans were chased out with a whoop. Pablo Chaves, one of the leaders in the uprising, was killed in the short battle.

So, after twice beating and scattering the Mexicans, Price reached Taos, on the afternoon of February 3rd. It was the day of reckoning. The Taos Indians, deserted by most of their quondam friends, faced the white men alone.

Taos Pueblo consisted then, as now, of two large buildings, both several stories high, flanked by a church and some smaller structures, such as stables and granaries. The sparkling waters of Taos Creek splashed and bubbled between the main structures. The whole was at that time surrounded by a high wall of adobe brick and pickets. It was the larger northern pueblo which the Indians selected in which to make their final stand.

There were, of course, no doors or windows in the pueblo's first story. Ladders gave the only way up and these had been withdrawn. The church, also of thick adobe construction, had been adapted for defense by piercing its walls with loopholes. Part of the Indians were inside of this structure. All in all the Pueblos presented a formidable appearance as Price deployed his army before them.

So confident were the Indians that they wasted some energy and breath in shrill yells of defiance. But Price went into action at once. Lieutenant Dyer, commanding the battery of artillery, was ordered up with his howitzers. The guns were unlimbered, and for two hours they bombarded the west side of the old church, but its thick adobe walls swallowed up the cannon balls in their spongy mass and refused to breach. Evening was approaching. The troops were exhausted by their long march. Price decided to withdraw to the town to rest.

As his soldiers drew away from before the pueblo, the Indians thought they were retreating. Loud were the taunts and jeers they sent after the Americans.

THE PUNISHMENT OF THE PUEBLOS

With some consternation they saw the troops returning next morning and realized they had been mistaken in supposing that Price was in retreat the previous evening. The American leader made his dispositions carefully

Cochise, great chief of the Chiricahua Apaches.

Jemez Pueblo, as it looked in the middle of the last century. Many of the pueblos resemble Mexican villages instead of the communal houses of which Taos is typical.

The North Pueblo at Taos. This was the scene of the battle with Price's soldiers.

The South Pueblo at Taos, with mountains in the background.

this time. He placed Burgwin's veteran dragoons, with two of the howitzers, west of the pueblo. St. Vrain and his "Avengers," their hard jaws grimly closed, sat their horses on the east, to prevent the escape of any fugitives to the mountains. The infantry formed north of the pueblo with the remaining guns in front of them.

With thunderous booms and white clouds of smoke, the first shots of the artillery were fired at 9 o'clock that morning of February 4th. For two hours the dull, shattering reports of the heavy guns echoed from mountain to mountain. Then Price, at 11 o'clock, ordered a charge. It was an old-fashioned military charge, with ranks dressed, officers waving flashing swords in front, drums rolling and fifes squeaking. Captains Aubrey and Barber, and Lieutenant Broon stepped forward gallantly at the head of the infantry. At the same time Captains Burgwin and McMillin surged forward from the west with their heavy dragoons.

Instantly the Indians in the pueblo and church opened a furious fire. The charging infantry and the dragoons alike made for the church, whose high, bluff walls offered shelter from the galling fusillade from the pueblo. There the whole contingent took refuge, safe for the time being under the western walls, since the loopholes above were so cut that the guns of the defenders could not be depressed sufficiently to shoot men immediately below them.

The soldiers were busy. Some of them, with axes, began an attack on the thick wall. Others hastily constructed a makeshift ladder and, climbing to the roof, set it on fire. Holes were presently chopped through the church walls and through these the men tossed lighted shells by hand into the interior, the projectiles bursting murderously inside.

The church door faced the corral, and the pueblo to

the east. Captain Burgwin decided that if he could batter down that door, he could more quickly win the fight. Calling to his men, the reckless young officer clambered over the adobe wall of the enclosure and tried to beat down the door. A number of the dragoons joined him. But the move was both foolish and fatal. What Burgwin had done placed his detachment at the mercy of the Indians behind them in the pueblo. A storm of bullets and arrows beat on the troops. Burgwin reeled with a bullet in him, then fell. Several other soldiers were hit. The Indian shooting was wickedly deadly at this point. It did not take the troops long to realize that. Carrying their wounded, the survivors tumbled over the fence again and ran to the safety of the church wall. The attempt to batter down the door had been a costly failure.[1]

Meanwhile Price had sent the big guns up to within sixty yards of the church, where by shooting at places already breached by the axes of the soldiers, a gaping hole was blasted at last. Through this the troops crowded. They found the church full of smoke from the burning roof and the bursting shells. Gasping for air they groped forward. But the enemy was gone. The defenders had scuttled out of the east side as the soldiers entered the west.

Part of the Indians, fleeing from the church, attempted to reach the main pueblo. But the rest ran for the mountains—a tragic decision. For there, grim and deadly, waited St. Vrain and his "Avengers."

Now rose the long trapper yell and the mountain men rode down their foes. In vain the wretched Pueblos

---

[1] Burgwin was shot, not by a Pueblo, but by a Delaware Indian known on the frontier as "Big Negro" who was trapping in the country at the time and espoused the cause of the Taos insurrectionists. He escaped after the fight, to the Cheyennes. This warrior killed five Americans in the corral before the church door. His wife, Pin Dassa, a Mexican woman, stood on top of the pueblo and loaded guns for her lord throughout the fight.

doubled and dodged and tried to hide. With his own hand
St. Vrain shot down Jesus Tafoya, a Mexican who had
been one of the chief factors in bringing the Taos Pueblos
into the revolt. Tafoya was wearing the coat and shirt of
the dead Governor Bent when he was killed. Later, seeing
an Indian lying by the roadside apparently dead, St. Vrain
dismounted to examine him. Only shamming, the savage
leaped up and grappled with the leader of the mountain
men. The Indian was a powerful athlete; the chief of "the
Avengers" was slight and growing old. It might have
meant St. Vrain's death had not another famous trapper,
Uncle Dick Wooton, ridden up behind and brained the
warrior with a tomahawk. Out of fifty-three or -four fugitives who left the church and tried to reach the mountains,
fifty-one were killed.

Night fell and hostilities ceased. Price quartered his
troops in the church and other buildings west of the
pueblo, prepared to resume battle in the morning. But the
Pueblos had more than enough. They saw now how they
had been duped by the Mexicans. Already they had lost
one hundred and fifty killed out of six hundred and fifty
persons in the pueblo, to say nothing of the wounded. At
dawn the Taos Indians, men and women, came out bearing
white flags and crucifixes, and on their knees begged for
mercy. Price granted it. But he spared them only on condition that they surrender the chief Tomasito and a number of other leaders, to stand trial for the murder of
Governor Bent.

In the following weeks a grim tribunal sat in Taos Village. On the bench was flint-faced old Judge Beaubien,
whose son had been killed by the Indians. Among the witnesses against the prisoners were the widow of Governor
Bent and the wife of Kit Carson, who had witnessed the
governor's death.

With unmoved countenance Tomasito heard these women point him out as the slayer of Bent. He did not intend to hang for the deed. Nor did he. Before the date of the execution, Tomasito made a break for freedom and was shot to death by the guards.

It is not likely that the Indians had much chance with the carefully hand-picked jury which included only Americans and New Mexicans whose sentiments were well known and "safe." [2] On February 9th, six of them, found guilty of the murders in Taos, were hanged from the same gallows, in the presence of the army and the people. It was the final act in the tragic drama. Never again did the Pueblo Indians deviate from the strict path of peace and loyalty to the United States government.

[2] Illustrating the attitude taken toward the prisoners is the case of Juror Baptiste Brown, a trapper by trade, and a French-Canadian. Juror Brown slept through most of the proceedings, but as soon as the jury room was reached, and without consulting the rest of the veniremen, shouted: "Hang them all! They may not be guilty now, but they soon will be!" (Colonel Henry Inman, "The Old Santa Fe Trail," p. 136.)

III.

AN EYE FOR AN EYE
1846–1862

CHAPTER VI

THE COMING OF THE PINDA LICK-O-YI

APACHERIA AGAIN

EVEN before the Taos Indians made their one wild bid for independence from the white man in northern New Mexico, uneasy word of the American invasion reached the Apaches in the southern part of the territory. Mangus Colorado received the news perhaps by messenger from his ally Gian-na-tah (Always Ready), chief of the Mescalero Apaches to the east of the Mimbreno country. The word was that the Mexicans had fought the white men from the other side of the plains and had been beaten. And the soldiers of the victorious Pinda Lick-o-yi, the White Eyes, were marching upon Apacheria.

Such news must sorely have troubled the Mimbreno chief. Not that he was surprised at the defeat of the Mexicans; his own fierce warriors had whipped them so often that his respect for them had long departed. But Mangus Colorado had tested the mettle of the American trappers and miners and found them of tougher fibre than the Mexicans. The White Eyes, for example, were not given to panics. Even when taken by surprise, their movements had a surety and a deliberate, deadly purpose.

Apache scouts paralleled the column of General Kearny every foot of the way after he reached southern New Mexico in the autumn of 1846. Marching rapidly from his almost bloodless conquest of Santa Fe, with California as his objective, the American general stopped briefly at the Copper Mines. He was met by Mangus Colorado and some of his chiefs near the mines, at San Lucia Springs.

The Apaches thoroughly approved of the American war on the Mexicans. One of the chiefs spoke thus: "You have taken New Mexico and will soon take California; go, then, take Chihuahua, Durango, Sonora. We will help you . . . the Mexicans are rascals; we hate and kill them all." [1] Greatly to the relief of the Indians, Kearny moved on after buying from them some mules and horses. The first American invasion ended bloodlessly.

But not for long were the Apaches unmolested. The great tide of empire was about to move west. On February 9th, 1848, the little daughter of a man named Marshall, overseer of a grist mill in California, brought him a "pretty stone" she had found in the mill race. It was a gold nugget, as her father instantly knew. The mill belonged to Captain John A. Sutter, and was situated on the American River, an affluent of the Sacramento. Sutter and Marshall tried to hush up the matter, but to keep such news from spreading was impossible. By May, 1848, the whole nation knew that gold had been found in fabulous quantities in California.

At once began the strange, hysterical stampede known as the "California Gold Rush." Cold, heat, hunger, and every imaginable peril failed to stop it. Trampling their way westward, the gold seekers thrust out of their road the Indians who lived in the country, or slaughtered them out of hand. Almost overnight life changed for the aborigines. They found themselves in the path of a crazed typhoon of humanity, charging desperately west, deaf to

[1] J. P. Dunn, "Massacres of the Mountains," p. 365.

every consideration except the desire to get to the coast
to dig gold—gold—gold.[2]

Inevitably the Indians fought back. They began to attack the wagon trains, and lurid tales come down to us
from those days when the emigrants fought for their lives
on the way to California across the desert country.[3]

The California Gold Rush did not at first directly affect
the Mimbrenos. Their country was out of the line of
travel. But after the Guadalupe-Hidalgo treaty closed the
Mexican War, the work of surveying the Mexican-United
States border began, and in 1851 J. R. Bartlett, at the
head of the American Surveying Commission, reached
Santa Rita.

The arrival of the surveyors, with their strong military
guard and large retinue, was a complete surprise to at
least one redoubtable Mimbreno chief. Cuchillo Negro,
seeing a lone white man riding through the country, ambushed him in a little grove of trees. The rider, all unconscious of peril, came into the net spread for him, and
suddenly found himself surrounded by a score of Apaches,
as deadly as so many rattlesnakes coiled to strike.[4]

---

[2] "What effect did this discovery (of gold in California) have on the Indians?
It was fraught with greater evil for them than any other one event in the history
of America, except the discovery of America itself." (*Ibid.*, p. 125.)

[3] The famous Oatman massacre, which has received so much attention from
writers of Southwestern history, was typical. The Oatman family was attacked by
a band of nineteen Tonto Apaches, as it was crossing the Gila at what is now
known as Oatman Flat, April 18th, 1854. The father and mother, two daughters
and one son, were killed. The other son, Lorenzo, was left for dead. With the loot
from the wagons and the two surviving Oatman girls, Olive and Mary Ann, the
Apaches slunk away. Lorenzo was rescued by friendly Pima Indians. Nursed back
to health, he began a search for his sisters. It was five years before he once more
saw his sister Olive. The other girl, Mary Ann, died of hardships and exposure.
Olive's strange and fascinating story of captivity among the Indians has been the
subject of many books and articles.

[4] Cuchillo Negro was not on the war path but hunting. That made little difference to him, however. It was too good an opportunity to overlook. An Apache,
particularly this one, could change at any time, on a moment's notice, from a
peaceful hunter to a warrior.

The lone white rider was Captain John C. Cremony, interpreter for the Bartlett expedition. He had every reason to be frightened out of his wits, but he acted calmly, if instantaneously. Jerking his revolver from its holster, he sank his spurs into his horse's flanks, causing the animal to bound forward right beside the Indian whom Cremony took to be chief. The captain's judgment was unerring. Cuchillo Negro found himself looking down the barrel of the officer's pistol. At his signal, knowing death was near him, the warriors stopped their stealthy, circling approach. An astonishing colloquy followed.

Surrounded by Apaches, and preserving his existence only as long as he kept Cuchillo Negro under the muzzle of his pistol, Cremony had the temerity to jeer at the chief because he had been so lax in his watchfulness as to allow a party of white men to enter his country without knowing it. He told the Mimbreno that he was the forerunner of a large body of Americans. The Apache replied that Cremony lied; that, if there were many with him, he would never have wandered thus foolishly through the Mimbreno country alone. But presently the glint of many rifle barrels showed through the trees, and the doughty captain allowed his *vis-à-vis* to slink away.

Bartlett's party camped near the ruins of Santa Rita. The commissioner was visited shortly by Mangus Colorado himself. The chief told Bartlett he had been following the commission several days: that the Apaches had been near the white encampments throughout the journey. The Indians were uneasy, fearing the Americans had come to stay. Bartlett assured them he was there only temporarily. For a time things went along peacefully. But that ended as might have been expected.

WHITE LAW AGAINST APACHE LAW

Taking advantage of the presence of the Bartlett party, three Mexican traders came to the Copper Mines, as they would otherwise never have dared to do, bringing with them a beautiful fifteen-year-old Mexican girl named Inez Gonzales. She had been captured by the Pinal Apaches and later sold to these traders. The Mexicans were taking her to Santa Fè, probably to sell her or keep her for immoral purposes, the usual fate of such slaves. Bartlett interfered and released her, restoring her to her relatives a few weeks later.[5]

Without emotion the Apaches watched this little drama. But a few days later it came directly home to them. Two Mexican boys, Savero Aredia, thirteen years old, and Jose Trinfan, eleven, were prisoners in the Indian camp. They saw the rescue of Inez and decided to take advantage of the same opportunity.

One evening they darted into Cremony's tent, begging for his protection. The captain heard their story and took them to Bartlett. Almost on his heels came the Apache chiefs to demand the return of their property. Mangus Colorado, in person, headed the delegation and was its chief spokesman. He outlined the position of his people as follows:

"You came into our country. You were well received. Your lives, your property, your animals were safe. You passed by ones, by twos, by threes through our country. You went and came in peace. Your strayed animals were always brought home to you again. Our wives, our women

---

[5] The sequel to the fair Inez's adventures is interesting: "Inez was returned to her parents by the commissioner when he arrived in Santa Cruz. She subsequently became the mistress of Captain Gomez, who commanded the troops in northern Sonora. He married her at the death of his wife, and after his death, Inez married the *alcalde* of Santa Cruz, her social standing not having been at all affected by her romantic adventures."—Dunn, "Massacres of the Mountains," p. 366.

and children came here and visited your houses. We were friends—we were brothers! Believing this, we came among you and brought our captives, relying on it that we were brothers and that you would feel as we feel. We concealed nothing. We came not secretly nor in the night. We came in open day, and before your faces, and showed our captives to you. We believed your assurances of friendship, and we trusted them. *Why did you take our captives from us?*" [6]

Bartlett was in an awkward position from the standpoint of logic. At the very moment there were millions of Negro slaves in the South. He did his best to explain the attitude of the United States on slavery—as practiced by somebody else. Finally, in desperation, he offered to pay for the captives. The reply was surprising:

"The brave who owns these captives does not want to sell. He has had one of these boys six years. He grew up under him. His heart strings are bound around him. He is as a son in his old age. . . . Money cannot buy affection. His heart cannot be sold. He taught him to string the bow and wield the lance. He loves the boy and cannot sell him."

The boys, apparently, were being adopted into the tribe, a common practice among the Indians of that time and section. But there was nothing Bartlett could do about it. The United States had bound all its officers, by the Treaty of Guadalupe-Hidalgo, to release all Mexican slaves and stop the traffic in them. At last he prevailed upon the Apaches to accept about two hundred dollars' worth of trade goods for the boys. The Indians departed in ill humor, but still remained non-hostile.

[6] These conversations are quoted verbatim by Cremony. ("Life Among the Apaches," pp. 62-66.)

Once more things moved serenely. Mangus Colorado, with some three hundred Mimbreno warriors and their families, camped on a rise four miles from Santa Rita. Delgadito, with another band, was at the Warm Springs. Four hundred Navajos moved down presently and established a village in the Gila Valley, twenty-eight miles from the Copper Mines. Still the white men of the boundary commission, in twos or threes, hunted or carried on their various errands, moving through the Indian country without molestation.

A climactic incident occurred July 6th. Jesus Lopez, a Mexican laborer employed by the commission, causelessly shot an Apache warrior during a petty argument. Many Indians were in the camp at the time, including Mangus Colorado himself. As the Mexican's shot sounded, they ran out and mounted their ponies, riding wildly away in panic. Too well they remembered the massacre by Johnson at this same place. Bartlett placed the murderer under arrest and sent word to the Apaches that he had done so.

The chiefs cautiously reappeared. As soon as they saw that Bartlett was sincere in his friendly position, they demanded the murderer's life. The commissioner, hampered by law, could not summarily execute the man, guilty as Lopez was. Bartlett could only promise a trial in Santa Fe and an execution there. But that did not coincide with Apache ideas.

"This is all very good," said Poncé. "The Apaches know the Americans are their friends. . . . They know that the Americans do not speak with two tongues. . . . They know that you will do what you say. But the Apaches will not be satisfied to *hear* that the murderer has been punished in Santa Fe. They want to *see* him punished here, at the Copper Mines, where the band of the dead brave may see him put to death—where all the Apaches may see him put to death." [7]

Bartlett made a counter-proposal that he keep the murderer in chains and make him work, giving the money he earned to the family of the slain man.

"Money will not satisfy an Apache for the blood of a brave," exclaimed Poncé with scorn. He could not understand such reasoning at all. Did the White Eye think one could purchase honor with gold? Or bribe an Apache to forego his vengeance? Poncé simply could not follow the reasoning.

In the end, Bartlett had to refuse the Indians' demands. Every face was sullen as the Apaches left camp. Within a few days horses and mules began to disappear from the commission's herd, so fast that within a month nearly two hundred were gone.

Proof that the Mimbrenos were guilty of stealing the animals came when Delgadito was seen leading one of the raiding bands. The Americans did not retaliate. There was, indeed, no time for it. The commission had to move on about its business.

Almost afoot Bartlett's party went on its way. And to Mangus Colorado and his chiefs, there could be but one reason for the departure: they believed they had driven the White Eyes away.

[7] Cremony, "Life Among the Apaches," pp. 68-69.

CHAPTER VII

THE WAY OF THE WHITE MAN

DURING the stay of the United States Boundary Commission at Santa Rita that summer of 1851, gold was discovered at Piños Altos, northwest of the Copper Mines. Men at once flocked thither and began to work the diggings. By the time Bartlett moved on, there was a settlement of one hundred and forty miners, and they remained behind, fully confident of their ability to maintain themselves even in the heart of the Apache country.

Their presence was a cause of keenest anxiety to the Apaches, particularly Mangus Colorado. The Red Sleeves had succeeded beyond all expectations in removing the Bartlett party, using—from an Apache viewpoint—most pacific means. He now turned his diplomatic talents to removing the miners.

By long hours of observation from cover, he became convinced of a puzzling truth. The strange white men labored and sweated among the sizzling rocks for nothing more important or usable than the yellow metal which the White Eyes called gold and which the Mexicans knew as *oro*. Since getting gold was their sole desire, his reasoning ran, the best way to induce them to leave the Apache country would be to show them where there was more gold than at Piños Altos.

It was good reasoning, but Mangus Colorado failed to

count upon the suspiciousness of the White Eyes. Pursuing his plan, he one day ventured near the mining camp and spoke to one of the miners. He had a smattering of Spanish and perhaps the miner knew a little Apache. At any rate he succeeded in making the white man understand that if he would accompany Mangus Colorado, he would be shown where there was much *oro* to be found— far more than could be scratched out of the rocks at Piños Altos.

The miner had no intention of trusting himself alone with this fierce savage. He put the Indian off with an excuse. Later, Mangus Colorado, still working under his great idea, approached a second miner with the same proposition.

It is quite probable that the Mimbreno was telling the truth. There was much gold in the section and it would not be strange that he knew where some of it was. But no Piños Altos miner would believe that an Apache would take so much interest in him, unless for the purpose of luring him out of the reach of friends and murdering him. And that idea stuck in their minds in spite of Mangus Colorado's patient, oft-reiterated explanation that he only wanted them to leave Piños Altos and go peacefully to the country of the Mexicans.

After a time one of the miners, probably drunk, suggested that they tie the chief up and whip him. It sounded like a capital idea; it appealed to the brutal frontier sense of humor. One kept the Apache in conversation. Others sneaked behind him. All at once a dozen men leaped on him. In spite of his bull strength he was borne to the ground.

Rawhide cords were lashed about the great wrists. The straining arms were spread-eagled on a tree and a brawny miner rolled up his sleeves as he picked up a blacksnake whip . . .

There is no record that Mangus Colorado winced or uttered a sound while the lash bit deeper and deeper into his flesh, cutting the skin of his back to ghastly ribbons, bringing the blood in streaming rivulets to trickle down his legs. He was no longer young, but an Apache knew how to bear agony without a sign. They finished at last. Then they released him and jeered at him as he staggered out of camp.

They could not have made a greater mistake. Better for the whole white population of the Southwest would it have been had they finished by killing him. Mangus Colorado stumbled forth from the Piños Altos settlement a changed man. In spite of Johnson's massacre at Santa Rita; in spite of Bartlett and the Mexican murderer; in spite of a score of other causes for action, he had tried to remain friendly with the White Eyes. But that whipping changed all that. He never forgot it. Deeper than the wounds on his lacerated back were the wounds in his heart. It was the greatest insult that could be inflicted even on an ordinary Indian. And Mangus Colorado was a great chief. He devoted the rest of his life to avenging his shame.

Thereafter Mangus Colorado wore a shirt to conceal the puckered weals. And each day he sought with savage concentration to wipe out the dishonor in blood. Never before had the Apaches seen a chief so single-purposed in destruction. Never before had they seen one who raided so incessantly, harrying the settlements in New Mexico and Arizona and even going out into the plains of Texas in search of ease for his scarred back. The White Eyes and Mexicans who died slowly, lingering out their mortal

hours in agony under the Apache torment, were many.[1]
And even more were those who died quickly, in the heat
of a rush, with lances running red.

THE AFFRONT TO COCHISE

Among all the Apache chiefs, Cochise, the snake-like
Chiricahua, was closest to Mangus Colorado's heart. The
Chiricahua Apaches lived to the west of the Mimbrenos
and shared with them the grazing lands between the
Warm Springs and the Chiricahua Mountains, a broad
stretch of fine pasture unequalled in all of Apacheria.
They were war partners of old with the Mimbrenos and,
in the old, good days before the Pinda Lick-o-yi descended on the desert country like grasshoppers for numbers and like lobo wolves for grimness, had shared often
with Mangus Colorado's people in the fierce, bloody raids
down into Mexico.

Mangus Colorado had bound to him by diplomacy or
fear all of the great Apache leaders. There was Gian-na-
tah, who led the Mescaleros in the flat, bitter alkali, east
country, and Piah, of the White Mountains, who dwelt to
the northwest, and Hash-kai-la of the Coyoteros, whose
land stretched north toward the cold Navajo plateaus,
and others. These men waited on Mangus Colorado's
word. But to Cochise only did the Red Sleeves give his
friendship. The great Mimbreno's comeliest daughter,
offspring of the lovely Mexican *señorita* for whom he had

[1] The following from Cremony ("Life Among the Apaches," p. 267) is a good
description of a typical piece of Mangus Colorado's work: A party of Mexicans
having been captured, "each man was seized, bound to the wheel of a wagon, head
downward, about eighteen inches from the ground, a fire made under them and
their brains roasted from their heads. The women and children were carried off
captive. . . . As I was the first to pass through Cooke's Canyon after this affair, the
full horror of the torture was rendered terribly distinct. The bursted heads, the
agonized contortions of the facial muscles among the dead, and the terrible destiny
certain to attend the living . . . were horribly depicted in my mind."

fought a double duel, was given to Cochise for wife. Often the two blew a cloud together in council.

At first Cochise hung back from warring against the White Eyes, although he had always been willing to foray into Mexico. But one day a thing occurred which made him as eager as was ever Mangus Colorado himself for the blood of the invaders.

Living on the Sonoita River was an Irishman named Johnny Ward [2] with his Mexican mistress and her son. The woman had been a prisoner among the Apaches and the boy was born while she was thus a captive, the father being an Apache warrior. After her rescue with the child, Ward gave her a home in his ranch shack.

One October day, in 1860, while the Irishman was away, a raiding band of Apaches rode up to the house, plundered it, and drove off a herd of cattle. They also carried away the child.[3] Ward returned to find the destruction wrought, and rode a horse "into the ground" to reach Fort Buchanan, twelve miles away, and get help.

Sixty men were promptly dispatched by the commandant of the post, Colonel Pitcairn Morrison, with orders to search for the missing cattle and child. Lieutenant George N. Bascom, fresh out of West Point, with all of a newly created shavetail's cockiness, commanded the detachment.

Through the heart of the Chiricahua Mountains slashes the deep and narrow Apache Pass, up which went the stage road. Best proof of the peacefulness of the Chiricahuas at this time is the fact that the stage line was in operation, without molestation, through the middle of their range. About half way up the pass was a stone stage station. The station keeper, a man named Wallace, was

---

[2] The name is also given as Wadsworth.
[3] This boy grew up among the Apaches. He is believed to be Mickey Free, who later became an interpreter and scout for the United States Army during the Geronimo days.

one of Cochise's friends and had contracted with the chief and his people to supply the wood for the station. To better furnish this wood, the Chiricahuas camped near, at some springs about six hundred yards away.

Bascom knew of the peaceful camp at the springs and headed straight that way. When he arrived with his troops, Wallace offered to go to Cochise's village and tell him why they had come. Presently the chief himself, accompanied by several of his people, came to Bascom's camp. The lieutenant was sure the missing cattle were in Cochise's village—on what evidence nobody knows. He opened his negotiations by ordering the chief to surrender the cattle and child, threatening him with military punishment unless he did so. Cochise seemed at a loss to know what cattle or what child Bascom meant. As for the soldier's threat, he treated that as a joke at first—he could not believe that the officer was serious in such an absurd declaration.[4]

Bascom was short tempered and grew furious. So sure was he that Cochise's band was guilty that he made a move which was dangerous, impolitic, even fatal. He ordered the arrest of Cochise and all his warriors, in spite of the fact that they had come into his camp under a flag of truce, and announced his intention of holding them as hostages for the return of the cattle and the boy.

Now for the first time Cochise realized that the officer was in earnest. The whole complexion of the affair changed from the jocular to the deadly serious.

Arrest Cochise? Not while he was able to fight. A war whoop like a panther's scream burst from his lips, and like a panther he leaped for freedom. So instantaneous was

[4] Brigadier General B. J. D. Irwin, writing of this incident in "The Infantry Journal," April, 1928, says that Cochise "scoffed at the idea of force being brought there to compel obedience on his part." This is perfect proof of Cochise's failure to understand Bascom's attitude.

his charge that the ranks of the soldiers failed to hold him. Right through them he dashed, with part of his warriors at his heels. A volley fired after him wounded him, but did not disable him. Five of the slowest braves were seized by the soldiers and imprisoned.

Wounded though he was, Cochise ran like a deer up the slope with the bullets spatting around him. His people rallied. A ragged volley broke out from the heights. Bascom began to realize that he had a serious battle on his hands. Heavier and heavier grew the Apache fire. Several soldiers were hit. The rest dove behind the rails of the mail corral from which they fought off the Indians until dark.

Late that night the Overland Mail coach from California struggled up to the corral. One horse had been left dead on the trail behind, the driver's leg was shattered by a bullet, and a passenger was shot through the chest. Apaches had attacked it down the pass. By a miracle the plucky driver succeeded in cutting the dead horse loose and getting the rest of the frightened animals to pull the stage up the pass. That was the last Overland coach to traverse Apache Pass in many long months.

There were several wounded men in the corral by this time. As night fell, a daring soldier volunteered to attempt to reach Fort Buchanan, which lay to the westward, with a message for help. He led a mule over the steep hillside of the canyon wall after dark, and actually succeeded in reaching the mail station at Dragoon Springs, from which he rode in safety to the post with news of Bascom's peril.

REPRISAL

Early next morning an Indian woman, who had been held prisoner overnight, was freed and told to inform

Cochise that the hostages held by the troops were to be taken to Fort Buchanan. A few minutes later the chief himself appeared with a white flag—whose protection he still seemed to trust—and asked for a conference. Accompanied by two soldiers and the stage employees, Wallace, Jordon and Lyons, Bascom went forward. The stage men could not believe that Cochise had really turned hostile. They knew him so well that they went along voluntarily to mediate. But it was a different Cochise they found. Gone was the friendly, quiet, affable Indian. In his place was a savage with a flint-rock face and a burning heart. Their friendly pleadings fell on deaf ears.

Suddenly a lookout on the roof of the station house signalled that some Indians were hiding in a ravine close behind Cochise. Bascom smelled treachery and began a retreat. At the movement the hidden Apaches leaped out and dashed forward to surround the party. Rifles crackled. Several bullets cut the young lieutenant's clothing, but he was unwounded. Wallace and his two companions had mingled with Cochise's party. They were seized and dragged away.

While this was taking place, Cochise's imprisoned warriors in the soldiers' camp made a bold attempt to escape. One slashed a slit in the tent which held them, and led the dash. But the guard was alert. A bullet laid one ducking, buck-jumping fugitive low. Another was knocked down and horribly transfixed to the ground by a bayonet. The rest were overpowered and bound.

Bascom and his two soldiers had reached the corral safely. The situation was desperate. There had been a heavy snowfall and all the nearer snow was gathered and melted to water the men and horses. But it lasted only a few hours. The springs were six hundred yards away. By the third day the stock was going crazy for water. Bascom divided the herd and sent a part to the springs, holding the rest at the corral. As the horses approached the springs, the Apaches pounced down upon them. There was a sharp roll of rifle fire and the guard fell back, carrying several wounded. The horses were in the hands of the Indians.

But help was on the way. When the first news reached Fort Buchanan, Captain B. J. D. Irwin volunteered to lead fifteen men to Bascom's relief. Colonel Morrison sent a courier to Fort Breckenridge, a hundred miles northwest, asking for two troops of cavalry to be sent to Apache Pass. Irwin started at once on his ride toward Bascom. As his small detachment approached the pass, it ran into a handful of Indians driving off some cattle. There was a sharp brush, the soldiers captured the cattle and took three warriors prisoners. Then they resumed their journey.

That night Cochise placed a cloud of braves at each end of the pass. A small train of five wagons, whose teamsters knew nothing of the sudden hostility of the Chiricahuas, blundered into the hands of the Apaches. Next day, when Irwin passed the place, he found the wagons burned and plundered. Lashed to their wheels were the charred remains of eight human bodies—the first victims of Cochise's reprisal. And the Indians had carried off into the mountains three prisoners from the same train, who were to be found later.

A stroke of uncanny good luck saved Irwin's party from the same ambush. After the herd of horses was captured from Bascom, part of Cochise's warriors drove the animals down the pass and out on the west side of the mountains. While they were running them toward the level country, the Indians saw a company of infantry on the march, changing station from Fort Breckenridge to Fort Bliss. The troops did not see the Indians, but the warriors followed the command, thinking it might be marching to the east side of the pass to attack Cochise from the rear. In doing so, they left the western entrance open for a few hours. During that brief period Irwin entered the pass, marched up it and reached Bascom with his reinforcements and the three Indian prisoners.

Stories vary as to what next took place. One account says that Cochise brought his trembling captives—the three stage attendants and the three men from the captured wagon train—to a place in full sight of the white camp and called out that he would exchange them for the warriors held in Bascom's camp. This is not mentioned in Irwin's story. In any case no exchange was made. A little later the two troops of cavalry arrived from Fort Breckenridge and Cochise withdrew to the high peaks.

Next day the soldiers left the pass. As they marched down it they noticed a flock of buzzards circling in the heights some distance to the right of the trail. Scouts were sent to investigate. At their approach more of the obscene birds flopped heavily up among the trees. And now the horrid feast upon which they had been gorging was seen. There were the remains of the six unfortunates Cochise had captured—Wallace, Lyons, Jordon and the wagon train men—tortured to death and left for the vultures.

Bascom and Irwin, at the insistence of the latter, immediately executed six of their prisoners on the same spot and left them hanging there for Cochise to cut down.[5]

[5] "It was then and there that it was determined to execute an equal number of Indian warriors confined at the mail station. The silly fabrication that a game of chance decided their fate is as absurd and groundless as the ridiculous assertion that I objected to their execution and wanted to take them to the post of Fort Buchanan. So far from having remonstrated against their merited punishment, it was I who suggested their summary execution, man for man. On Bascom's expressing reluctance to resort to the extreme measure proposed, I urged my right to dispose of the lives of the three prisoners captured by me, after which he then acceded to the retaliatory proposition and agreed that those prisoners and three of the hostages taken by him should be brought there and executed, which after full and deliberate consideration was accordingly done. . . . The punishment was an extreme mode of reprisal but was demanded and justified by the persistent acts of

One of the Apaches hanged was the warrior who had been stabbed in the stomach by a bayonet when he attempted to escape. In spite of the terrible nature of his wound, he was forced to walk a mile and a half to his place of execution.

The old Mosaic law had been obeyed. An eye had been demanded for an eye, and a tooth for a tooth. It was war to the knife now between Cochise and the white man. The Apaches never really ceased fighting for a quarter of a century after that. Thousands of lives and an inestimable amount of property were destroyed because of the treachery toward Mangus Colorado and Cochise.

---

treachery and the atrocious cruelties perpetrated by the most cowardly tribe of savages infesting the territory."—General B. J. D. Irwin's article, "The Apache Pass Fight," in the April, 1928, issue of "The Infantry Journal."

This article, written by General Irwin in 1887, was published posthumously. The general's contention that the hanging of the six prisoners was "merited punishment" is hard to follow. None of the six had anything to do with torturing the six white men. Three of them were imprisoned when they came to Bascom's camp under a flag of truce. The other three were captured out on the desert, in the fight over the stolen cattle. The names of four of the Apaches killed by Bascom and Irwin were later given by the Apaches as Sanza, Kla-de-tahe, Niyo-kahe and Gopi.

Chapter VIII

MANGUS COLORADO EVENS THE SCORE

THE CIVIL WAR BEGINS

When Beauregard's guns opened their thunderous bombardment of Fort Sumter, April 12th, 1861, they loosed consequences so far-reaching that people even so remote as the white frontiersmen of Arizona and New Mexico, and the Indians who lived in those territories, were affected.

Soon after the Civil War began the North was forced to abandon practically all the forts in Arizona and New Mexico. The Apaches took instant advantage of the circumstance. Believing they had driven the soldiers away, Mangus Colorado and Cochise, with the enthusiastic cooperation of all the other Apache leaders, systematically laid waste to the whole Southwest. The mines were abandoned, even the large workings at Tubac, and cities were deserted, until practically the only settlement remaining in Arizona was Tucson, whose population was reduced to two hundred persons living in daily fear of their lives. The Indians made a smoking desert out of a country as large as all of New England with New York State included.

The Confederacy was quick to invade southern New Mexico. A small army of Texans followed hard upon the heels of the retreating Union troops and occupied Fort Davis, in Texas, Fort Stanton, in New Mexico, and other posts. Fort Davis, built on Limpia Creek, Texas, in 1854, as a safeguard for the Chihuahua Trail, had always led a hectic existence. When Lieutenant Colonel Washington Sewell first came with his detachment of four hundred men to establish the fort, he had to fight his way into camp through an Apache ambush. Throughout its existence thereafter the fort was a constant center of seething trouble.

The Mescalero Apaches,[1] in whose country the fort was established, always resented its presence. Their chief was the famous Palanquito, but he died the year after Fort Davis was built, and his son, Gian-na-tah, known also to the Mexicans as Cadéte (Volunteer), succeeded him. There were numerous sub-chiefs, such as old Nicolas, notable for their energy and singleness of purpose when it came to slaughter. In the twenty years following its establishment, Fort Davis was attacked more often than any other post in the United States.[2]

Fort Davis was garrisoned by six companies of the 8th United States Infantry when the Civil War opened. Most of the officers of the regiment joined the South, and the enlisted men were forced to surrender to the 2nd Texas Confederate Mounted Rifles under Colonel John R. Baylor.[3]

The Mescalero country was now occupied by Confederates in gray instead of United States troops in blue, but the color of their uniforms failed to exempt them from the common hatred for all white men which the Apaches felt.

[1] The Mescalero Apaches ranged between the Rio Grande and the Pecos in New Mexico, and extended their country into the Staked Plains and southward into Coahuila, Mexico. (F. W. Hodge, "Handbook of American Indians," p. 846.)

[2] C. G. Raht, "Romance of Davis Mountains," p. 137.

[3] Colonel Baylor was later named governor of Arizona by President Jefferson Davis of the Confederate States of America and became a storm center when he made the initial suggestion of an "Extermination Policy" against all Apaches, a suggestion which lost him his position.

Gian-na-tah and his warriors killed every White Eye they met. The Texans found themselves in a hornets' nest. The Mescaleros literally wiped out the settlements along the Rio Bonita. Then they turned their attention with bloody effect to those along the Rio Grande. In large war parties the Apaches prowled through the Big Bend country of Texas. The white ranchers learned to look with what philosophy they could upon the loss of their live-stock, and the deaths of their families or friends.[4] The whole region was depopulated.

Within six miles of Fort Davis was the beautiful ranch of Don Manuel Musquiz, a wealthy Spaniard. Like most ranchers of his day, he had a number of peons, and these, with his family, made up a little settlement of approx-imately twenty persons. Because of the number of people at the ranch and its proximity to the fort, it was deemed safe from attack. But soon after the arrival of the Texas troops, while Don Manuel was on a business trip to Pre-sidio del Norte, a large Mescalero war party, led by old Nicolas, swooped down, killed three of Don Manuel's men, and drove off every one of his fat cattle.

Colonel Baylor ordered Lieutenant May, a dashing young Texan, to pursue. May had twelve mounted rifle-men and four civilians with him. Nobody knew the size of the Mescalero raiding party [5] so a messenger rode to Fort Stockton for reinforcements.

[4] To show the strange equanimity with which Indian depredations were viewed, the following quotation is given from a business letter, written by Pat Murphy, a storekeeper at Fort Davis, to John W. Spencer, at Presidio del Norte, December 29th, 1861. In the last paragraph, thrown in as if it were a matter of little interest or an ordinary event, is this statement: "Night before last, the Indians came to my corral and drove off a number of my cattle. A party of thirty-three men pursued them yesterday, hot on the trail, and I hope will be successful. Yours, P. Murphy."

[5] Raht ("Romance of the Davis Mountains," p. 146) says there were two hundred and fifty warriors in this party, but the writer questions whether such a number could have made a raid that close to the fort without being detected. Only one man survived after May's fight, a Mexican guide, and he probably estimated the number of Apaches through the eyes of fear.

War Department

Old Fort Bayard. The barracks are on the left. The continuous row of buildings on the right consists of the guard house, quartermaster's storeroom, commissary, administration building, and office and storeroom. Taken in 1877.

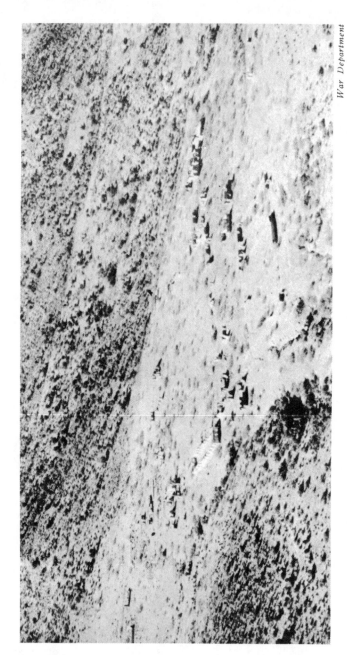

War Department

A typical stretch of Arizona scenery, with the ruins of old Fort Thomas in the foreground. This is an air photo made in 1924 by the U.S. Signal Corps.

Hot on the plain trail left by the large herd of cattle, galloped May and his men. The track led toward Mitre Peak, ten miles northwest of the present Alpine, Texas, then south toward Cathedral Peak, where it plunged down a canyon leading to the Rio Grande. Eager for distinction, the young lieutenant perhaps failed to read correctly from the signs the odds against him. But it is more likely that the wily Nicolas purposely kept his main body of warriors to one side of the cattle trail where the number of their ponies' tracks would not be noticed.

After a day's ride May caught up with the Apaches. As he spurred down the canyon he caught sight of a small band of Indians, perhaps a dozen or so, fleeing ahead. The men cheered and whipped their horses in pursuit. No attempt to fight was made by the red men, who seemed concerned only with escape. Closer and closer drew the Texans. They seemed about to catch the Apaches, but they could not quite close the last gap.

Then the roar of a volley from above awakened shattering echoes. White smoke fluffed out from the cliffs high on either side. Arrows glinted in the sunlight. Too late the white men saw that they were in a cunning trap laid by old Nicolas. The Indians they had been pursuing were a decoy. Before May's men could turn, their retreat was cut off by a swarm of vicious Mescaleros.

There, in the bottom of the gorge, ringed around by deadly enemies, the Texans fought it out, game to the last man. And one by one they died.

Only a Mexican guide escaped. As soon as the fight started this man dismounted and hid among the rocks. He found a cave in the canyon wall and lay in it for a night and a day. The Indians knew he was in the vicinity and hunted for him, but the saints were good. The Apaches failed to find him.

Next day Nicolas and his braves gave up the search for the Mexican and moved leisurely on with their booty. The guide walked to Presidio del Norte with news of the tragedy.

PIÑOS ALTOS AGAIN

Thus continued the war all over the desert country. The Chihuahua Trail was abandoned. Only the settlements of Presidio and El Paso remained in the Big Bend area. Presently conditions became even more tense for the few whites, because the Confederate troops were withdrawn for the fighting to the north. The Apaches roamed free, literal masters of all they surveyed.

They even carried out their long ambition of sacking Fort Davis. Nicolas again was the leader in this raid. There were eight persons in the post at the time, a stage agent named Diedrick Dutchover, four Americans, a Mexican woman and her two children. These took refuge on the flat roof of one of the adobe houses which had a small parapet around it. The Indians, not knowing of their presence, never thought of climbing to the roof of that particular house, and for two days as they looted the place and destroyed the post buildings, the eight persons crouched behind the low wall which alone hid them from their enemies. During this entire time the refugees existed on a sack of flour and two barrels of water. The third night, after the Indians left, Dutchover, the woman and her children, and three of the Americans began the ninety-two mile journey to Presidio on foot. The other American, too sick to move, was left behind and died at the fort. But the rest of the party eventually reached safety.

All this time Mangus Colorado and his Mimbrenos, aided by the Chiricahuas, Mogollons and Tonto Apaches, were indefatigably active, interspersing their constant destruction in the United States with frequent raids deep into Mexico.

Once the Red Sleeves paid his compliments to the Piños Altos mines, strong as they were. With two hundred warriors he suddenly descended upon the settlement early on the morning of September 27th, 1861. Had he struck twenty-four hours sooner, he might have carried the place, but, on the night before the attack, Captain Martin, with a detachment of Arizona Guards, arrived at the mines. The Apaches were outnumbered and after several hours fighting, drew off. As they retreated they attacked a government wagon train, coming out from Piños Altos toward the Mimbres River, and besieged it for fourteen hours. But the appearance of troops saved it.

These two checks were about the only ones suffered by the Apaches during the year, but since they touched his dearest hate, they disappointed Mangus Colorado bitterly. The Red Sleeves felt it was time now to extirpate the blot at Piños Altos. Too long had the miners scratched at the rocks in the valley. It was a plague spot in Apacheria. Mangus Colorado's great back smarted all over again every time he neared the place. Only the rubbing out of the settlement would bring easement to his scars.

The chief understood the serious nature of his task. The White Eyes at Piños Altos differed from the Mexicans at Santa Rita. Every Apache knew this. They had studied the habits of the miners at length and with deliberation. Above all they were interested in the white men's great efficiency with the rifles without which they never moved. It was well known that these men were very difficult to kill; and that even in dying they thought of only one thing—to take with them as many of their enemies as possible into the land of shadows.

So Mangus Colorado, considering the numbers of his own warriors, sent to his friend Cochise for help. But Cochise's word was that he could not come. He had troubles of his own.

Forgetting his own present problem, Mangus Colorado, with two hundred fighters at his back, rode to learn what was wrong with the Chiricahua. He found Cochise high in the fastnesses of his mountains, watching a towering dust cloud far out in the desert to the west. Instantly the Red Sleeves understood. And when he learned that the approaching dust cloud was made by many white soldiers, Mangus Colorado settled back on his haunches like a great beast. He would stay and have dealings with these white men.

And then, unexpectedly as come most of the desired things of life, the huge Mimbreno had his chance to scotch the Piños Altos miners after all. Word that a party of fourteen miners was rambling across the country toward Apache Pass was brought to him by his scouts. At that moment the Mimbrenos were waiting in that very cleft through the Chiricahua Mountains, for the soldiers advancing from the opposite direction.

The Red Sleeves knew that the keen eyes of the hard-rock men would be doubly sharpened when passing through such a patent Indian stronghold as the pass, and that to bring about their deaths would be costly to his people unless some unusual stratagem was employed. He was equal to the occasion.

Out on the plain, two miles from the foot of the mountains, was a ragged gully which ran right across the flats, cutting the trail to the pass. Here Mangus Colorado placed a party of warriors, instead of planting the ambush in the pass itself. The gulch could not be seen unless one came right upon it. From in front the entire terrain appeared open and unobstructed.

On came the miners. Suddenly the earth seemed to open before them. Half the party was downed by the first Apache volley. The rest fought with despairing bravery. But one swooping rush wiped out all of them.

The fourteen bodies, mutilated, pin-cushioned with arrows, were left where they lay, to be found days later by Captain Cremony's command, a bloody record on the ledger that Mangus Colorado had evened his long account with Piños Altos.

CHAPTER IX

THE FIGHT IN APACHE PASS

THE ATTACK ON THE CALIFORNIANS

THE detail of the miners having been attended to, Mangus Colorado turned with Cochise to meet the advance of the soldiers from the west.

Nobody knows exactly how many warriors the two chiefs commanded. Cremony's estimate was seven hundred [1] but that is probably extremely generous. There is no record, so far as the writer can find, of any Apache force of seven hundred braves ever being assembled for battle. The Chiricahuas may have been able to muster, at an outside figure, three hundred warriors. If to this number is added the two hundred Mimbrenos brought by Mangus Colorado, the total of five hundred is still probably somewhat greater than the number of Indians actually in the battle.

It was the advance guard of General J. H. Carleton's California Volunteers, marching east to fight for the Union in the Civil War, which was creating the dust cloud out to the west. Captain Thomas Roberts, 1st California Infantry, was in command of the force, which included three companies of infantry, a troop of cavalry under the Apaches' old acquaintance, Captain John C. Cremony, formerly of the Bartlett Boundary Commission, and two

---

[1] "Life Among the Apaches," p. 161.

howitzers—a total of about three hundred men and two cannon.

Roberts apparently never thought of danger, although he should have known that the way through the Apache Pass had long been closed to the stage route. He blundered into the canyon with his infantry, the howitzers, and a few troopers, as if he were marching through his own peaceful California hills. Without any particular precautions in the way of flankers or scouts, the command began the steep ascent of the pass, heading toward the springs and the abandoned stage station at the top of the divide. Two-thirds of the way up, the dread Apache yell echoed from canyon wall to canyon wall, and from both sides of the battlemented gorge, bullets and arrows rained down among the troops.

Roberts' position was impossible. His command was strung along, route marching, with no semblance of fighting formation. Well-nigh unassailable rocks, high up the mountain sides, were occupied by the Indians. The soldiers fought back courageously enough, but Roberts' order came just in time to save them from being cut to pieces. Back out of the pass they tumbled. The triumphant yells of the Apaches followed them.

The first attempt to go through the mountains had been repulsed, but not for long. Far up the pass lay the springs, the only available water supply. The Californians had to reach them or die of thirst. They had marched forty miles that day under the Arizona sun, over an alkaline desert, with their throats parched and their eyes blinded by the dust fog. It was forward or perish.

Bringing up his two howitzers, Roberts sent the infantry into the pass once more. This time they were in battle order. With the Apaches fighting like wild-cats, the Californians pushed forward until they reached the abandoned stage station [2] but the springs were still six hundred yards farther on.

Here the advance stopped. Mangus Colorado knew the importance of holding the water supply. On two steep peaks which commanded the springs, one to the east and the other to the south, he had posted strong parties of warriors. Rocks were piled for breastworks on the summits by the Apaches. There was no way to return effectively their fire from below. The soldiers were completely worn out by their long march and the hard fight.

It was a critical situation. The springs had to be carried. Roberts still had one trump card and now he played it. At his order, the howitzers were brought up. There was some bungling at first. One of the guns was so badly handled that it was overturned right under the heights where it was exposed to enemy riflery. The gunners scurried away from it.

Sergeant Mitchell, of the cavalry, and six of his men, ran forward under the Apache fire, righted the howitzer and brought it back down the hill to a position where it could be used. By some miracle nobody was wounded in performing this exploit.

And now the heavy reports of the cannon echoed ear-splittingly up and down the cliffs. For the first time the Apaches faced shell fire. To their astonishment and alarm, the missiles which landed among them exploded when they struck, scattering fragments in every direction, and adding the shock of their terrific detonations to the fear of death.

The artillery was too much. After a few minutes of shelling, the Indians began to retreat over the mountains.

[2] This was the very spot where Cochise was arrested the year before and where Bascom had his fight with the Apaches. Not a mile and a half away was the place where the six white men were tortured to death and the six Indians hung in retaliation.

Roberts found himself in possession of the springs, where, preparing for a still harder fight in the morning, he camped that night.

THE EXPLOIT OF PRIVATE JOHN TEAL

No one can predict what might have happened in Apache Pass the second day of the fight, had not an incident during the night changed the whole aspect of affairs.

Roberts, believing that some of the most dangerous fighting was still ahead, and expecting even fiercer resistance from the Indians in the morning, sent messengers back to Cremony, who was following with the supply train, warning him to protect himself. Then he inspected his camp, stationed sentries, and prepared for the morrow.

Early next morning the Californians' bugles sounded, and the men examined their weapons and grimly surveyed the heights before them. Presently the advance began. Indians were seen on the distant cliffs, but when the howitzers wheeled into action and sent a shell or two screeching in that direction, the red men disappeared. Roberts went on through the pass without further molestation. The Apache resistance had ended.

What happened between sunset and sunrise to change the Mimbrenos and Chiricahuas from fierce wolves to fleeing sheep? It is a story of the courage of a single man, coupled with strange good fortune—the kind of an incident upon which history often turns.

As we have seen, Roberts sent messengers back to warn Cremony the evening before. The small detachment of cavalry, led by Sergeants Mitchell and Maynard, was assigned to the perilous duty of going back down the pass.

Scarcely had these messengers left the command, when Mangus Colorado's scouts informed him of it. The chief wanted to cut off such messages, hoping to destroy Roberts' men in the morning, and fearing the coming of reinforcements. With fifty or more of his best-mounted warriors, he rode in pursuit.

It was a stern chase. The Apaches, some of whom had splendid horses, gained ground and after a time it became a running fight. Sergeant Maynard's right arm was shattered by a rifle ball. Two horses were killed, but the riders were pulled up behind their comrades and the flight continued.

Private John Teal's horse was lagging. He had fallen behind the main body two hundred yards or so, in spite of his rider's whip and spur. A dozen of the Indians on swiftest ponies had gained ground so that Teal was forced off toward the left, riding south at an angle with the line of his companions' flight. An Apache bullet brought his mount to the ground, shot through the body. The trooper was afoot, surrounded by his enemies. So completely outnumbered were Mitchell's men, that they were forced to ride on, leaving Teal to his fate.

There was no thought of escape in the soldier's mind. He only hoped to kill at least one Apache before they finished him. Crouching behind the carcass of his horse, he began shooting with his carbine, one of the newly issued breech-loaders. Because he could keep up a much more rapid fire than the old muzzle-loaders were capable of, the Apaches were disconcerted, and at first did not close in upon him.

Around him they galloped, at fairly long range, shooting and yelling. Their leader was a giant. Teal knew from his every movement that he was a chief of consequence, although he did not dream that it was the dreaded Mangus Colorado himself. He aimed at the giant with all possible care, however, and pulled the trigger.

To his delight, the huge warrior fell out of his saddle. The Apaches instantly seemed to lose interest in the fight. It had grown dark and Teal could hear the exclamations as the Indians gathered about their leader. After a time he could "hear their voices growing fainter in the distance," as he subsequently reported to Cremony.

For a long time Teal waited where he was. The Indians were certainly gone. He arose at last. It was eight miles to Cremony's camp, but the trooper was a thrifty soul. He took the saddle and bridle from his dead horse and walked the entire distance, carrying them. Not an Indian was seen on the way.[3]

. . . .

The panic of the Apaches at the wounding of their leader proved his high standing. No man stood higher. It was Mangus Colorado himself who received Teal's bullet in his body.

With wonderful care the warriors hurried south, carrying the chief, across the mountains and into Mexico. Fifty miles or so to the south of Santa Rita was the Presidio del Janos, a fortified post, with a village near by. Indifferent to the presence of the Mexican soldiers at the fort, the Mimbrenos bore their leader right into the town. Their dark figures occupied the streets. Mexican women and children cowered behind closed doors as they peered out in frightened awe at the harsh faces of the desert destroyers. A Mexican doctor was known to live in Janos. Straight to his door the Indians carried the great, limp body of their chief.

"You make Indian well," said the spokesman. "He no die, everybody live. He die, everybody in Janos die, too."

[3] Private John Teal's own story of this affair, and the events which succeeded it may be found in detail in Cremony's "Life Among the Apaches," pp. 158-160.

It is probable that no physician ever went about the practice of medicine with greater care than did this one. Upon his skill depended not only the life of the patient, but his own life and the lives of his family and all the people of Janos as well. Fortunately the rawhide constitution of the sufferer was in his favor. The bullet was extracted, the wound bound up, and great care lavished upon Mangus Colorado.

He lived.

After a time he was well enough to leave the *presidio*. But it was too late then to prevent the white man from passing through the mountains. Without Mangus Colorado the Apaches were nothing. And that is why on the second day of his advance through Apache Pass, Captain Roberts found it easy, without fighting, to do what he had been unable to do with the hardest kind of battling the day before.

IV.

EXTERMINATION
1862–1871

Chapter X

THE END OF MANGUS COLORADO

NORTHERN *versus* SOUTHERN ETHICS

APACHE tactics, which swept Arizona and New Mexico bare of civilized life during the early days of the Civil War, aroused bitterness in Union and Confederate officers alike. As they fought each other they found time to wish that the Indians would let them alone, and later they devoted their energies to fighting the desert nomads.

Independently both Confederate and Union leaders suggested a policy of extermination toward their common enemies. Late in 1862, Colonel John R. Baylor, appointed by Jefferson Davis governor of Arizona for the Confederacy, proposed that every Apache man, wherever found, should be killed on sight, and the women and children sold into slavery. This proposal was promptly and emphatically disapproved by President Davis, and an explanation demanded of its author.

In an attempt to justify his recommendation, Baylor wrote on December 29th to General J. B. Magruder, commanding the Confederate district of Texas, New Mexico and Arizona. He cited past cruelties of the Indians, their depredations and their untamable nature. He even included, as a ghastly exhibit, the scalp of a Miss Jackson, which had been taken by the Indians, and asked that it be sent to the President.

"Arizona has been kept in poverty by Indian depredations," he wrote. "Not a cow, sheep, or horse can be raised there now except by being herded day and night. As the Indians there live almost exclusively by stealing, depredations are a daily occurrence, and the people are kept poor from want of protection. Treaty after treaty has been made and broken, and the general belief among the people is that extermination of the grown Indians and making slaves of the children is the only remedy. This system has been practiced in New Mexico. There is not a family of wealth in that country but has Indian slaves derived from that source. In fact so popular is this system of civilizing the Indian that there have been several efforts made to pass a law in the New Mexican legislature, making all Indians slaves for life. It is a knowledge of this custom among the people of Arizona that to some extent induced me to give the order that has been the cause of complaint against me."

This letter, forwarded by Magruder to Jefferson Davis, was given by him to his secretary, J. A. Seddon, with the curt note:

"This letter requires attention. It is an avowal of an infamous crime and the assertion of what should not be true in relation to troops in Texas, &c. (Signed) J. D." [1]

Shortly afterward, G. W. Randolph, Secretary of War, ordered Magruder to revoke Baylor's authority to raise

[1] Other cogent arguments for this method of "civilizing" the Indians are contained in the following letter, written by M. H. McWillie, delegate to the Confederate Congress from Arizona, to President Davis, January 10th, 1863:

"With further reference to that clause in his (Baylor's) order directing the women and children to be sold into slavery, I can only say that it has been the unvarying custom of the country from the time of the Spanish colonists to the present day; and I cannot recollect a single instance wherein Indian captives have ever been set free by the people of that country. In Mexico the long-continued practice has acquired the force of law. The usage was recognized and guaranteed by a treaty between the United States and Mexico. From this custom originated the peonage system of New Spain and Mexico and that admixture of European and Indian races which for nearly three centuries has been slowly but gradually absorbing and civilizing the once powerful aboriginal tribes of Spanish America. Captive Indian women and children are reckoned in the same caste as peons, perform similar duties and are treated with moderation and humanity. This state of servitude, it would naturally seem, is infinitely preferable to the only other alternative of having them perish of starvation and exposure among the mountains and deserts." To his credit be it said, President Davis saw no more value to McWillie's arguments than those of Baylor.

troops for the Confederacy. The order was put into effect at once. Thus the Confederacy's high command dealt with the first attempt at an "Extermination Policy."

The North, however, was not so meticulous. Soon after General Carleton took over the command of the Southwest from General E. R. S. Canby, he instituted the very policy which the South had refused to sanction. There was no disapproval from Washington as there had been from Richmond.

With Colonel Kit Carson to help him, Carleton began a relentless war against the Apaches. Fort Stanton, recaptured by the Union, was Colonel Carson's post. He had five companies of New Mexican volunteers and instructions to campaign against the Mescalero Apaches and the Navajos. Captain William McCleave, with two California companies, was sent to hunt Indians toward the south, while Captain Roberts, the hero of the Apache Pass fight, marched with two more companies on a different route. The orders of command were the same: *"The men are to be slain whenever and wherever they can be found. The women and children may be taken prisoners, but, of course, they are not to be killed."*

The results of the extermination campaign were at first indecisive. The troops attacked a few Apache *rancherías*, burned a few *jacales*. There was some fighting of a haphazard character. Riding along a dry washout, a small detachment of soldiers would hear a spiteful volley, and a few of them would be down. Usually that would be the extent of it. By the time the troops were ready to return the fire, they would only see the dirty breech clouts of the Apaches fluttering among the rocks high up the mountain side and know there was no chance to overtake them. Sometimes there was a real battle. Then the carbines whanged, the bullets kicked up little puffs of dust and ricocheted, and now and again a tawny warrior, dressed in his soiled white garments, flopped and kicked among the scrabble. But most of the time it ended in flight—weary plodding through the burning sand; Apaches popping up from God knew where, blazing away, and then disappearing to God knew where again.

It was long before the extermination policy yielded its first-fruits.

DEATH COMES TO THE RED SLEEVES

Now the sands were running low for Mangus Colorado. He was more than seventy years old—very long for an Apache warrior to live—and age had taken from him some of his hardness. His giant size, his cunning, above all his implacable hatred distilled out of that day when he was spread-eagled and flogged by the miners at Piños Altos, had given him a prestige unequalled among his people. But he began to wish for peace in his old age.

The Red Sleeves had made a vast contribution to the history of his race. Cremony, who knew him better than any other white man, wrote of him: "He was the greatest and most talented Apache of the Nineteenth Century. . . . His sagacious counsels partook more of the character of wide and enlarged statesmanship than those of any other Indian of modern times. . . . He found means to collect and keep together, for weeks at a time, large bodies of savages, such as none of his predecessors could assemble and feed . . . and taught them to comprehend the value of unity and collective strength . . . Take him all in all, he exercised influence never equalled by any savage of our time." [2]

It was his old age and his eagerness for something

[2] "Life Among the Apaches," pp. 176-177.

Old Fort Apache, Arizona, as it looked in 1880.

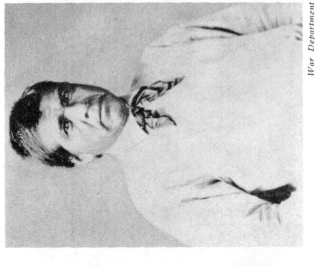

Left: Colonel John R. Baylor, Confederate governor of Arizona, who proposed for the first time the policy of extermination against the Apaches. Right: Eskimo-tzin, Aravaipa Apache chief, whose band was destroyed in the Camp Grant massacre.

which in his prime he would have scorned—peace with the White Eyes—which was Mangus Colorado's undoing. Early in January, 1863, Captain Joseph Walker, with a party of prospectors, was in central Arizona, looking for gold. This was in line with Carleton's policy, which was to encourage miners to come into the country so that the government would be forced to send additional troops to protect them, thus gradually crushing the Indians out.

While camping near Fort McLean, Walker's party learned that Mangus Colorado was not far away with a portion of his Mimbrenos. At the same time that this information was received, Captain E. D. Shirland, with a company of Californians, came into Walker's bivouac. Calling the officer to one side, the prospector suggested a plan to take the Mimbreno chief prisoner—a plan which would have made a Judas blush. Shirland, however, was no Judas. He agreed promptly.

Word that the *nan-tan* (chief) of the soldiers wished to see him was carried to the Red Sleeves by a Mexican. The great Apache eagerly accepted the invitation.[3] He was ready for a treaty.

Very soon he was on his way, accompanied by about fifteen warriors. He left his people over their own protest. There were many misgivings as he rode away. But Mangus Colorado believed he was doing the best thing for his band.

Riding up the trail, he saw a white man, Jack Swilling, a member of the Walker party, standing ahead of him and motioning for a conference. The gimlet eyes of the old Mimbreno must have detected the rustlings in the bushes

---

[3] This is according to the story of Geronimo who was a young warrior in the Mimbreno camp at the time. If it be true it shows a great change in the chief's spirit. A few years before, that Mexican messenger would have been flayed alive and bound on an ant hill to die in agony.

where Shirland's troops crouched in hiding, but he showed no sign of fear or suspicion as he went forward to talk with Swilling.

They conversed in Spanish. Then Mangus Colorado turned and spoke to his warriors in the Apache tongue, telling them to go back to their camp. Obediently they turned and trotted away down the trail.

Now the huge Indian came on into the camp alone with Swilling. He did so in good faith. He came of his own free will and alone. He believed he was protected by a truce, and that he would have a chance to discuss terms of peace with Shirland in safety.

Quickly he learned his mistake. When he was inescapably within the toils of the ambush, the concealed soldiers rose and surrounded him. As Mangus Colorado proceeded to Walker's camp, he was a prisoner and knew it.

That was the afternoon of January 17th, 1863. As soon as he heard the news that the Apache leader had been captured, Colonel J. R. West, in command at Fort McLean, rode to Walker's camp to see the prisoner. He arrived after dark. It was chilly and there was a big fire. Beside this Mangus Colorado had calmly stretched his huge form, wrapped in his blanket.

West walked up to the lounging giant and surveyed him from head to foot as he lay there. Then he ordered two guards with fixed bayonets to stand watch over the Apache. Before he left the campfire for his own tent, he inspected the two guards, Privates James Collyer and George Mead, and then gave them their final instructions for the night.

"Men," he rasped, "that old murderer has got away from every soldier command and has left a trail of blood five hundred miles on the old stage line. I want him dead or alive tomorrow morning; do you understand? *I want him dead.*" [4]

He tramped away. The soldiers glanced at each other, then at the prostrate prisoner. One of them began to stir the embers of the fire with his bayonet. Presently he allowed the point of the bayonet to remain in a bed of glowing coals. Now and then he took it out and looked at it.

Mangus Colorado, apparently dozing by the fire, seemed not to see the action. It is not probable, however, that any movement of the soldier escaped him. He must have clearly divined the guard's purpose.

When the bayonet became white hot, the soldier thrust it suddenly into the Apache's leg. Mangus Colorado leaped up. The reports of both the soldiers' rifles rang out simultaneously.

The Red Sleeves fell in a great, sprawling heap. Collyer and Mead came closer and emptied their revolvers into him.

By the time the sergeant of the guard arrived, the chief was dead.[5]

[4] This conversation was quoted by Clark B. Stocking, a California soldier, who was present and heard it. Frank C. Lockwood cites it. ("Pioneer Days in Arizona," p. 159.)

[5] In his report, Colonel West said that he left the old Indian under a guard to make sure that he should not escape and that he was killed at midnight "while trying to get away." A disgusting detail is that the dead man's head was severed from his body by a surgeon and the brain taken out and weighed. The head measured larger than that of Daniel Webster and the brain was of corresponding weight. The skull is said now to be in the Smithsonian Institution in Washington, D. C. We should hesitate long before we criticize the Indians for mutilating dead enemies.

CHAPTER XI

MURDER BY WHOLESALE

WHITE MAN'S WAR

THE murder of Mangus Colorado gave new impetus to
Carleton's campaign of extermination. Presently the dogged persistence of his troops began to obtain results.
Within two days of the Red Sleeves' death, Captain William McCleave fought the Mimbrenos near Piños Altos
and killed eleven of them. On January 20th, 1863, Captain Shirland, who had received credit for capturing Mangus Colorado, surprised an Indian *ranchería* and killed
nine Apaches besides wounding many more.

McCleave, now a major, with seventy-nine men, took
the trail of a band of Indians which had run off the post
herd of horses from Fort West. After he had exhausted
his men and practically worn out his horses, he reached
Canyon del Perro (Dog Canyon), on March 27th, 1863.
There he was suddenly rewarded. Quite to his own surprise, he located a *ranchería*, charged and completely destroyed it and killed twenty-five Indians. Only one soldier
was wounded. Later the Apaches attacked McCleave's
column, wounding Lieutenant French and one private
soldier. The troops charged up both sides of the canyon,
driving away the Indians and killing three.[1]

[1] The following from the military report of this battle gives an interesting side-
light: "As an illustration of the way in which our men are able to beat the Indians
at their own game in fighting, Corporal Charles E. Ellis crept up to a rock behind
which an Apache was hidden. When he got to this place, he coughed. As the
Apache raised his head, he (Ellis) shot him."

The Apaches were completely routed. A few days later this band appeared at Fort Stanton and begged for peace. They were Mescaleros and at their head was Gian-na-tah himself. To Colonel Carson the chief said:

"You are stronger than we. We have fought you so long as we had rifles and powder; but your weapons are better than ours. Give us weapons and turn us loose, we will fight you again; but we are worn out; we have no more heart; we have no provisions, no means to live; your troops are everywhere; our springs and water holes are either occupied or overlooked by your young men. You have driven us from our last and best stronghold and we have no more heart. Do with us as it may seem good to you, but do not forget that we are men and braves." [2]

A warrior speaking to a warrior. Carson had his orders, direct from Carleton: "The men are to be slain, whenever and wherever found. The women and children may be taken prisoners . . ." But the old scout and trapper had lived too long among the Indians. He was unable to look upon them as wild animals. To him they were human, and he took them under his protection. They were sent to a newly created reservation at the Bosque Redondo, on the Pecos River, in eastern New Mexico, and placed under the control of Captain Cremony, who also understood Indians. For a time the Mescaleros ceased to be a troublesome factor.

But there were other Apaches. Captain Walker's prospecting party, which had trapped Mangus Colorado, went on to interior Arizona where Pauline Weaver had discovered gold placers, and there the prospectors found large gold fields, which brought a rush of people into the country. Although this was the invasion of lands which had immemorially belonged to the Apaches, Carleton had no

[2] Dunn, "Massacres of the Mountains," pp. 383-384.

scruples against ejecting the red owners in favor of white interlopers.

He proposed to the Mexican governors of both Sonora and Chihuahua, that they cooperate in running down and killing all the Apaches in their joint provinces. The general further enlisted as scouts the miners in the gold and silver districts, and the friendly Pima, Maricopa and Papago Indians, all hereditary enemies of the Apaches.

Then began a huge man-hunt in Apacheria, with orders always the same: "Kill every Indian man capable of bearing arms and capture the women and children." From every direction moved the hunters, the military and civilian forces of two great nations. It is impossible to give even a list of encounters which took place. Six pages of fine type were required to enumerate them in the General Orders for 1865. The figures show that three hundred and sixty-three Indians were killed and one hundred and forty wounded; seven soldiers killed and twenty-five wounded; eighteen civilians killed and thirteen wounded. Much livestock was recaptured from the Indians.

And how were these results achieved? An example, the famous "Pinal Treaty" will show:

Colonel King S. Woolsey, aide to the governor of Arizona, started with a party of thirty Americans and fourteen Pima and Maricopa Indians, from the Pima villages on January 24th, 1864, to hunt for some livestock which had been stolen, supposedly by the hostile Indians. About sixty miles northeast of the villages, Woolsey's party saw smoke signals dotting upward from a mesa, and a little later observed Indians on the eminence.

Colonel Woolsey believed in subtleties. He devised a scheme on the spot by which he could avoid fighting and yet carry out General Carleton's wishes. One of the Pima scouts was sent forward to tell the Apaches, who proved to be Pinal Coyoteros, that the white man wanted to make peace with them and invited them to his camp.

Led by their chief, Par-a-mucka, a harsh-faced savage, the Apaches accepted the invitation and thirty-five of them came in. Par-a-mucka loftily demanded a place to sit. Woolsey silently handed him a folded blanket.

The colonel addressed the Indians through an interpreter, telling them that he would make a treaty with them and give them certificates of good conduct which no white man would ever question.

By this time Woolsey's followers had gathered closely about the sitting Apaches. The colonel himself gave the signal. Whipping out his pistol, he shot Par-a-mucka dead. In an instant every white man was shooting. Part of the Indians got away, some of them wounded. But nineteen bodies remained behind, mute witnesses to the dependability of the white man's promises.

THE AFFAIR AT CAMP GRANT

A little to the east of where Woolsey "signed" his treaty on the dead bodies of his conferees, another drama was taking place. The Aravaipa Apaches, under their chief, Eskimo-tzin, had been harried from one end of their country to another. Eskimo-tzin himself, a rim-rock Apache if there ever was one, had a gall-bitter hatred for everything white.

Throughout the dreadful sixties when Carleton's Indian-hunters pursued his people up and down the desert, Eskimo-tzin had managed to keep clear of the troops. He watched Carleton bring the Mescaleros under control and then subjugate the Navajos. Kit Carson performed the last-named feat. He marched with four hundred men through the depths of the Canyon de Chelly, the stronghold of the Navajos in northeast Arizona. He did not find much resistance. The soldiers laid waste the peach orchards, and the corn fields they found, rounded up the sheep and cattle, destroyed the villages and killed a score of Navajos. Then the Indians sued for peace and Carson sent them down to the Bosque Redondo, where they were to remain until 1878 when they were removed to their present reservation. Exit the Navajos from the arena of history.

Much time passed and the pressure of the army on the Apaches grew more severe each month. One by one Eskimo-tzin's sub-chiefs were killed. At last he himself saw that there was no longer any hope.

It was February, 1870, when five old Aravaipa squaws crept into Camp Grant and timidly asked to see a little child who had been captured from their band on the Salt River months before. The permission was granted. The old women received such good treatment that they returned to their people with gifts and with glowing descriptions of the white man's generosity. Even Eskimo-tzin was impressed. Perhaps, after all, he had not been well informed about the *Americanos.*

Presently, through the same squaws, Lieutenant Royal E. Whitman, in command at Camp Grant, began negotiations with the chief, the result of which was that the Aravaipa leader surrendered. By March 11th, more than three hundred Indians, among them the most dangerous of the Apaches, had come in to Camp Grant and were living there in peace.

Lieutenant Whitman understood Indians far better than most of his military associates and took deep interest in his wards. He found them terribly poverty-stricken, many being nearly naked and almost starved. Wisely humane, the officer looked about for some way to employ them, and hit upon a plan which was later used with much success at other posts—he set them to cutting hay for the fort, using their knives and bringing it in on their backs, and being paid for it at the rate of a few cents for each fifty pounds they delivered.

It was almost pitiful to see the joy of the Apaches at having something to do. They worked with a zest which within little more than two months produced nearly three hundred thousand pounds of hay, all of it cut with butcher knives and carried in on the Indians' backs. Under Whitman's policy the numbers of Apaches at Camp Grant gradually increased, until they totalled five hundred and ten.

Then, on April 1st, Captain Stanwood arrived at the post and took command. He approved of Whitman's methods, but he had been ordered to make a long scout through the southern part of Arizona, and for this he needed nearly all the soldiers at Camp Grant. Almost immediately he departed, leaving Whitman only fifty men to garrison the post.

Arizona in those days possessed some of the most precious scoundrels in the whole world. Driven out of California by the Vigilantes and flocking wherever mining camps promised easy pickings, a shifty population of gamblers, "road agents," [3] cattle "rustlers," [4] and loafers hung in a cloud about every lively town in the Territory. Tucson at this time was infested by some of the worst of these, and news that the bulk of the soldiers had left Camp Grant reached their ears almost at once. Within four days a mob of Americans, Mexicans and Papago Indians started toward the post with the expressed determination of killing the Apaches camped there.

---

[3] "Road agent" was the expressive western expression which included highway robbers of all types, particularly those which made a specialty of "standing up" stage coaches from mining towns for the gold shipments carried by them.

[4] "Rustlers" were cattle or horse thieves.

Captain Penn, at Fort Lowell, discovered the plot, and sent a warning to Whitman. But the messenger arrived too late. Whitman received the word on April 30th, and immediately sent instructions to the Apaches to come in closer to the post—they were then camped about five miles away. His messenger was back in an hour. The Apache camp was a mass of burning ruins, he reported to Whitman, and there were no living Indians in it, while the ground was strewn with dead and mutilated women and children.

AN APACHE OBJECT LESSON

To see his months of patient work brought to nothing was a terrible shock to the officer who had done so much for these people. He at once dispatched the post surgeon, Dr. C. E. Briesly, with a guard of twenty men, to see what could be done.

The surgeon, as he approached the camp site, could see the smoke from the burning dwellings. Then horrid scenes began to unfold themselves. Here and there, scattered about in the contortions of death, were the bodies of twenty-one women and children. Some were shot. Others were stabbed and their brains beaten out with stones. Two at least of the squaws had been first ravished, then killed. At one point an infant only ten months old was discovered, shot twice and one of its legs nearly hacked off from its tiny body.

"There was little for me to do," Dr. Briesly wrote in his report. "The work had been too thoroughly done."

The scene was deserted except for the dead; the mob from Tucson had departed, on the way back to the saloons and gambling houses which had spawned it.

Next morning Whitman sent a burial party to the place, and the work of interring the slaughtered unfortunates began.

"I thought the act of caring for their dead would be evidence to them of our sympathy at least," said the lieutenant sadly, "and the conjecture proved correct for while at the work many of them came to the spot and indulged in their expressions of grief, too wild and terrible to be described. That evening they began coming in from all directions, singly and in small parties, so changed in forty-eight hours as to hardly be recognizable, during which time they had neither eaten nor slept." [5]

Two wounded women were found and taken to the post. When the totals were summed up, it was discovered that eighty-five persons had been killed, of whom only eight were men. Twenty-nine children had been carried away into slavery. "Get them back for us; our little boys will grow up slaves, and our little girls," pleaded the Indians concerning the kidnaped children. "Our dead you cannot bring back to life but those that are living we gave to you and we look to you to get them back." [6]

Lieutenant Whitman did what he could. Two of the twenty-nine abducted children escaped and five were later recovered from Arizonans. But the other twenty-two were all sold into slavery in Mexico and were never again seen by their families.

And what of Eskimo-tzin? His eyes had been fully opened. As a climax to his woes, he and some of his people were shot at by troops on June 8th, under the mistaken notion that they were hostile. He fled to the mountains with the remnants of his band, crazed with grief, since he had lost two wives and five children in the massacre.

[5] Lieutenant Whitman's statement in Vincent Colyer's report, p. 32.
[6] *Ibid.*, p. 33.

During this flight an incident occurred which has been much and often quoted as proof of the lack of all human feelings in an Apache. But let the reader consider the background and then judge of the question for himself: A few miles out from Camp Grant, there dwelt an elderly trapper named Charles McKenny, who had often befriended Eskimo-tzin. For many years they had known each other, and even before his surrender, the Aravaipa chief had frequently been a guest at the white man's cabin. The trapper remained the one white friend Eskimo-tzin possessed.

On the day that he fled from the troops following the massacre, the Apaches' line of flight took the chief right past his friend's dwelling place. He stopped on the way and ate a meal with the trapper. When he had finished, he coldly raised his rifle and shot the white man dead. Then he continued his journey.

Years later he was asked by Sam Bowman, assistant chief of scouts under General George Crook, why he had performed such an extraordinary act of treachery. His reply gives one food for thought:

"I did it to teach my people that there must be no friendship between them and the white men. Anyone can kill an enemy, but it takes a strong man to kill a friend."

The Romans lauded Brutus who sent his sons, whom he loved, to the execution block to uphold the Roman law, because he thus set the example of placing Rome above all human considerations. Eskimo-tzin's act was not unlike that of Brutus in its final analysis. By it he cut himself off from all communication with the white man, and, as he believed, taught his people a lesson.

Not long afterward he was captured again. For three

years he worked hard in chains, before he was freed on the order of General O. O. Howard.[7]

And so the war of extermination progressed. But while many Apaches were killed, and for a time their activity decreased, it became more and more evident as time passed that the complete extermination of the Indians would take too long and was too expensive to be practical.

Life burned too deep in the Apache's body.

[7] Misfortune followed Eskimo-tzin to the last. By General Howard's order he and the seven or eight families remaining in his band were given a small piece of supposedly worthless land at San Carlos.

There he was visited in 1873 by Lieutenant Britton Davis, who commented on the great progress the Indians had made. At that time they had adobe houses, fenced fields, farm implements, good teams and cows. They dressed like Mexicans and resembled a prosperous Mexican community. Davis dined with Eskimo-tzin and particularly praised the cleanliness of the dining table and the excellence of the meal.

At this time all seemed well. Eskimo-tzin had apparently solved the problem of following the white man's road, but appearances often deceive. Somebody discovered, under this apparently worthless land, a vein of coal. Then a reservation lawyer found that the lines of the reservation had been inaccurately surveyed and finally it was proved that the farms of Eskimo-tzin were south of the reservation line.

And so the robbery of the red man progressed. Eskimo-tzin was removed from his farm, and his friends from their homes. All fixed improvements were turned over to white settlers, while the despairing Indians were marched to another dreary waste.

Shortly after this Eskimo-tzin died. His spirit could not survive this last blow.

V.

THE WAR IN THE LAVA BEDS
1871–1873

Chapter XII

WHEN THE MODOCS REBELLED

RED MASSACRE AND WHITE DUPLICITY

WHILE the troops in Arizona and New Mexico were fighting out their never-ending war with the Apaches, another episode was taking place far to the west, which for two years or more took the attention of the nation from the Southwestern theater and focussed it on truly spectacular events in northern California.

The first settlers who drove their high-pooped covered wagons over famed South Pass into Oregon found there a beautiful, tree-covered, smiling country, and also some of the deadliest enemies on the continent. These were the Modocs, a unique people, hunters and fishers, but primarily warriors. In one respect they resembled the Arabs of North Africa. They were fierce and predatory slave-drivers,[1]

---

[1] The slave traffic was so well organized in Oregon that it was recognized by the Hudson's Bay Company and even encouraged. The price of a slave ranged from five to fifteen blankets, according to Slocum, with the women valued higher than the men. If a slave died within six months of his purchase, the seller returned half the purchase price to the buyer. These slaves did menial work such as cutting wood, fishing, and digging camas roots for food. Employees of the Hudson's Bay Company generally owned two or three of these slaves each, which saved the company from employing an additional large number of workers in its operations. One chief, Casino, of the Klickitat tribe, was followed by a retinue of at least one hundred slaves wherever he moved. The fate of the slaves was often terrible. According to Hodge ("Handbook of American Indians," p. 598), they were often killed and buried under the corner posts of their huge houses by the Tlingits, while among the Makahs a chief's favorite slaves were buried with him when he died. Their masters had the power of life and death over them and sometimes killed them outright in moments of passion. Slaves could not hold property or have part in ceremonials. They married other slaves, or, occasionally when a free Indian married a slave woman, their children did not have the full rights of free people. Among the Tlingits at one time, one-third of the population was slaves. Not even Africa equals this record.

periodically raiding down into the desert regions of California and Nevada, where dwelt the miserable and degenerate Digger Indians. Sweeping out on the wastes, they rounded up the helpless natives, marched them north and sold them to the wealthy tribes such as the Klickitats, Tlingits and Haidas.

This haughty, fiercely independent tribe resented immediately the calm assumption of the white man that the beautiful land was his. Aided by their former enemies, the Umpquas, the Rogue River Indians, the Klamaths and the Pitt River Indians, they fought the paleface from the beginning. As early as July 14th, 1834, the Umpquas attacked a party of fourteen men sent to the coast by the trading firm of Smith, Jackson and Sublette and headed by the famous Jedediah Smith himself. Eleven of the trappers were killed. Smith and two others escaped and finally found refuge at the Hudson's Bay Company post of Fort Vancouver.[2] The following year the Rogue Rivers slew four out of a party of eight led by Daniel Miller, wounding the others. Frémont's Third Expedition was attacked by the Klamaths at Klamath Lake, in August, 1845. The Indians crept into camp and killed three men before Kit Carson's wilderness-trained ears heard their silent movements, warning him to leap to his feet and give the alarm which saved the rest of his party.

There were many other attacks. Major Phil Kearny fought a short campaign with the allied tribes in 1851, defeating them and taking about thirty prisoners. Shortly afterward the Rogue Rivers signed a peace treaty, which, however, was never ratified by the United States.

In the meantime the other tribes in the section kept on fighting. The war was climaxed in August, 1852. Led

[2] Leroy R. Hafen and W. J. Ghent, "Broken Hand," pp. 67-68.

by their chief, Old Schonchin, the Modocs attacked an emigrant train containing thirty-three persons and massacred everybody in it. A volunteer company of Californians under Captain Ben Wright, and one of Oregonians under Captain Ross, marched into the Modoc country. They saved another train from annihilation, by beating the Modocs off after they had surrounded the wagons for several hours. A dozen or more warriors were killed in this fight, in which eighteen white men lost their lives.

After that, with Ben Wright at the head of the combined forces, the volunteers scoured the country, trying to catch and punish the Indians. They found they had undertaken a task which they could hardly complete. For three months the Modocs played hide-and-seek with Wright and his men, and the white men were always "it." At last Wright fell back upon treachery of the blackest kind to accomplish what he could not accomplish by open warfare.

That November he sent a captured squaw to summon the Modocs to a feast, after which they were to talk peace. The Indians attended the council in good faith. They did not know that the food placed before them was poisoned with strychnine. Wright and his men watched them eat, but for some reason the poison did not take effect.[3] Finally, the Californian grew impatient. Drawing his revolver, he shot twice, killing two of his Indian guests. At the signal every white man opened fire. Thirty-six more Indians fell. Only ten escaped. And that murder was committed under the sacred symbol, a flag of truce.

As it chanced, Old Schonchin, due to illness, had not

[3] "Some say that the squaw got an inkling of what was going on and informed the warriors, who thereupon refused to eat. Others say that they ate, but the poison did not operate; that Wright used to swear afterwards over the way he had been imposed upon by the druggist."—Dunn, "Massacres of the Mountains," p. 193.

been able to attend the council. One of the ten who escaped was Schonchin John, his younger brother, who was destined to play an important part later in the Modoc War of the 'Seventies.

Whatever we may think of Wright's act [4] it broke the power of the Modocs. They never again were a threatening factor to settlement. By 1871 they were little more than a band of mendicants in their own land. They had been reduced to only a fraction of their former numbers. They were living in southern Oregon, on a miserable reservation, hectored and abused by the Klamaths, over whom they had formerly lorded it, and despised by the white settlers around them.

Yet in proof of the fact that the meanest of men can stand only so much and will then fight like tigers, these same ragged tramps gave the United States its most costly war, from the standpoint of losses and expense, when the number of enemies is considered.

AT LOST RIVER

When their treaty, signed in 1864, was not ratified for six years, the Modocs reached the end of their endurance. Grim Old Schonchin complained to Agent A. B. Meacham and the agent, a good friend to the Indians, consented to their removal to a new reservation in the Sprague River Valley. But conditions failed to improve. So tormented were the Modocs by white and Indian neighbors that they

---

[4] Wright's treachery, of course, should be condemned by every right-thinking person. But, as was the case when Colonel J. M. Chivington perpetrated his massacre of the Cheyennes at Sand Creek in 1864, the people of the section were so wrought up over the Indian troubles that they made him a popular hero. He was given a great ovation at Yreka, when he returned to California, and the California Legislature paid the volunteers for their services. Wright was given a position as an Indian agent. But retribution finally overtook him. Four years later when the Rogue Rivers again went on the war path, they killed him in his own agency.

Left: Captain Jack (Kientpoos), who was the leader of the Modocs during the war in the Lava Beds. Right: Scarface Charlie, Modoc warrior, who fired the first shot in the war.

Left: Hooker Jim, Modoc sub-chief and leader of the murderous element in the Modoc War. Right: Schonchin John and Captain Jack, chiefs of the Modoc Indians, photographed the day before they were executed.

could not harvest the crops and were on the verge of starvation. The agent consented to another move.

But a new power had arisen among the Modocs. Kientpoos, known to the whites as Captain Jack, refused to go on the new reservation. There was a display of power by the government and Old Schonchin, with the bulk of the tribe, submitted. Captain Jack, however, with his small group of bitter-enders, moved thirty miles up the Lost River to their old home near Tule Lake.

Their arrival was the signal for a general outcry from the settlers in the vicinity who visioned an immediate massacre. So much pressure was brought to bear that the situation came to the attention of the commander of the department, General E. R. S. Canby.[5]

Canby was a sincere friend to the red man. He had repeatedly forestalled moves against the Modocs, because he knew they were badly treated. He tried once more on this occasion to smooth matters out. But this time he failed. A new agent, F. B. Odeneal, now held the reins. The friction grew until it culminated in a formal request from Odeneal to Major John Green of the 1st Cavalry, commanding Fort Klamath, to put the Modocs on their reservation, "peaceably if you can, forcibly if you must." On the night of November 28th, 1872, Captain James Jackson, with twenty-eight soldiers and ten civilian vol-

---

[5] "Brigadier-General Edward R. S. Canby . . . began his career as a cadet at West Point in . . . 1835 . . . continuously served thirty-eight years, passing through all the grades to major general of volunteers and brigadier general of the regular army. He served . . . with marked distinction in the Florida and Mexican Wars, and the outbreak of the Civil War found him on duty in New Mexico, where . . . he remained in command and defended the country successfully. . . . Afterward, transferred east, he had the honor to capture Mobile. Since the close of the Civil War he had been repeatedly chosen for special command by reason of his superior knowledge of law and civil government, his known fidelity . . . and his chivalrous devotion to his profession, in which his success was perfect."— General Orders issued to the Army at the announcement of Canby's death, April 14th, 1873.

unteers, marched silently to the Modoc camp on Lost River.

Two years before Captain Jack had killed a Klamath medicine man. The chief's daughter was ill, and he, passionately fond of his children, summoned the medicine man to attend her. The shaman was highly renowned among his own people but in spite of his most solemn incantations, the girl died. Captain Jack showed little emotion when he was told she was dead. But he went into his hut, came out with his rifle, and without a word of explanation, shot the medicine man dead.

Captain Jackson was authorized to arrest the Modoc leader on a charge of murder based on this incident. Of course the murder charge was only a pretext and all the Indians knew it.

Jackson reached the Modoc village shortly after dawn of November 29th. The Indians were camped on both sides of the river, the larger band on the near side, and the rest, headed by Curley Headed Doctor and Hooker Jim, just opposite. Jackson approached the larger camp, while the ten civilians crossed the river and headed for the smaller one. The Indians came out of their huts and listened with astonishment to the white commander's order to surrender. Captain Jack remained inside his lodge.

Surprised though they were, the Modocs were not ready to comply. Among them was a particularly ferocious looking savage called Scarface Charley. His had been a sad and bitter experience with the whites. With his own eyes he had witnessed the lynching of his father.

Lieutenant F. A. Boutelle, with a squad of men, started toward the Indians at Jackson's order. With a harsh cry, Scarface Charley threw his rifle to his shoulder and fired. The soldiers halted, then returned a scattering volley. The Modoc War was on.

At Scarface Charley's shot, Captain Jack stepped out of his door for the first time, and calmly took command. Almost at the same moment the civilians across the river opened fire on Hooker Jim's village.

Short, sharp and fierce was the battle. Captain Jack had only fourteen warriors, who were hampered by the presence of their women and children. Hooker Jim had even fewer. But on his side of the river, the ten civilians were badly beaten. Three of them were killed and another wounded. The survivors were driven for refuge to Crawley's ranch which was near. On the opposite side of the river, Jackson's troops fired volley after volley into the smoke of the Modocs' guns, hitting several women and children. Sergeant Harris was killed in the fight and seven enlisted men wounded.

The Modocs retreated. With eight of his twenty-eight men disabled, Jackson could not pursue. He also retreated, ferried his wounded over to Crawley's ranch, and sent for help.

.   .   .   .

Near Tule Lake, in northern California, exists a peculiar geological freak, known as the Lava Beds. Some time during remote ages, a volcanic eruption spread hot lava over an area about fifty square miles in extent. The formation which resulted is thus described by Captain Lydecker of the United States Engineers, who surveyed and mapped it:

"The beds present the appearance on first view of an immense sagebrush plain, with no obstructions to easy movement in any direction. A closer examination, however, develops the fact that the plain is broken at irregular intervals by sections of low, rocky ridges. The ridges are not isolated, but occur in groups, and form a perfect network of obstructions, admirably adapted to a defense by an active enemy; they seldom rise to a height of ten feet above the bed, and are, as a rule, split open at the top, thus giving continuous cover along their crests."

To these Lava Beds, one of the most perfect natural fortifications to be found in the whole American continent, Captain Jack led his people. His band molested nobody on its march. Hooker Jim's people, who went in a separate division, killed every male settler they met—seventeen in all—but even they harmed no women.

In the northern end of the congealed mass of lava, near Tule Lake itself, the Indians established their camp in what are now known as the Modoc Caves. Captain Jack was soon joined by Hooker Jim and his braves, together with other warriors who came in, raising the Modoc leader's fighting force to fifty.

Meanwhile Lieutenant Colonel Frank Wheaton marched for the Lava Beds. He found the Modocs in a natural fort, almost as impregnable as the Hindenburg Line of World War fame, every inch of which they knew so well that they could traverse it blindfolded without being seen at any time by watchers from outside. Wheaton camped his four hundred soldiers and a battery of howitzers at the edge of the Lava Beds. The men were all well-armed and equipped, eager to attack and confident of victory.

The Modocs were equally confident. They boasted they could hold off a thousand soldiers. The boast was shouted to the white men when they arrived at the Lava Beds. It was laughed at then, but events proved it literally true.

WHEATON'S DEFEAT

Cold and foggy dawned the morning of January 17th. Wheaton believed that with the fog to mask his move-

ments he would have little difficulty in brushing the Indians out of their stronghold. He ordered three companies
of troops to attack. "If the Modocs will only make good
their boast to whip a thousand soldiers all will be satisfied," he had written airily two days before.

Joyous at the prospect of action, the soldiers started out
across the slag heaps. A stunning surprise awaited them
there. As they entered the Lava Beds, they were met by a
sudden deadly fire, which left numbers of them crumpled
among the rocks. Forward they went, but it was no brisk
charge such as they had anticipated. The razor edges of
the volcanic rocks, tortured into weird whorls and gullies
by the long-dead fires from the bowels of the earth, hampered them so that they moved forward at a bare walk.
All day they fought. They scrambled over seemingly im-
passable crevasses. They shot blindly and saw their comrades struck down at their sides by a continuous withering
fire which came from they knew not where. The fog, upon
which Wheaton had counted to hide their movements,
proved the Modocs' best friend. Throughout the whole
long day the soldiers never saw an Indian.

Forward they still stumbled. Their shoes were slashed
to ribbons by the sharp needles under their feet. Occasionally they saw a puff of smoke, but when, after half an
hour's creeping on bleeding knees, they reached the place,
the Modoc whose rifle had spoken there was gone. Bullets
whined constantly about their ears. They lost and lost,
without wounding a single enemy. The long day dragged
its course. At evening Wheaton ordered them to withdraw.

The men were utterly exhausted. They had lost thirty-
nine, nine of them dead. The wounded were carried out of
the Lava Beds but it was impossible to move the dead.
Even the unwounded were cut and bleeding from the dia-

bolic rocks. Practically a fourth of the battalion which began the battle was on the casualty list. Included in this number were three wounded officers, Captain Perry and Lieutenants Kyle and Roberts.

The Modocs had made good their boast, but Wheaton was not through. All the more he was determined to drive those Modocs out of the Lava Beds at any cost. A message was sent for reinforcements and his changed opinion and new respect for his enemy was revealed in the report he made with his request for help:

"In the opinion of any experienced officer of regulars or volunteers, one thousand men would be required to dislodge them from their almost impregnable position, and it must be done deliberately with a full use of mortars."

What a compliment was that report to the tattered handful of Indians with their muzzle-loading rifles and their few revolvers. It brought General Canby down to take command in person. As has been said, Canby's sense of fairness was never limited by the color of a man's skin. He knew that the poor, hectored handful of humanity now besieged had been shamefully treated and his first thought was that things might be adjusted peaceably.

A suspension of hostilities was ordered by the general on January 30th, to permit a peace commission to treat with the Indians. Nothing came of it. The Indians refused to meet where they would be in the power of the whites—they remembered too well the lesson Ben Wright had taught them. The whites equally cautious about going into the power of the Indians. So February passed without results.

In the meantime reinforcements had been brought up until between one thousand and twelve hundred troops were camped at the edge of the Lava Beds. Canby made one last effort for peace. He changed the personnel of the peace commission which had been composed of men not trusted by the Modocs, and included in it the following: Judge Roseborough, Reverend Eleazer Thomas, L. S. Dyer, and A. B. Meacham, the former agent of the Modocs. To this group the general added himself.

Negotiations dragged. Captain Jack showed a desire for peace. He sent a letter by his sister Mary to the commission on March 6th in which he said:

> "I am very sad. I want peace quick or let the soldiers come and make haste and fight. . . . Let everything be wiped out, washed out, and let there be no more blood. I have got a bad heart about these murders. . . . I want the soldiers to go away . . ." [6]

Canby knew that with the civil authorities to satisfy he could not accede to the request of the chief that the troops be moved away, until the leaders of Hooker Jim's band, —Curley Headed Doctor, Bogus Charley, Shacknasty Jim, and Hooker Jim—were surrendered to stand trial for their murders of settlers while on the march to the Lava Beds.

In the Indian camp an evil leaven was working. The proscribed leaders, of course, wished the war to continue. Well they knew that their shrift would be short if they surrendered. Captain Jack, who thus far had waged a war which was well within the limits of civilized rules, was torn between conflicting desires. His people demanded that he continue to fight. Yet he knew that peace was best for them. As the debate raged, tense scenes were enacted in the Lava Beds.[7] Finally the chief gave in. And when he

---

[6] Dunn, "Massacres of the Mountains," p. 562.

[7] It is said that Captain Jack's warriors finally put a woman's shawl on the chief and told him he was nothing but a squaw. This insult, coupled with his inability to agree upon anything with the commissioners, broke down his resolution. He threw the shawl to the ground and told his tormenters that if they wanted war they should have it—and he, Kientpoos, would not be the one to ask for peace.

submitted to the wishes of his tribe, he seemed to decide that he would stop at nothing.

General Canby was invited to enter the Lava Beds with his peace commission—unarmed of course—to treat with the Indians. Canby knew his danger, but resolved to risk it. On March 10th he and the commission entered the Lava Beds, to deal with Captain Jack and the Modocs in their stronghold.

Chapter XIII

THE TAKING OF THE LAVA BEDS

GENERAL CANBY'S MURDER

REPEATEDLY the peace commission appointed to treat with the Modoc Indians in the Lava Beds had been warned by well-wishing friends, that it stood in peril of death. Knowing that the warnings were not based on fancy, the members of the body nevertheless braved the danger to do their duty by the government and by the poor, desperate, badly advised savages who were cornered like wild beasts in the stony wastes.

On the morning that it started on its perilous mission, the treaty group contained the following persons:

General E. R. S. Canby, commander of the department and a proved friend of the Indians; Reverend Eleazer Thomas, a Methodist Episcopal minister who had devoted his life to them; A. B. Meacham, former Indian agent, famed for his just treatment of the Modocs; L. S. Dyer, another agent of character and standing; Riddle, an interpreter; and Winema, his Modoc wife, called Toby Riddle by the whites. With them, too, were Boston Charley and Bogus Charley, two of Captain Jack's warriors, who had gone to the soldiers' camp during the night to invite the commission out for the conference.

At the edge of the Lava Beds, in an open space near the foot of the bluff, a tent had been pitched. It was about half way between the army lines and the Modoc lines, and its location was level enough so that a horse could be ridden to it. Three of Canby's party were, therefore, mounted—Meacham, Dyer, and the woman, Toby Riddle. Captain Jack met the commissioners with five braves, Schonchin John, Black Jim, Hooker Jim, Ellen's Man and Shacknasty Jim, who were joined by Boston Charley and Bogus Charley at the council tent.[1]

It was observed that the Indians carried revolvers contrary to agreement—as a matter of fact, Meacham and Dyer also had derringers [2] in their pockets—but the consummately planned treachery was not suspected. Within fifty feet of the gully where the council was held were hidden twenty armed warriors, awaiting a signal to begin killing.

The parley opened. Canby's terms were that the Modocs should surrender the murderers and return to their reservation. Captain Jack, as before, insisted upon the removal of the soldiers and stoutly refused to give up his followers. He should have turned over those cowardly murderers without a moment's hesitation. The very men he thus defended were to be his eventual undoing. Hooker Jim's actions were insolent throughout. Several short speeches were made, the commissioners growing more and more nervous. Suddenly two Indians, named Barncho and Slolox, jumped forward from the ravine where the warriors were concealed, carrying three guns, while Steamboat

---

[1] The curious names of the Indians were not their native titles. They were named by the whites with whom they came into contact. Captain Jack was so called because of his fondness for brass buttons. Hooker Jim had worked for the Hooker family. Shacknasty Jim's shack was always in an unclean condition. Boston Charley was light in color, hence like the white men or "Boston People." Black Jim, on the other hand, was very dark. Scarface Charley had a deep, ugly, three-cornered scar on his right cheek which disfigured him. Schonchin John was the brother of Old Schonchin, the chief. And so on.

[2] A derringer was a small, single-shot, pocket pistol very popular at one time in the west. It was named after the American gunsmith who invented it.

Frank and another Modoc appeared from another direction.

Captain Jack gave the prearranged signal, *"At-we!"* (All ready)—and shot General Canby full through the face.

Instantly the hollow was filled with bounding Indians. Reverend Mr. Thomas was shot in the left breast by Bogus Charley. With the fear of death in his eyes, he staggered to his feet and ran, followed by two savages. A rifle shot stretched him dead within a few yards. Canby, horribly wounded by a ball which tore a ghastly hole under his left eye, fell but rose and tried to get away. Ellen's Man, one of the Modoc warriors, shot him and Captain Jack stooped over him to see if he was dead. The great-hearted general, friend of the men who were murdering him, groaned. At that feeble moan, Captain Jack plunged his knife again and again into the prostrate back, until Canby lay still and lifeless. Meacham was missed by the first bullet, although Schonchin John fired at less than four feet. The former agent whipped out his derringer and fired back, but missed. Then a second ball struck him in the head and he fell unconscious to the lava floor. Riddle, his ear burned by a rifle bullet, and Dyer, the agent, ran for their lives with Hooker Jim in pursuit. At about two hundred yards Dyer pulled out his derringer and pointed it at the Modoc. He did not fire, but Hooker Jim drew back and permitted the two to escape.

Only brave Toby Riddle, the Indian squaw, remained behind. Slolox, one of the warriors who had been hiding in the ravine, hit her across the back with his rifle, but Captain Jack harshly ordered her left alone. The Modocs were stripping the clothing from the dead. Boston Charley stooped and began to scalp Meacham.

"Soldiers! Soldiers!" It was Toby Riddle's voice. Boston Charley desisted and ran for cover. The shooting had been heard by soldiers at the army camp. Troops were actually coming at the double-quick, although Toby had not seen them when she called. The quick-witted woman used the ruse to save Meacham from being scalped.

As the troops approached, Scarface Charley, posted at the edge of the Lava Beds, shot down Lieutenant Sherwood. In spite of that the soldiers came right on. The Indians slipped away to their retreats like ghosts.

In the little hollow which was to have been dedicated to peace the ghastly wreckage of treachery was found. A few feet apart lay the bodies of General Canby and Reverend Mr. Thomas. Further on was Meacham, wounded five times and partly scalped. It seemed impossible that he should recover, but he finally did so. The dead and wounded were carried back to camp. Lieutenant Sherwood died three days later.

THE BEGINNING OF THE ATTACK

The army was crazy for revenge. But revenge, it was to find, was hard to obtain. Colonel Alvin Gillem, who took command at Canby's death, took prompt action. Mortars were brought up on March 14th, and all next day shells were thrown into the lava fields. A few Indians were killed.[8] Then the troops went through three days of fighting exactly like that experienced by Wheaton at the start of the war.

It was hard—terribly hard—but bull-dog tenacity finally had its effect. Captain Jack was forced at last to

---

[8] The chief damage was due to the Modocs' own curiosity. One of the shells failed to explode. The Indians gathered around and examined it. One tried to draw the fuse plug with his teeth. The shell exploded and blew the group into eternity. This was shortly before nightfall on the 16th.

withdraw to another part of the Lava Beds. On the morning of March 17th, three months after the fighting began, the soldiers entered the Modoc Caves, and found them deserted. A small Modoc rearguard fired a few derisive shots and disappeared. In the three days' attack the troops had lost eight men killed and seventeen wounded. They found the bodies of three warriors and eight squaws in the stronghold which had been so gallantly defended.

And where were the Indians now? It was six days before the Modocs were found—and when the soldiers found them they had cause to regret that they had done so. A party of Warm Springs Indians [4] headed by their interpreter, Donald McKay, reinforced the soldiers and took charge of the scouting. By this time the overconfidence of the soldiers had been converted to a respect which was almost fear.

Early on the morning of March 26th, Captain Evan Thomas, with eighty-five men, began a reconnaissance of the Lava Beds, to try to discover if mortar batteries could be taken far enough into them to shell the new Modoc stronghold which had been discovered just three days before.

Thomas marched toward a sand hill which he had marked near the center of the Lava Beds as a possible artillery emplacement. He was not hunting for Indians at all, but he found them. As the command halted for lunch at noon, a sudden, completely unlooked-for volley lashed into them from the ridges about. The soldiers found themselves in a valley of doom. On both sides lay the hidden Modocs, their bullets cutting the troops down.

[4] These Indians, from Warm Springs, Oregon, are not to be confused with the Warm Springs Indians of New Mexico. The Oregon Indians were excellent scouts, but were extremely religious. They absolutely refused to scout or fight on Sunday, which considerably impaired their effectiveness since the Modocs possessed no such scruples.

There was a panic. "We're surrounded!" was the cry. Commands were not heeded. Some of the men sneaked away and retreated to the main camp. The rest took refuge on the sand hill near them.

With a handful of soldiers, Lieutenant Wright advanced toward a ridge on the west. Lieutenant Cranston with five soldiers attempted to reach another ridge to the north. Every man in Cranston's detachment was killed. The rest of the troops, about thirty including the surviving officers, followed Wright within a few minutes. They could hear heavy firing. By the time they reached Wright the Indians had cut his platoon to pieces. As the main body came up to a hollow which he was supposed to occupy, it was greeted by another death-dealing Modoc fusillade.

About this time McKay and his Warm Springs Indians, who had been scouting far out ahead, slipped back and attempted to join the soldiers. But the fear-stricken troops, mistaking them for Modocs, began shooting at them. The scouts tried every possible device to show who they were. They even captured an escaping bugler and at the points of their rifles forced the craven to sound the whole gamut of bugle calls. Thomas' men could not understand. McKay's Indians had to remain concealed between two fires, until the fight was over. Miraculously not one of them was hit.

Only twenty men now remained with Thomas. The captain kept steadying the survivors. "We're surrounded, but we can die like brave men," he said over and over. Although they fought as best they could behind the volcanic rocks, the Modocs had them at their mercy. Thomas was killed. Lieutenant Howe also fell dead. Lieutenant Harris was already dying from a wound.

But help was coming at last. Major Green had heard

the firing and was rushing all available reinforcements to what was left of Thomas' command. The relief reached the battle ground late in the afternoon, in time to save the remnant. All that night they held the position, yet in spite of their watchfulness the snake-like Modocs crawled through the lines to scalp the dead and rob the bodies. In the morning the Indians were gone. The troops also retired, carrying their dead and wounded.

In that day's fighting, eighteen enlisted men had been killed and seventeen wounded. Captain Thomas was dead as were Lieutenants Cranston, Wright and Howe. The only other line officer, Lieutenant Harris, died in a few days, and Surgeon Semig, who heroically performed his duties without regard to flying bullets, suffered a shattered knee which necessitated the amputation of his leg.

The most astonishing thing about the affair, as the whites later learned, was that the Modocs had only twenty-one warriors in the fight. Not one of them was hit. With less than one-fourth of the total number of their enemies, they had inflicted a crushing blow, and had killed or wounded nearly twice their number of foes.

GENERAL DAVIS TAKES COMMAND

Within a few days General Jefferson C. Davis arrived at the Lava Beds to take command. He found the troops dispirited, half convinced that they could not whip the Modocs. The utter invisibility and silence of the Indians was fearsome. Davis spent days rebuilding the morale of his men. Then he went to work to squeeze out the Modocs.

Fortune favored him. Hooker Jim, who had been one of the leading advocates of war to the hilt, was tiring of it. Some time early in May he separated from Captain Jack. Davis drew his cordon tighter each day. Numerous skirmishes were fought. Finally Captain Jack resolved to leave the Lava Beds for the open country.

A pair of friendly Indian squaws first reported the departure. Soon afterward the news was confirmed by the Warm Springs scouts. Then came word that the Modocs had captured a supply train of four wagons outside of the Lava Beds near Tule Lake, wounding three of the escort. Major H. C. Hasbrouck, with two squadrons of cavalry and some Warm Springs Indians, rode in pursuit.

He camped the night of May 10th near Sorass Lake. At dawn the same fierce warriors who had so often defeated the white men charged down upon him. Captain Jack himself, clad in General Canby's uniform, led the rush. Behind him were thirty-three warriors.

Momentarily in confusion, the cavalry soon rallied and fought back. The first charge scattered the troopers' horses and pack mules, but Hasbrouck led a counter-attack which drove the Modocs from the adjacent hills. Most important, a pack train of twenty-four mules, carrying practically all the Indians' ammunition, was captured. And all this with the loss of but three killed and seven wounded on the white side. One Modoc was killed.

The Modocs, who had fought well together in victory, now began to find how much harder it is to stand defeat. After Hasbrouck's repulse of their attack, there was a violent quarrel between Captain Jack and Hooker Jim. The latter accused his leader of being tyrannical. All of the Indians concerned in the murders of the settlers during the march from Lost River to the Lava Beds at the start of the war, sided with Hooker Jim. The separation, already begun, became final. Hooker Jim, with the men whom Captain Jack had defended and in whose behalf he had committed the act of treachery which made him a marked man, went away, deserting their leader. There were thirteen warriors and sixty-two women and children in this band. The best part of the fighting men, however, thirty all told, with fifty-two women and children, remained staunchly with their chief. This separation occurred about May 15th.

As soon as the split in the Modoc band was discovered, Davis ordered pursuit. The trail of Hooker Jim's band was picked up by Hasbrouck, who overtook the Indians after a hard march of fifty miles. For seven miles the Modocs kept up a running battle before they scattered. Next day, May 22nd, all of Hooker Jim's followers came in and surrendered.

Where now was the resolution which the Indians had shown in the three months' heroic resistance under Captain Jack? Hooker Jim, Bogus Charley, Shacknasty Jim and Steamboat Frank, all involved in the murders which had caused Captain Jack to refuse Canby's peace terms because he did not wish to see them hanged, displayed overweening eagerness to be of service to the white man. One after another they suggested that they be allowed to go to Captain Jack's camp to secure his surrender. On Willow Creek, where the turncoats found the chief and his people, there was a stormy interview. Captain Jack was full of intense scorn.

"You are cowards and squaws," he hurled at them. "You got me into this war and now you desert me. Kientpoos will never surrender; he will die with his gun in his hand."

Back to the troops slunk Hooker Jim and his partners. The next day they were leading the soldiers to the hiding place of their fugitive leader—traitors to him and their people.

At 2 o'clock on the afternoon of May 29th, Hasbrouck's cavalry struck Captain Jack's camp. Rifles rattled briefly.

Then Boston Charley came out of the brush with his hands up. Seven women, including "Princess Mary," the chief's sister, were captured. The rest of the band escaped by running down a canyon where horses could not follow.

But the end was very near for Captain Jack. His band, harassed and pursued by the cavalry, was captured, one by one. The inevitable came at last. With but two faithful warriors and several women and children, the chief was surrounded a few miles above the mouth of Willow Creek, by Captain Perry's cavalry squadron on June 1st.

There was nothing to do but surrender—Captain Jack saw that. One of his two warriors was sent forward with a flag of truce, a white rag tied to a stick. He told Captain Perry that Kientpoos wished to give himself up. Perry consented.

A few more minutes and a solitary figure stepped from the woods. He gazed about him with an expression of utter hopelessness, then came forward and held out his hands for the manacles to be put upon them.

"My legs have given out," was all he said.

With him surrendered the last of the Modocs, two warriors, fifteen squaws and seven children.

CAPTAIN JACK'S EXECUTION

That ended the Modoc War but it did not complete the tragic drama. The Indians had dealt a stunning blow to the white man's prestige.[5] Examples must be made.

[5] The summary of losses in the Modoc War is as follows:

Whites	Killed	Wounded
Officers	8	5
Enlisted men	39	60
Civilians	16	—
Scouts	2	—
Settlers	17	18
	82	83
Indian (Men) killed	5	

Several women and children were also killed.

General Davis was for hanging the leaders out of hand, but was stopped by a telegram from Washington ordering their trial by a military commission. That body sat at Fort Klamath from July 5th to July 9th. And here occurred the crowning act of infamy on the part of Hooker Jim and his worthies—they turned state's evidence.

The Indians arraigned were Captain Jack, Schonchin John, Black Jim, Boston Charley, Barncho and Slolox. Ellen's Man was dead. Hooker Jim had bought immunity with his promise to testify. The prisoners were charged with the murders of General Canby and Reverend Thomas, in violation of the rules of war.

The trial was a travesty. The Modoc prisoners saw the men they had defended sitting with the tribunal as their accusers. They knew there was no mercy there. In spite of the fact that the trial was conducted with the utmost fairness, the verdict was a foregone conclusion. Little testimony was introduced by the Indians.

Captain Jack made one halting speech in his own defense. Not gifted with any natural eloquence, he tried to tell the commission about his early life.

"I have always lived like a white man and wanted to live so," he said. "I have always tried to live peaceably and never asked any man for anything . . . have never gone begging; what I have got I have always got with my own hands, honestly . . . I don't know how white people talk in such a place as this; but I will do the best I can."

Told by the Judge Advocate to "talk exactly as if you were at home, in council," he went on to say that the whole trouble was caused by Captain Jackson's attack; that his people feared treachery and fled. When he reached the place where he had given in to the demands of the murderers, he choked and could not finish—emotion strange for an Indian. Then he asked the court to adjourn until next day. The request was granted.

By the next day his full composure was restored. Captain Jack was every inch the warrior again. Short, sharp and pointed were his words. He pointed out that his accusers—the wretched, spineless tribesmen, who to save their own worthless lives had turned state's evidence and given their leader to the gallows—were the very men he had refused to surrender to the commission to be tried for murder.

That was all. It was inadequate. The prisoners were found guilty and sentenced to death.

At 10 o'clock on the morning of Friday, October 3rd, 1873, Captain Jack, Schonchin John, Boston Charley and Black Jim were hanged before the assembly of Klamaths and their own people. The sentences of Barncho and Slolox were commuted to life imprisonment on Alcatraz Island.

The four condemned men met their deaths with typical Indian stoicism. As he stepped out on the gallows platform, Captain Jack took one last, long, lingering look which swept far to the horizon of the country he loved and for which he had fought. His eyes descended from the hills and rivers of his beloved land to a high stockade at the foot of the gallows. In it he saw the faces of his people—penned up like cattle to see his execution. He must have seen his wives and children there, children he loved with the deep fervor of fatherhood, a fervor which induced him to kill the man who failed to save the life of one of his little ones.

Not a word did he speak, although there was much, very much, which clamored to be said. The treachery of Ben Wright still went unpunished. One of the men who stood with a noose about his neck beside the chief—Schonchin

John—could have told first-hand of that massacre. Other wrongs heaped upon the Modocs by the white man cried for utterance. Captain Jack was silent. His was not the gift of tongues.

The hoods were adjusted over their heads. At a signal the traps were sprung. There was an involuntary cry of horror, even from the spiteful onlooking Klamaths, as the men died.

The prestige of the white man was upheld.

But was it quite upheld?

VI.

NAN-TAN LUPAN
1871–1876

Chapter XIV

THE DEATH CAVE

COCHISE SURRENDERS

While the events described in the past two chapters were taking place in northern California, the Apache War, with varying fortunes, still swung back and forth in the South-western deserts. After a decade the celebrated "Extermination Policy" had failed. And when, in July, 1871, the government decided to try a policy of conciliation, the situation was very bad.

Cochise, chief of the Chiricahuas, was in particular a problem. In May, 1871, he ambushed and killed Lieutenant Howard B. Cushing, one of the ablest, most tireless, and most successful Indian fighters of Arizona.[1] In three years the young officer had led his 3rd Cavalry detachment over thousands of miles of desert mountains and desert country, fought scores of skirmishes, killed a number of Indians, and destroyed several *rancherías*, laying waste to the small fields planted by the squaws, wherever they were found.

But Cochise at last stopped his campaigns.

It was May 5th. With twenty-two men Cushing was

---

[1] Cushing came from a famous family. One of his brothers was renowned for his exploit in blowing up the Confederate ram "Albemarle" during the Civil War. Another died leading a charge at Gettysburg. Still another had a distinguished service record in the U. S. Navy. This member of the family was typical of the lot. His relentlessness in fighting Apaches was due to the death at their hands of a close friend, Lieutenant Franklin Yeaton, in the fall of 1869. Cushing brooded over this and was positively ferocious in his pursuit of the Indians.

following like a blood-sleuth on the trail of Cochise. The track led toward the Bear Springs in the Whetstone Mountains. There lay Cochise, the serpent-like. In spite of all his experience, Cushing ran right into the trap, laid along the sides of a canyon leading to the springs.

Before a shot was fired, the whites were surrounded. Sergeant John Mott, a veteran Indian fighter, first detected the presence of the Apaches and called Cushing's attention to it. The warning came too late. At the first tearing volley from the bushes, Cushing dropped, a bullet through his body. Down the sides of the gorge bounded the Apaches. It was hand to hand. Mott finally extricated a few survivors from the canyon, but he left behind the bodies of the lieutenant and several men. Days later troops from Fort Crittenden found the mangled corpses. By then Cochise and his warriors were safely across the international boundary in Mexico.

On July 21st, 1871, President Grant appointed Vincent Colyer his personal representative in Arizona and sent him to the Southwest with plenary powers to "locate the nomadic tribes upon suitable territories, and bring them under control of the proper officers of the Indian Department." [2] Colyer knew the President's kindly attitude toward the Indians. He worked hard, trying to conciliate them and actually succeeded in bringing about friendly relations with some. But the Camp Grant massacre, the Pinal treaty, and the Extermination Policy were too fresh in the minds of most Apaches to permit them to listen to white promises of peace. [3] Had Colyer gone to

[2] Order of authorization from the War Department, July 21, 1871.

[3] "This report shows plainly that . . . the Apache Indians were the friends of the Americans when they first knew them; that they have always desired peace with them . . . the peaceable relations continued until the Americans adopted the Mexican theory of 'extermination,' and by acts of inhuman treachery and cruelty made them (the Apaches) our implacable foes; that this policy has resulted in a war which, in the last ten years, has cost us a thousand lives and over forty

Arizona ten years earlier, he might have had much greater success.

Most important of the chiefs who quit the war path under Colyer's policy was Cochise himself. After some negotiations, he met a peace commission headed by General Gordon Granger at the Cañada Alamosa, early in September. The great Apache appeared with his warriors around him. Apparently he at first suspected treachery, but he finally joined the council circle and blew a cloud of smoke with General Granger. The conversation was in Spanish.

Granger told the chief he must stop raiding, expressed the President's great desire for peace, and ended by offering the mountains and valleys in which they were then conferring as an all-time reservation for the Chiricahuas. It was part of their favorite country, and the terms were acceptable to Cochise. Dr. A. N. Ellis, who was present, thus describes him as he looked that day:

"While he was talking we had a fine opportunity to study this most remarkable man. Evidently he was about fifty-eight years of age, although he looked very much younger; his height, five feet, ten inches; in person lithe and wiry, every muscle being well rounded and firm. A silver thread was now and then visible in his otherwise black hair, which he wore cut straight around his head about on a level with his chin. His countenance displayed great force." [4]

Cochise's speech was a striking example of Indian oratory and logic. The essential sadness of the red man and his perplexity in facing the unsolvable problem presented by the white encroachment were all included. Toward its conclusion he said:

---

millions of dollars, and the country is no quieter nor the Indians any nearer extermination than they were at the time of the Gadsden purchase."—Report to the Board of Indian Commissioners on Peace with the Apaches, made by Vincent Colyer, 1871.

[4] Kansas Historical Society Collections, Vol. XIII, p. 391.

"When I was young I walked all over this country, east and west, and saw no other people than the Apaches. After many summers I walked again and found another race of people who had come to take it. How is it? Why is it that the Apaches want to die—that they carry their lives on their finger nails? They roam over the hills and plains and want the heavens to fall on them. The Apaches were once a great nation; they are now but a few. . . . Many have been killed in battle. . . . Tell me, if the Virgin Mary has walked throughout all the land, why has she never entered the lodge of the Apache?" [5]

He ended his extraordinary address by saying firmly that he would never go to the Tularosa reservation in New Mexico.

"That is a long ways off," he said. "The flies in those mountains eat out the eyes of the horses. The bad spirits live there. I have drunk of these waters. . . . I do not want to leave here."

In spite of the specific promise made by General Granger, Cochise was ordered within a few months to take his people to the hated Tularosa reservation. The Chiricahuas went into galvanic action. Cochise took to the mountains and war flared all over the Southwest. Less than half of the sixteen hundred Apaches at Cañada Alamosa travelled to Tularosa. The rest followed Cochise. And even those who did go had to be transferred soon to Ojo Caliente, New Mexico.[6] In exactly a year, September 1st, 1871, to the same date in 1872, the Apaches made fifty-four separate attacks, killed forty-four persons, wounded sixteen, and ran off much livestock. The white man's inability to keep his promises was reaping its usual harvest.

[5] The full text of this speech is well worth reading. It is quoted by Dr. Ellis in his article in the Kansas Historical Society Collections, Vol. XIII, pp. 387-92.
[6] This occurred in 1874.

Rose Collection

Three of the condemned Modoc leaders, taken just before they were hanged on Friday, October 3rd, 1873. Left to right they are: Black Jim, Captain Jack, and Boston Charley.

General George Crook, Nantan Lupan (Chief Gray Wolf) to the Apaches, taken while he was commander of the Department of Arizona.

War Department   *War Department*

Left: General E. R. S. Canby, killed in the peace commission massacre by the Modoc Indians. Right: General Jeff Davis, the final conqueror of the Modocs.

THE TONTO BASIN

General George Crook, known to the Indians as Nantan Lupan (Chief Gray Wolf), took command in Arizona in July, 1871. He was an experienced Indian fighter and knew the red men thoroughly. His attitude toward the Apaches was refreshingly different from that of his predecessors. Said he: "I think the Apache is painted in darker colors than he deserves and that his villainies arise more from a misconception of facts than from his being worse than other Indians. Living in a country the natural products of which will not support him, he has either to cultivate the soil or steal, and as our vacillating policy satisfies him that we are afraid of him, he chooses the latter, also as requiring less labor and being more congenial to his natural instincts." [7]

Crook's first act was to call the troops of his department together for an inspection and practice march. When he assembled them there were just five troops of cavalry and one of scouts. The general had planned an immediate move against the hostile Apaches, but Vincent Colyer was then in Arizona, with powers from the President which exceeded those of the army. Crook marked time while long conferences took place and nothing was accomplished. The general took advantage of this delay to reorganize his forces for hard campaigning.

Lieutenant Cushing had employed friendly Apaches as scouts against their hostile relatives to some extent, but Crook amplified and worked out this branch of the service in a manner never before conceived. In its ranks he put Navajos, Apaches, Opatas, Pimas, Yaquis, Pueblos, Mexicans, Americans and half-breeds of all kinds and pedigrees. This corps was to prove tremendously effective in the

[7] Annual Report of the Secretary of War, 1871, p. 78.

months to come. Skillful as he was it is doubtful if Crook could have accomplished much without his scouts. There were hatreds among the Apaches and after the days of Mangus Colorado they never presented a united front to the white man. This was taken advantage of by Crook.

The general also reorganized the pack train service to the highest state of efficiency it had ever known. He knew mules and he knew packing and he insisted on the utmost efficiency from his men. As a result of his care in this department the pack trains of his troops gave the finest service in the entire army.[8] By the time Colyer's policy late in 1871 had been proved impractical, Crook was ready to strike.

Well to the north in Arizona is the famed Tonto Basin. It is really a mountain plateau, surrounded on all sides by the high ranges of the Mogollons, the Mazatals and the Sierra Ancha, heavily timbered and snowy topped. Into this area, then comparatively little known, many of the hostile Apaches had retreated.

After Colyer had been given every chance to try persuasion and had given up his project, Crook announced in September, 1872, the new policy of "proceeding at once to punish the incorrigibly hostile." He knew that there were Tontos, Coyoteros, Yampais and Hualapais in the Tonto Basin, and that they were led by various daring chiefs, such as Del-she, Chuntz, Nata-totel, and Naquinaquis.

[8] On one occasion a packer who had never seen Crook was visited by the general, who was in the habit of personal inspections. The packer saw an individual dressed in the ordinary manner, who looked able bodied, and the following conversation ensued: Packer—"Say, mister, do you understand packing mules?" General Crook —"I think I do." Packer—"Have you had any experience in that line?" General Crook—"Well, considerable, here and there." Packer—"I'll give you forty dollars a month and grub to help us in this campaign." General Crook—"I'm much obliged for the offer, but I already have a job." Packer—"Is that so? What kind of a job is it?" General Crook—"Well, my friend, I am at present commander of this department."

For several reasons he set November 15th as time to start the campaign. It marked the beginning of winter, making it harder for the enemy to climb into the higher mountains because of the snow; causing the Indians to be unwilling to move if they could avoid it; and making campfires necessary, with resultant smoke which could be spotted by the keen eyes of Crook's scouts.

Promptly on the day, Crook started. The troops marched on plateaus where cold weather had already set in so hard that all the springs and small streams were frozen solid, making it difficult to water stock. Each morning the sleeping soldiers were aroused at 2 o'clock. By 4 the whole command was on the march and they did not halt until late in the afternoon.

Crook's plan was to sweep the Tonto Basin clean of hostile Indians by sending out several converging columns, each self-sufficient, but all cooperating in a central scheme. The orders were simple: The Indians were to be induced to surrender wherever possible; where they would not surrender, they were to be hit hard and hunted down until the last one in hostility was killed or captured; every effort should be made to avoid the killing of women and children; no excuse was to be accepted for leaving a trail; if horses played out, the enemy was to be followed on foot.

The Tonto Apaches were among the most dangerous of the Indians in the basin, and Crook especially wished to find the *rancheria* of Chief Chuntz, a fierce and tireless raider. This particular task was assigned to Major William H. Brown and his battalion of the 5th Cavalry. Somewhere Crook had found a young Apache called Nantahe, who had been a member of Chuntz' band and knew his favorite lairs. The general sent this scout with Brown. As events transpired, Nantahe was destined to be the decisive factor in the success of this expedition.

In addition to Nantahe, there were forty Apache and
a hundred Pima scouts, the latter deadly hereditary enemies of the Apaches, under their crafty, daring chief Bocon
(Big Mouth). All told, including the scouts, Brown had
three hundred and twenty fighting men, with whom he set
out to capture a band—as it was later learned—of ninety-
four men, women and children.

THE FIGHT IN THE SALT RIVER CANYON

Brown's men spent Christmas day on the march, cold,
pinched and tired. On the night after Christmas, December 26th, the command began to ascend on foot the rugged
gorge of the Salt River Canyon in the Mazatal Mountains.
The night was exceptionally frosty and the men, who had
left all unnecessary baggage and clothing behind them,
climbed fast to keep their blood circulating. After a time
a whispered command was passed back to lie down and
remain silent. Far up ahead the Indian scouts had dis-
cerned the flickering of distant campfires. The scouts returned shortly with word that the fires were at an abandoned camp, where they also found fifteen foot-sore
horses, recently stolen from the Pima villages on the Gila
and abandoned as useless.

Again the advance began. Every precaution was taken
to avoid making a noise.[9] Toward morning of December
27th, one of the scouts, ranging far ahead, smelled smoke.

---

[9] To illustrate the wonderful perceptive powers of these Indians, during the
march up the canyon, in blackest night, Nantahe suddenly threw both arms around
Major Brown and stopped him from stepping forward. The Apache's moccasined
foot had fallen on a depression in the trail and although he could not see it, he
knew it was a footprint. With his fellow scouts holding blankets over him to
screen the light from any possible watchers up the trail, Nantahe lay down, lit a
match, and inspected the sign. In a moment he was up again, grinning in the dark.
It was not a human track but a bear track, very similar in size and shape. The wonderful thing about the incident is that the Indian, although he could not see a foot
ahead of him, could tell in an instant that he had stepped into a track which was
like a human footprint.

No Apache, knowing an enemy was on his trail, would have been guilty of so colossal a breach of woodcraft as to kindle a fire. But these Indians did not dream of the proximity of their pursuers. The keen nostrils of the scout —sensitive almost as those of a blooded hound—caught the tell-tale taint while the command was still a mile away. Nantahe now took charge of the troops' movements.

They were within a few minutes' climb of a cave where Chuntz' band often camped. Nantahe asked Major Brown to send a detachment of picked men with him to climb over the precipice up the canyon and head off escape from above. The officer whispered his instructions. Within an hour every man was in his place.

Lieutenant William J. Ross led the men who went over the precipice. And it was he who opened the battle. Creeping to where he could see, Ross descried in plain view a large rock shed, in which were many Apaches engaged in their early morning activities. The sun had just risen and he could see women cooking, children playing about, and men smoking. On a sort of shelf in front of the cave a party of returned raiders was dancing. So peaceful was the scene that it required an effort of mind to realize that here was as bloody a band of savages as the world contained.

By now the unsuspecting Apaches were all "bottled up". Ross' men chose the warriors as their targets and the lieutenant gave the order to fire. The crashing volley, which re-echoed a dozen times from the canyon walls, was the first intimation the Indians had that danger was near. Six of them, killed instantly, never knew what enemy had fired.

It was wonderful how quickly and smoothly the Apache mind worked in a crisis. Without stopping to take a look in the direction of the shooting, warriors, women and children sprang for the one haven of safety—the cave, which had a natural parapet of boulders along its front. Not a moment's hesitation, not a bit of confusion, but before the troopers could fire a second volley, the face of the cliff was vacant except for six huddled heaps of rags and gaudy finery which represented the corpses of six men who had a moment before been full of life.

Now Nantahe, calling out in the Tonto tongue, shouted across the canyon a summons to the Indians to surrender. A yell of defiance was the reply. With the first shots sputtering out the battle began.

Brown's experienced eye saw at once that a direct charge and an attempt to scale the parapet would be too costly. The rock wall was at least ten feet high at its lowest point and smooth and slippery as well. The Apaches could have clubbed the climbing soldiers as they mounted, even had the Indians not possessed modern firearms with which to shoot them.

Assault was out of the question. Attrition seemed the better plan. At vantage points on the wall of the canyon opposite the cave, Brown placed picked sharpshooters. A first line of battle was arranged, in a sort of half moon, with flanks resting on the canyon's rocky walls, about fifty yards from the Indian position. Back of this line were more marksmen, carbines ready, watching to prevent the escape of a single warrior.

The men in the first line could not reach the Apaches by direct fire. Brown directed them to aim against the granite roof of the cave so that the bullets would glance down among the Indians massed behind the rampart. It was like shooting with the eyes shut, but the men opened fire with enthusiasm and results were soon apparent. The Apaches, goaded into desperation by the glancing bullets, began to return the soldiers' fire. Squaws loaded the warriors' guns. Now and then a baby's wail or a woman's cry showed that the leaden hail was taking effect on others besides men behind the bloody rampart.

After thirty minutes of continuous firing, Brown gave the order to cease. Again the Apaches were offered a chance to surrender or let their women and children come out unharmed. In the silence which followed, a peculiar chanting sounded from the cave. Nantahe listened intently. "Look out! That's their death song; they're going to charge!" he cried sharply.

At the words, twenty almost naked brown figures catapulted over the rampart, their hair bound back from their faces by red turbans, their bodies splashed with war paint. They came shooting. Half stood upright on the rocky wall and blazed away at the soldiers below as rapidly as they could work the levers on their guns. The others went bounding like catamounts down the slope toward the right flank. For a moment it looked as if they might break through. But the troopers flung themselves into a hand-to-hand mêlée. Six or seven men were killed in a space only a few feet square. The sortie was over. Back into the cave ran the survivors. In a few minutes only the blank wall of the parapet presented itself to the eyes of the besiegers.

One of the charging Indians did break through. He got beyond the first line and, not seeing the second line behind him, was in the act of giving a war whoop of encouragement to his friends, when he saw death staring him in the eye. Twenty carbines were concentrated upon him. In an instant it was over. The poor devil tried to say something: "No! No! Soldados!" was what it sounded like, but the twenty guns rang out and the warrior was dead. His body was almost pulverized by the volley, and the force of the bullets was such that he seemed to be lifted clear off the ground and hurled back by them.

Brown redoubled the fire on the cave. Feebler and feebler was the Apache reply. And now came the turning point. Captain James Burns, with two men, climbed the canyon above the cave. By leaning over they could see the Apaches behind the rock wall which jutted out somewhat from the cliff. Burns had an idea. Sending for more men, he reverted to stone-age warfare. Within a few minutes he had his men throwing and rolling boulders down on the rampart. Many of the rocks hit on top of or directly behind the wall. The havoc was fearful. Men, women and children were smashed into wet pulp beneath the huge, bounding stones.

That boulder barrage ended the battle. After ten minutes the soldiers stopped rolling rocks, and skirmishers cautiously advanced from below. Corporal Hanlon, of Troop G, was the first man over the top. Even to the hardened old soldier, the sight was sickening. In an indescribably shocking mess, the wretched Indians lay mangled, dead or dying. Only eighteen persons, all women or children, were found living and practically all of these were wounded or injured by the boulders. Seventy-four were dead. Brown had carried out his orders. The band was wiped out.[10]

[10] Six or seven young women escaped at the start of the fight and made their way to their friends in other bands. They had been sent to examine a mescal pit at dawn and the first volley warned them not to return. One other person escaped. A warrior, badly wounded in the leg, had lain down behind one of the great slabs of stone which leaned against the rear wall. As the fight progressed more and more corpses piled about him, and when the soldiers entered, they completely overlooked him. After they left, he improvised himself a pair of crutches and crawled and hobbled to Tonto Creek where he met and turned back another band of Indians which might have run into the soldiers.

CHAPTER XV

CONCENTRATION

SWEEPING OUT THE TONTO BASIN

WHILE it was by far the most crushing blow given by
Crook's forces during the campaign, the destruction of
Chuntz' band was only one of several victories for the
soldiers. Chuntz himself had escaped—a big disappointment to Crook. Warned, either by the escaping girls or by
the wounded warrior, he was able to elude Brown, having
been away when the soldiers struck. The following day
after the fight in the cave, he joined Del-she's band with
the few warriors left to him. But in doing so he selected
anything but a haven.

There still remained, in the Tonto Basin, two strong-
holds where Crook believed large bodies of Indians were
lurking. One of these was the almost inaccessible top of
Turret Butte. The other was in the fastnesses of the
Superstition Mountains.

Brown marched toward the last named place. With all
the care which had characterized his former efforts, he
combed this area, but the Apaches were alert. Time after
time they eluded him. Once, in the early morning of January 15th, 1873, he "jumped" a small *rancheria* and captured it, killing three Indians and capturing thirteen, all
women and children. But the main body escaped.

It was bitter cold and the troops suffered in the high
mountains. Still Brown grimly held to his purpose. Three

143

days after the capture of the *rancheria*, some yells were heard from the high shoulder of a mountain near the trail. Like hounds slipped from their leashes, a dozen or more lean Apache scouts detached themselves from the column and melted into the underbrush. The soldiers halted. Every ear was strained for the opening reports of the rifles. Minutes stretched into half an hour or more. Still not a sound was heard. It was as if there was nobody on that mountain side, yet every man in the detachment was morally certain that there were scores of Apaches there.

Suddenly the sibilant, warning scout hiss: "Tssit! Tssit!" sounded down the trail. Every eye turned in that direction. The bushes parted and the scouts stepped into view—with a captive.

But what a captive! The cruel faces of the scouts expanded into broad grins. In their midst was a tiny, black-eyed boy. Not more than eight years old was he, yet he carried himself with the pride of a chief. And well he might—he was the emissary of his people, sent down by them to interview the white commander. With all his pride the lad was badly frightened. He trembled as he confronted the major. Yet there was an edge of defiance to his voice as he delivered his message: His people wanted no more war, but wished to make peace.

It was Brown's turn to grin. Food was brought to the youngster, and then tobacco with which the eight-year-old filled a pipe and puffed away with all the gravity and satisfaction of an octogenarian. Having filled the young emissary's belly with beans and given him a smoke, Brown provided him with an old army blouse—the boy was naked to the waist in that bitter weather—and sent him back to his people, with a message that while the lad was too young to talk with men, he could see for himself that the troops would receive favorably real peace talk, and not harm any Indians who were sincere about wanting to surrender.

Up the mountain side scurried the boy, mightily relieved to be out of the reach of the white men. An hour later the soldiers in Brown's column heard another series of shouts. This time it was unnecessary to send out scouts. It was the boy again. He brought with him a wrinkled old squaw to talk with the major. Once more Brown refused to discuss terms with anyone less than a warrior. The squaw in turn was fed and sent back.

For the third time shouts up the mountain warned of an envoy. This time it was an aged and very decrepit old man. Down the slope he came, using a long walking-stick to support his feeble body. And now Brown consented at last to talk. He told the old chief that Nan-tan Lupan was determined to bring every Apache to peace or hunt him down, and indicated that only an immediate surrender would save the Indians. The old man replied that his band could not surrender on the instant. It was scattered too widely to be assembled at once, having separated in every direction at the approach of the troops. He added that if the soldiers would march directly to Camp Grant, he would gather his people together and they would follow, catching up at the junction of the Gila and San Pedro Rivers, and there surrender.

Major Brown agreed. He marched slowly across the mountains to the appointed place. But there was not a sign of an Indian. It was a bitter disappointment. The army saw itself tricked again. But the Indian scouts were unperturbed. "Wait and see!" said they.

Just at evening, the old chief came cautiously sidling into camp, accompanied by a few warriors. He wanted to know what would be done with his people when they surrendered. Brown replied that only Crook himself could decide that. Another smoke, and the Apaches vanished again into the mountains.

Next morning as the troops started up the San Pedro there was not an Apache in sight. But as the march progressed, a furtive Indian appeared from behind a cluster of mesquite and slipped in among the scouts. Another and another emerged from behind sage brush, or *palo verde* or cereus cactus. Each newcomer's face was a study in anxiety and fear. *"Sisquisn"* (My brother) was the greeting of each, uttered in a manner half supplicating, half defiant. By the time the troops reached Camp Grant, one hundred and ten men, women and children had joined the column. It was a decisive and bloodless victory and cleared the Superstition Mountains of hostile Apaches.

THE CAPTURE OF TURRET BUTTE

Meanwhile a blow almost as crushing as the debacle at the Salt River Canyon cave had been struck by Major George M. Randall of the 23rd Infantry.

After Chuntz joined Del-she's band, the Tonto Apaches raided south again, toward Wickenburg, near which they overwhelmed a party of young Englishmen, headed by a man named Taylor, who, lured by visions of wealth in cattle raising or mining, had recently crossed the ocean. The Indians killed most of the party immediately, but two were captured and tortured to death.[1]

Following their usual tactics, the Tontos retreated rapidly to their coverts, across the Bradshaw Mountains, then to the Tonto Basin. They had twenty-four hours' start

---

[1] "The assailants . . . tied two of them to cactus, and proceeded deliberately to fill them with arrows. One of the poor wretches rolled and writhed in agony, breaking off the feathered ends of the arrows, but each time he turned his body, exposing a space not yet wounded, the Apaches shot in another barb."—John G. Bourke, "On the Border With Crook," p. 208.

of the troops, but Randall knew where he was going, and what he would do when he got there.

Turret Butte is named from the fact that it is shaped much like the turret of an old-style battleship or castle, with steep walls and a comparatively flat top. It was almost inaccessible, and the Apaches, believing themselves secure there, neglected to take their customary precautions against surprise. At the base of this Gibraltar of savagery, Randall and his battalion, weary with a long march, arrived the night of April 22nd. Randall understood his danger in climbing that natural fortress. If warned, the Apaches could easily hold it. Even boulders, rolled from the top, would be deadly weapons on the treacherous slope. Everything depended upon his making the climb without the knowledge of the enemy above.

Leaving every bit of superfluous baggage at the foot, the men began the crawl up the steep slope in the darkness. Every soldier was cautioned to take the greatest care not to dislodge a stone, or even strike the metal barrel of his rifle against a tree or rock. For hours they scrambled upward. Every minute was tense. It seemed almost impossible for so large a body of men to make the climb without being discovered. But in some way they did. At last they were on the top.

It was midnight and off to one side Randall could see the red eyes of campfires at the Apache village. It was a welcome sight. It meant that his quarry was still there. The soldiers had to sit down and wait until daylight, since in the night it would have been easy for most of the Indians to escape. So with what patience they could muster the men shivered through the long hours before dawn.

The sudden, brazen blare of a bugle, sounding the charge, was the first knowledge the Apaches had that the troops were upon them. With startled yelps they ran this way and that. But Randall's men cut off every retreat.

A few ripping volleys. The Indians knew they were helpless. They could not escape or even fight. Some of the warriors in despair leaped over the edge of the precipice near their camp and were dashed to death hundreds of feet below. But the rest of the band surrendered. Among the captured were the chiefs Chuntz and Del-she.

The Turret Butte fight completed the cleaning out of the Tonto Basin, and abated forever the threat of the Tonto Apaches. They never again as a tribe went on the war path.

Crook as usual dealt fairly and yet firmly with the Tontos. Most of them were sent to Fort Apache. The Apache-Mojaves, under Chali-pun, surrendered early in April. Their chief appeared with his head men at Camp Verde, and took Crook by the hand with the words, *"Demasiadas cartuchos de cobre"* (Too many cartridges of copper). He meant that he had never been afraid of fighting the Americans but that they had too much fixed ammunition while most of the Apaches were still using antiquated muzzle-loading guns, or bows and arrows.

The problem of how usefully to employ his captives was Crook's next study. He set them to work under military supervision, building irrigation ditches and breaking the ground for farms. He also arranged for a cash market for their products, so that the Indians had the comfortable assurance that when their products were harvested they would receive real money for them. The Indians worked with astonishing zeal. They seemed relieved to find something to which they could turn their hands. Since they had no tools or implements of their own, Crook let them use every axe, spade, pick, hatchet and shovel not in actual service in the army cantonments. These the Apaches supplemented with sticks, pointed and hardened in fire. With their crude implements, by infinite labor, they dug a ditch five miles long, averaging four feet wide by three feet deep. The men dug; the women carried away the earth in their conical wicker baskets.

SEVEN HEADS ON THE PARADE GROUND

Crook kept under the most rigid observation the Indians on his several reservations. There was a system of tagging under which each male old enough to bear arms wore a numbered disk and was checked at the agency periodically. This did much to prevent parties of outlaws from slipping away from the reservations. When small bands did go on raids, it was possible to find who the guilty ones were.

The scouts who had served Crook so faithfully and efficiently in the Tonto Basin remained on the payroll as police. Nan-tan Lupan called the chiefs of the various tribes into council and talked to them about maintaining order in their purlieus. The white man, he explained, forbade crime among his own people, and if any committed offenses against the law, was quick to punish. The Indians must do the same with their people. The appeal to the Apache race pride was a master stroke. Its results were soon forthcoming.

There was plenty of reason for discontent on the reservations. Many Indians objected to the tagging. Others resented the infringement on their liberties. But most of the bad feeling was caused by the grafting, unscrupulous white men who buzzed about every reservation like blowflies around carrion, using political influence to enrich themselves at the expense of the helpless red men.

A good example of this was the fate of the Camp Verde Indians. The labors of the Apaches to make that place habitable have already been described. After the Indians dug with sharpened sticks and a very few old implements an irrigation ditch, they began to cultivate a patch of ground. Some fifty-three acres were put under water. On this the Apaches soon had squashes, melons and other garden stuff. Directed by two army officers, Colonel Julius W. Mason and Lieutenant Walter S. Schuyler, both of the 5th Cavalry, they began next to plant corn, barley and other grains on a large scale. The outlook was brighter than it had been in years for the Indians.

And then the maleficent hand of the white man's graft showed itself. At Tucson there existed a political ring of federal officials, contractors and other interested persons. This gang of racketeers saw with alarm that under Crook's management the Indians at Camp Verde would soon be self-supporting. It meant that the white contractors would cease to furnish the government inferior supplies and thin cattle at exorbitant prices, to feed these Indians. But the Tucson ring had its own methods. Political influence was exerted at Washington. One day a peremptory order came to remove all Indians from Camp Verde to the barren San Carlos reservation.

The despairing people were once more driven out into the desert. From their melon patches and corn fields, the Apaches, shepherded by their only friends, the army officers, began their long, dusty journey to San Carlos. Overnight they changed from interested, industrious, cheerful people, into sullen, treacherous savages once more. Small wonder that the old, old cycle of death began to reappear in the desert.

The Camp Verde case is cited merely as an instance. There were many others. Chuntz, Chaun-desi, and Cochine [2] repented of their surrenders. On May 27th, goaded

2 Not to be confused with Cochise, the Chiricahua. Cochine was a Tonto.

to desperation, Chaun-desi tried to stab Agent Larrabee of San Carlos with a lance. Another Indian, Yomas, prevented him from doing it. Then Chaun-desi seized a gun and killed Lieutenant Jacob Almy. With their people the three chiefs took to the hills.

Crook called the remaining chiefs on the reservation together and told them the matter lay in their hands. They would have to trail down and bring in the outlaws, dead or alive. The leaders looked at each other and departed.

One day a group of scouts, carrying a large sack, presented themselves before the general. As he looked, they dumped at his feet seven bloody, grinning human heads. Then they explained. A few nights before a wagon train had halted near San Carlos and some of the teamsters gave whiskey to the Apaches. The Indians got ugly drunk. When the teamsters refused the Indians more liquor, every man in the train was killed.

The Apaches took to the wilds. But the reservation chiefs and scouts had their orders. Without even reporting to Crook they took the trail. The outlaws were surrounded. When they refused to surrender, the scouts simply killed them all. There was no other way of proving that they had disposed of the renegades, so they severed their heads, put them in a sack and dumped them at Crook's feet.

Meantime the hunt continued for the outlaw chiefs. One by one they were killed. Cochine was first. He was shot in the mountains May 26th, 1874, a year after he fled the reservation. Chaun-desi met his death June 12th of the same year. And finally Chuntz came to his end on July 25th. Del-she, too, after an abortive attempt at revolt, was brought to bay and killed by his own people on July 27th. The Tonto Apaches had entered a new era in their relations with the white man.

CONCENTRATION CONTINUES

But unbearable injustices persisted. The Tucson Ring kept its sinister forces at work in Washington.[3] Whenever a promising start was made by the Indians, the fruit of their labor was taken away from them and they were herded elsewhere. Wrote Captain John G. Bourke:

"Just as soon as a few of the more progressive people (Apaches) begin to accumulate a trifle of property, to raise sheep, to cultivate patches of soil and raise scanty crops, the agent sends in the usual glowing report of the occurrence, and to the mind of the average man and woman in the East it looks as if all the tribe were on the highway to prosperity, and the first thing Congress does is to curtail the appropriations. Next we hear of 'disaffection,' the tribe is reported as 'surly and threatening' and we are told that the 'Indians are killing their cattle.' But, whether they go to war or simply starve on the reservation effects no change in the system; all supplies are bought of the contractor as before, and the red man is no better off, or scarcely any better off, after twenty years of peace, than when he surrendered." [4]

In spite of all these circumstances, Arizona was now nearer to peace than it had been for generations. So much so that on January 6th, 1875, Governor Safford said in his message to the legislature:

"At no period in the history of Arizona have our Indian affairs been in so satisfactory a condition. Comparative peace now reigns throughout the Territory, with almost a certainty that no general Indian war will ever occur again."

Among the prophets of modern times, the governor

[3] The following significant paragraph from the annual report of General Schofield, in 1871, throws additional light on some of the motives and methods of the Tucson Ring:

"It is worthy of remark that these Indians (the Apaches) paid for a large part of the rations issued them by supplying hay and wood to the military posts, and the wood and hay thus furnished cost the government much less than before paid to contractors, and that the contractors, their employees and customers, thus lost the profits heretofore realized. It has been suggested that this may explain the Camp Grant massacre."—Report of the Secretary of War, 1871, p. 87.

[4] "On the Border With Crook," p. 223.

must stand out as one of the worst. There was going to be trouble, and that in plenty. And the "Concentration Policy," so called, as adopted by the Indian Bureau, was responsible.

The reservations of Arizona were transferred from the War Department to the Department of the Interior. The Indian Bureau at once began to concentrate its Indian wards. The fate of the Camp Verde Indians has been told. Next to go were the White Mountain Indians, who were driven down out of their healthful mountains to San Carlos, in the stifling valley of the Gila. Then the Indian Bureau turned its attention to the Chiricahuas. While Crook had been busy in the Tonto Basin, General O. O. Howard, guided by an intrepid white frontiersman, Captain Jeffords, made peace with Cochise. Howard pledged his solemn word that the Chiricahuas should be allowed to remain among their own mountains. Cochise died in peace, never dreaming that his treaty with the white men would be broken within eighteen months of his death, which occurred in June, 1876.

One fortunate circumstance there was. A man of exceptional tact, firmness and understanding, was made agent at San Carlos, destined to be the danger point for all the Arizona country. This man, John P. Clum, took his post in 1874. He served until 1877. During his term of office he handled, always with judgment and justice to the Indians, some tremendously difficult situations. With his company of twenty-five Indian policemen, he time and again walked right into a camp full of bitter, maddened savages and quieted them.

But no one man could make up for the accumulated wrongs heaped up by a whole bureaucracy. Very speedily was Governor Safford to see his optimistic prophecy proved futile and fatuous.

VII.

THE HUNTING OF VICTORIO
1877–1880

CHAPTER XVI

SUCCESSOR TO MANGUS COLORADO

CROOK LOOSENS HIS GRIP

IN THE middle of March, 1875, General Crook was transferred to the Department of the Platte, far to the north where already ominous signs foretold the outbreak of the dread Sioux. His place in Arizona was taken by General August V. Kautz, who found his hands immediately filled with complications arising from the myopic policy of the Indian Bureau.

The Chiricahuas were terribly disgruntled. Cochise's death had left them without a real leader. The true Chiricahuas were headed by Tah-sa, the old chief's son. The Mogollon division of the tribe recognized Juh, an old-time lieutenant of Cochise, as its chief. Over on the Ojo Caliente reservation in southwestern New Mexico, was Geronimo, born a Mimbreno, but now living with the Chiricahuas. With him on the same reservation was Victorio. Each of these men had his following.

Only a spark was needed to stir these ready elements into conflagration. That spark was supplied by an incident which took place in April, 1876. At Sulphur Springs, in the Dragoon Mountains, stood one of the stations of the Overland Stage route. The agent, a man by the name of Rogers, had been frequently warned against selling liquor to the Indians, but the temptation of easy profits was too

great. He made quite a little side income by bootlegging
whiskey to the Apaches.

That April the Chiricahua agent gave some of the warriors permission to take their families to the Dragoons to
hunt, because their supply of food was exhausted. During
their somewhat lengthy stay in the mountains, the Indians
became acquainted with the slippery Mr. Rogers, and
bought from him some liquor. Alcohol always had a bad
effect on Apaches. It made them ugly and brought to the
fore their undeniable talents for killing. The reaction in
this case was typical. That night the Indians got drunk
and had a fight among themselves which ended in the
deaths of two men and a child. Next morning, nursing a
terrible hangover and mourning the deaths of their
friends, most of them dragged themselves back to the
agency. A small band of a dozen warriors and their
families, headed by a sub-chief named Eskina, remained
in the mountains.

After Rogers found out what had happened in the
Apache camp because of his liquor selling, he was probably apprehensive. And he was anything but joyful next
day when two of Eskina's warriors, a sub-chief named
Pi-hon-se-ne and his nephew, rode up to the state station,
demanding more liquor. The Indians, by their blood-shot
eyes, twitching hands and irritable manner, still showed
the signs of their debauch of the previous night. Rogers
had grown cautious. Perhaps he began to fear word of this
might reach the ears of the authorities. He sold the two
warriors small drinks but refused to give them any large
quantity of whiskey.

Pi-hon-se-ne and his nephew stood in the stage station,
drinking the driblets the agent gave them and growing
uglier and more sullen every minute. Presently Rogers
quit selling them any liquor at all. He grew peremptory,

told them they could have no more whiskey, and ordered them to leave the station. Pi-hon-se-ne and his nephew, without moving a muscle of their faces, raised their rifles and shot the station agent dead, then killed his assistant, a man named Spence.

With all the liquor, horses and ammunition they could collect, the two Apaches rode back to Eskina's camp where the whole band got wildly drunk that night and decided to go on the war path. They killed a white man next day, wounded another, and stole four horses. A company of cavalry was sent to drive them back on the reservation, but failed to overtake them. And thus, because a profit-greedy station agent refused to obey the laws of his own nation, another bloody Apache war began.

Eskina's warriors raided several ranches. Early in June they were on the Chiricahua reservation again, trying to persuade the rest of the tribe to join them. Tah-sa, the chief, refused. In the fight which followed, six men were killed and three wounded. Eskina was among the dead and Pi-hon-se-ne, shot in the shoulder by Tah-sa, was among the wounded.

As a climax to this dangerous situation, officials from the Indian Bureau arrived with orders for the Chiricahuas to move to the hated San Carlos reservation. It was a tense hour. Tah-sa, unwilling to comply, but seeing the futility of resistance, at last agreed to go.[1] But on June 7th seventy-five or eighty warriors, with their women and children, some three hundred people in all, suddenly left the reservation and fled south into Sonora, killing as they went. They were led by Geronimo and Juh.

The war, now well started, progressed bloodily. Not less than twenty persons were killed on the United States

[1] Shortly after this Tah-sa was taken to Washington by Agent Clum. He died on the trip.

side of the international border in the next few weeks. And the record will never be complete of those who died at the hands of the stealthy Apaches in Mexico.

Not until the spring of 1877 were any of the hostile band apprehended. Then Agent Clum, with his faithful agency police, surprised Geronimo and Pi-hon-se-ne at Ojo Caliente and arrested them. Geronimo was lodged in the guard house at San Carlos to await trial. But the machinations of the Indian Bureau had grown too much for the intelligent, fair-minded Clum to stomach. He resigned. In the confusion which followed his replacement, Geronimo was freed.

THE MESCALEROS

The outbreak of Geronimo, Pi-hon-se-ne and Juh was watched with eager interest by the Mescalero Apaches. Since the days of Gian-na-tah, who will be remembered by the reader as an ally of Mangus Colorado, that people had suffered tragically at the hands of the whites. This, viewed from the white man's standpoint, was largely their own fault, because the Mescaleros never were what one might term tractable. They insisted upon their right to the land and continued to view the white men as interlopers.

After Gian-na-tah surrendered to Kit Carson, as described in an earlier chapter, the Mescaleros were held for some time at the Bosque Redondo. But the Navajos, more numerous than the Mescaleros and arrogant in their numbers, were soon moved down there. These newcomers made life so unbearable for the Apaches that by 1867 all the Mescaleros had left the reservation and wandered out on the plains of Texas and among the mountains of New Mexico, committing frequent depredations. It was

White Mountain Apache warriors. Seated, with the boy between his knees is Alchise, one of the famous White Mountain chiefs.

Left: Victorio, next to Mangus Colorado the greatest military figure in Apache history. He was killed by Mexicans in the Tres Castillos Mountains. Right: Chihuahua, Chiricahua leader and also a government scout later.

not until four years later, in February, 1871, that Captain Chambers McKibben, by negotiating with the sub-chief La Paz, induced the tribe to go on to the reservation at Fort Stanton.

They soon saw that they had made a mistake. The white settlers began charging that the young braves were leaving the reservation and raiding. If the Indians did so, they could at least say that there were plenty of vivid examples in cattle and horse theft set for them by the whites.[2] There is no doubt that much of the "rustling" in the territory, which was blamed on the Indians, was committed by white men. Add to this situation the fact that the Mescalero reservation was soon drained of game and the people were virtually starving, while at the same time unscrupulous white traders from La Luz and Tularosa constantly bootlegged whiskey to them,[3] and it is to be wondered why there was not more trouble than there actually was.

In the fall of 1874, a mob of white citizens crept up on a camp of Mescaleros, which was situated well within the borders of the reservation. Several women, children and men, peacefully sleeping in their tents, were massacred. The rest of the band, panic-stricken, fled to the mountains. Captain E. G. Fechet was sent with a detachment to bring the Indians back. Instead of trying to bring them peacefully to the reservation, he slipped up on the band, launched a surprise attack which killed more of them, and captured most of their horses. These same Indians were

[2] The Mescalero chiefs made frequent protests to W. D. Crothers, their agent, that white thieves were stealing their horses, in the fall of 1874. Crothers tried to catch the thieves, but was unsuccessful. (See Report of W. D. Crothers, in "Annual Report of Commissioner of Indian Affairs," 1875, pp. 329-330.)

[3] According to F. C. Godfroy, Mescalero agent from 1876 to 1879, the Apaches were so crazy for liquor that they frequently would trade a horse for a single quart and the unscrupulous traders sold them only the most inferior grade of whiskey, at that. ("Annual Report of Commissioner of Indian Affairs," 1876, pp. 105-109.)

later induced by two men, an Indian scout and an agency employee, to surrender without any use of arms.[4]

Still the Mescaleros were hectored and abused. Once more, in 1877, a body of the fragrant gentry who at that time infested the Texas border, made two raids on the reservation in which they ran off some forty horses belonging to the Indians. Again the Mescaleros saw the hopelessness of depending upon the government for protection and took to the hills. Some of them wandered as far north as the Staked Plains and joined the Comanches in their war against the buffalo hunters that year.[5] But at last the bulk of the tribe was induced to come back to the reservation by a new agent, S. A. Russell, who even managed to bring Victorio there for a time.

Numbers of the Mescaleros refused, however, to surrender to Russell and continued to rove the wilderness. A ceaseless campaign was waged against them by Colonel B. H. Grierson and General Edward Hatch. One band of the Indians fought and defeated a detachment under Captain S. B. M. Young near San Carlos on October 28th, 1877. But the following year even these were driven on the reservation.

VICTORIO

Among the old guard of warriors trained under the great Mangus Colorado was the Mimbreno chief Victorio. He had been one of the Red Sleeves' lieutenants, and was

---

[4] "On their return (to the reservation) it was heart rending to see a class of human beings so destitute of the common necessities of life; many of them were almost naked and bearing marks of an outraged class of human beings."—W. D. Crothers' report in 1875, p. 330.

[5] Captain P. L. Lee, with his detachment of the 9th (Colored) Cavalry, killed four and wounded several other Indians in a fight at Lake Quemado in 1877. He attacked what he thought was a Comanche camp. But some of the Indians killed were Mescalero Apaches. For a description of the Buffalo Hunters' War, see Paul I. Wellman, "Death on the Prairie," p. 211, et seq.

thoroughly grounded in every detail of Apache fighting tactics. In the years after his leader's death, Victorio was a constant menace to the white man and was frequently out on the war path. He agreed to settle on the reservation in 1877, but was soon thoroughly tired of his agreement.

At the time Clum arrested Geronimo and Pi-hon-se-ne, he had a talk with Victorio, who told him he would far rather die than go to San Carlos. All the Indians hated that place, and word was beginning to creep around among them of the "Concentration Policy" and its baleful significance.

Victorio's worst fears were realized in April, 1879. He was notified then that he and his people were to be moved to San Carlos. That was enough for the Mimbreno. Between sunset and sunrise he disappeared with thirty of his braves. Never again did he return.

With the troops hot on his trail, Victorio fled for Mexico, swinging around south of El Paso, and crossing the Rio Grande into the Big Bend Country of Texas, south of Fort Quitman. There he received reinforcements. Caballero, the aged chief of the Mescaleros, inspired by Victorio's bold move for freedom, also left the reservation with two or three hundred of his people and joined the Mimbrenos.

Victorio now had more than a hundred warriors. He began at once a series of the most baffling movements the United States army ever had to combat in Indian campaigns. The Mimbreno leader was a perfect master at deception. He pursued a settled policy with the Mexican sheep herders and small ranchers in the country over which he ranged. They were permitted to live on sufferance. So long as they furnished him with arms, food, and

ammunition, just so long he allowed them to exist.[6] All
of them knew this. Their lives were pitiable; they were in
constant terror. When the grim brown warriors with their
steel-trap mouths rode up to the little adobe *casas*, the
owners came forth with anything they demanded and were
glad to get off with their lives. Replenishing his supplies
in this manner and knowing every foot of the country,
Victorio matched his wits against the best in the United
States and Mexican armies and won for many months.

As soon as he entered Texas, the chief learned through
his scouts—who probably never had superiors in the history
of any warfare—that Captain Nicholas Nolan, with a detachment of the 10th (Colored) Cavalry, was headed
toward him. Too weak to fight any such body of troops,
the Mimbreno retreated. He turned and twisted, trying
to shake off the soldiers, but finally was forced to cross
to the south side of the Rio Grande when Colonel George
W. Baylor [7] and a company of Texas Rangers pressed him
too closely.

But it was only for a short time. In September the
Apaches appeared again—this time in New Mexico. Victorio never moved more secretly than he did that time.
The first hint anybody had that he was north of the border
was a message of blood. Captain Ambrose E. Hooker's
company of the 9th Cavalry was camped near Ojo Caliente. Victorio passed that way, headed north to give some
of the Mescaleros and Mimbrenos still on the reservation

---

[6] Colonel Grierson complained about this as follows: "There seems to be a tacit
understanding between Victorio and many Mexicans, that so long as he does not
make war upon them in earnest, he can take whatever food and other supplies he
may need for his warriors."—Report of Colonel B. H. Grierson, 1880, Old Records
Section, A. G. O., War Department.

[7] A former Confederate officer and the brother of John R. Baylor, one-time
Confederate governor of Arizona, who proposed the original policy of extermination for the Apaches and was removed from office as a result by Jefferson Davis.
Colonel George W. Baylor hated the Indians as much as did his brother. He
was one of the great figures among the Texas Rangers of the period.

a chance to join him. But he needed horses and, when he saw the troop herd grazing under a guard on the night of September 4th, he turned aside from his direct line of march. Victorio's shadowy skirmishers stole through the gloom. Orange flashes spurted out in the darkness as the rifles chattered angrily. With yells which sounded sharp and clear above the thunder of the stampeding horses, the Apaches were gone in a smother of dust.

Eight troopers were killed in the brief, bloody little battle, and forty-six of Uncle Sam's cavalry horses found themselves between the knees of Indian riders. Victorio did not lose a man.

The troops groped frantically through the desert for the Apaches but Victorio's people were gone almost as if they had disappeared into the air. Ten days later they struck again, suddenly, savagely.

It was near Hillsboro, New Mexico, this time. A posse of citizens, ranchers and miners had taken the trail. Victorio turned on them with a snarling fury which caught them unprepared. Ten of them were killed and all their horses were captured by the raiders.

All this time warriors were flocking to join Victorio, slipping away from their reservations and meeting him in the wilderness. He now had about one hundred and forty braves, including the Mescaleros under fierce old Caballero.

Lieutenant-Colonel N. A. M. Dudley, with two troops of the 9th Cavalry, rode hard to cut the Indians off following the Hillsboro fight, and found them on September 18th, in the canyons at the head of Las Animas Creek. Dudley attacked at once. But Victorio's desert wolves were posted in almost impregnable positions among the rocks.

The rattle of rifles had scarcely started when Captain Charles D. Beyer galloped up with two more troops of

the 9th, making a total of four companies in action. The
Apaches were now badly outnumbered, but in spite of this
the soldiers could not drive the Indians out of their position. Throughout the day the constant roar of the battle
echoed through the hills and canyons. When night fell,
Dudley discovered that in the day's fighting, from rock
to rock and bush to bush, he had lost five enlisted men,
two Navajo scouts and one civilian white scout killed, a
number wounded, and thirty-eight horses killed or crippled. The troops did not know of a single Indian they
had killed. It was clear to Dudley that Victorio was too
strong for him in his present position. In the darkness
the soldiers withdrew from the field, carrying their dead
and wounded. Victorio had won a convincing victory.

The chief's purpose was now fulfilled. He had fought
and beaten the white men three times, had killed twenty-
six of them, captured a large number of horses, and picked
up much booty. More important, he had been joined by
a good many warriors from the reservations. He therefore
began a retreat toward the border.

But the troops were still in the field. With one hundred and ninety-eight officers and men of the 9th Cavalry,
Major Albert P. Morrow struck Victorio near Ojo Caliente, and in a two days' running fight killed three Indians
and captured sixty horses and mules, among them twelve
of the animals taken from the hapless Hooker.

Four nights later prowling Apaches crept close enough
to his picket lines to kill a sentry walking post. But Morrow kept on the trail. With the aid of a captured squaw
he found and captured Victorio's camp. But the victory
was an empty one. The cunning chief had vacated the camp
before the troops arrived. That was on October 1st, 1879.
Morrow followed the Indians across the border into Mexico
and fought another skirmish October 27th, near the Cor-

ralitos River, a night fight in which he lost one scout killed
and two men wounded.

But the troops were at the limit of their endurance.
They had been without water for three days and nights
and their ammunition was nearly exhausted. If Victorio
had counter-attacked he might have wiped Morrow's
forces out. The troops were glad to retreat back to the
border, reaching Fort Bayard on November 3rd, completely worn out.

Chapter XVII

THE DOUBLE MASSACRE

VICTORIO INVADES TEXAS

Over in Texas the settlers and soldiers were congratulating themselves on having, for the time at least, rid themselves of the Indians. News came of the fighting in New Mexico and at last word was received that Major Morrow had driven Victorio down into Old Mexico. The frontier breathed freely again.

But late one afternoon the stage coach from Fort Davis dashed in to Fort Quitman with the driver and one passenger dead and arrows still quivering in the woodwork of its sides. Next came a report that the telegraph wires were cut and the poles chopped down between Fort Davis and Eagle Springs. The truth dawned on Texas: Victorio had in some manner eluded the troops who literally plastered the border those days, and was back in the Big Bend.

Colonel Grierson, at Eagle Springs, believed the Indians were headed for Fresno Springs and, knowing that this was an isolated watering place, he made a forced march by a short cut to get there first. He succeeded. When he reached the springs there was no sign of recent Indian visitation there. Grierson wasted no time. Soldiers were carefully posted around the springs in such a way that when the Indians came they could be permitted to reach the water, then surrounded and killed or captured. There were nearly a thousand troops concealed about the springs, and Grierson did not think that Victorio had more than one hundred and fifty. It looked as if the old wolf was reaching his finish at last.

Shortly before 11 o'clock next morning, the first cautious scouts of the Apache advance were seen. Grierson's men were nearly suffocating with excitement, but he held them in check while the Indians came slowly toward the spring.

Suddenly out of nowhere a wagon train appeared, also crawling toward the springs. The Indians took to cover at the first hint of this unexpected arrival. Helplessly the concealed soldiers watched the unfolding of an ambush within an ambush as the Apaches, wholly unconscious of Grierson's proximity, prepared to overwhelm the train. As the minutes passed it became increasingly apparent that unless Grierson rescued them the teamsters who had thus blundered into the situation would be massacred to a man.

Angry and disappointed, the colonel gave the order which sent his men to avert the attack on the wagons. The appearance of the troops, riding over the rise toward them was a complete surprise to the Apaches. But now they saw the trap into which they had almost fallen and began to retreat in earnest toward the Rio Grande. Grierson, before he took up the pursuit, probably used some warm language on the wagon master of that blundering train. In spite of his best efforts he could not overtake the Apaches, although he was so close behind them that his advance could see the Indians on the other side of the river when it arrived at the bank. There the soldiers were forced to turn back.

Victorio moved slowly down into Chihuahua. As they went south the Indians swept the country clean as far as the large ranches and prospectors were concerned, although they continued to observe the policy of sparing the sheepherders and small farmers. The first stop was at the Santa

Maria River, where there was an abundance of rich grama grass, together with plentiful wood and water—the three essentials of an ideal camping place. The location, however, did not satisfy the nervous Indians. It was too open and Victorio knew that Mexican troops might be expected at any time. In his present position he could easily be reached by them, and would be in a poor place for defense.

So Victorio ordered his people to break camp and moved them over into the wild and rugged Candelaria Mountains. There he took up a position which once more proved his genius as a leader. The new camp was not only perfectly located with regard to range for his horses and water and wood, but was beautifully strategic.

It was situated among almost inaccessible steeps, which would have been extremely difficult to attack successfully without serious loss to the enemy. Equally important, it afforded two or three towering peaks from which Victorio and his hawk-eyed scouts could see for twenty or thirty miles in every direction. Added to these advantages was the fact that it was near to the public road which ran between the city of Chihuahua and the Presidio del Norte —the Juarez of today—and all traffic could be observed.

THE FIRST MASSACRE [1]

Word of Indian depredations among the neighboring ranches soon reached Carrizal, the nearest settlement. Cattle and horses had been stolen and atrocities reported. The

---

[1] The word "massacre" is used because it is popularly applied to this affair, although it was not a massacre at all, but a battle in which all the members of one party were killed. No women or children or unarmed persons were involved. All the Mexicans fought until they were dead. The slaughter of Apache women and children by Mexicans and Americans at Santa Rita del Cobre and Camp Grant were true massacres. An Indian speaker once aptly phrased the common attitude in this respect when he said: "In the Indian wars, white treachery was always stratagem, and white massacre was always a victory; Indian stratagem was always treachery and Indian victory was always a massacre."

Mexicans at Carrizal deduced correctly that there was a band of Indians operating from some *rancheria* in the Candelaria Mountains. But they failed to grasp the idea of how powerful a band it was, or that it was led by the redoubtable Victorio himself. Had Carrizal realized this, the tragedy which followed might have been averted.

The general notion was that there was only a handful of Indians to deal with—possibly a dozen or even fewer, of the "broncho" [2] savages who were always wandering through the desert country. Early in November, Don José Rodriguez, one of the principal citizens of Carrizal and a member of one of the large land owning families, organized a posse to scout for the Indians and if possible exterminate them. The expedition set forth on November 6th, gay, confident, absolutely failing to comprehend the peril of its mission. Most of its fifteen members were from the better families of the district. It was a sort of a lark—dangerous but good hunting.

From his lofty watch tower in the Candelaria peaks, Victorio saw the small party of Carrizalistas while it was nothing but a tiny dust cloud, a score of miles away. That was November 7th. The Mexicans were coming up an old beaten track which led from the Santa Maria River to a big "tank" [3] on the northern slope of the mountains in which the Apaches were camped. The possemen were riding along carelessly enough, but Victorio knew that if they continued that line of march, they would be certain to strike the main trail made by his band when he moved it into the Candelarias. As wily a strategist as ever the

---

[2] "Broncho" Apaches were outlaws who held no allegiance either to the United States or to the Mexican government, or to any of the recognized chiefs among their own people. There were always a few of these bands on the prowl during this period.

[3] A "tank" in the Southwestern desert, was one of the infrequent places where rain water sometimes gathered in small pools or ponds, affording water until it dried out.

red race produced, he knew that once they saw the breadth of that trail, there was no chance of ever luring the Mexicans any further—and he wanted those rash Carrizalistas.

A delicate situation. But Victorio was equal to it. Calling forty or fifty of his warriors together, he laid a trap for the oncoming Don Rodriguez and his *compadres*. The trail led through a deep canyon which passed between two of the taller Candelaria peaks, both of which had done the Apaches good service as watch towers. In this gorge Victorio prepared as clever an ambush as ever an Indian devised; an ambush which was a psychological as well as a military masterpiece.

At the north side of the trail, among some large boulders, he posted some of his best marksmen—not many, but enough for his purpose. These would be the first to come into contact with the Mexicans, and Victorio counted on them to spring the real trap which was laid on the other side of the canyon, somewhat back from the trail itself.

On came the jaunty Mexicans, slouching with negligent grace in their saddles, chattering and smoking their corn-husk cigarettes, not dreaming of peril. A sudden spray of bullets from the boulders to the north greeted them. To the south of the trail lay some inviting rocks which would make excellent shelter. It was natural for them to seek the cover of these boulders—and that was exactly what Victorio had planned. Knowing human nature, he had not placed any braves among those particular rocks, but had posted his men *higher*, and back so that the very friendly hospitality of the boulders should convert them into a death trap worthy even of his sinister intelligence.

As Don Rodriguez and his men threw themselves behind the shelter, preparing to fight the Indians on the north side of the canyon, beady-eyed warriors watched them from behind. They had the Mexicans at their mercy, and knew it. At the perfect moment the first rifle sounded from above—possibly Victorio's own—and the slaughter began. There was no escape and no protection from the terrific fire which broke from the higher cliffs.

One poor devil of a Mexican managed to squeeze into a crevice where his body was protected, but his legs protruded; there was no room for them inside. The Apaches turned their rifles in that direction and began deliberately, remorselessly to shoot those legs to pieces. How the helpless wretch must have writhed and screamed as his twitching limbs were struck again and again by the bullets of those pitiless marksmen. It was the sort of thing which appealed to the macabre Apache sense of humor. The twitching ceased after a time. The Mexican had bled to death. But the Indians kept on firing until they literally shot both legs off at the knees.

By that time every member of Don Rodriguez' party, including that elegant *hacendado* himself, was dead. As they vainly tried to find cover, they had been picked off coolly and deliberately from above. Their horses, plunging and rolling in their death struggles, added to the confusion by breaking their lariats and crashing down into the deep canyon to the east, in a smother of dust far below.

After a time the shooting ceased. Then the first of the furtive Indians stole forward from rock to rock. No rifle sounded to greet him. Others came down, one by one, until Victorio's warriors all stood among the slain, looting the bodies and making sure that there were none left living.

THE SECOND MASSACRE

The failure of Don Rodriguez' party to return to Carrizal, caused grave alarm. As the days passed, the fear grew into a conviction that the men had met some terrible fate. There was no proof of this, however, and at last a party of fourteen citizens of the town volunteered to try to find what had happened to their kinsmen. It was a dangerous thing to attempt, but they probably counted on the fact that the Indians seldom lingered long near the scene of a fight.

Following the trail left by Don Rodriguez, they too disappeared into the mountains. Days passed. They failed to return. When, after a reasonable time, the party had not made its reappearance, Carrizal went wild with excitement, rage and grief. It dawned upon the town that the Apache menace in the mountains was far more serious than had been supposed. A courier was sent to the Presidio del Norte, to beg for help. While he was making his report to Señor Ramos, in command at del Norte, Colonel Baylor of the Texas Rangers in El Paso, on the American side of the Rio Grande, heard of it and crossed the river to offer the services of his hard-riding, straight-shooting daredevils—an offer which was thankfully accepted.

With true Latin courtesy, Señor Ramos offered to Baylor the command of the united forces, but the Ranger declined because the campaign was to be on Mexican soil. Then Ramos placed Don Francisco Escajeda of Guadalupe, a seasoned and experienced soldier, at the head of the allied array, giving second command to Baylor. A force of one hundred well armed, well mounted men was soon on its way south toward the Candelarias.

Straight south rode the rescue party. It halted beyond Samalayucca where scouts were pushed forward to reconnoitre. There was going to be no blundering into ambush this time. Night fell, bitter cold. Deep in the canyons where they could not be seen by watchful eyes in the peaks ahead, some of the men kindled fires of greasewood and mesquite and there tried to warm themselves.

The scouts returned late in the night. Going to the bivouac of Don Escajeda and Baylor, they reported they had not seen a sign of Indians. The commander immediately ordered his men to mount. It was an all-night march this time, and the foot of the Candelarias was reached early the next morning.

Shortly after dawn, for the first time, they saw Indian sign. A great, broad trail it was, whose width and plainness indicated that it was made by a very large band. It looked fresh. The scouts examined it and pronounced it only two days old. It led toward Lake Santa Maria to the north. Evidently the Indians were gone. Still, no chances of a trap were taken. As the command entered the canyon between the two Candelaria peaks, a detachment was sent over the crest to the south while another took the northward steeps. The rest then proceeded down the gorge itself.

Not far had the beaters in front progressed when a shout brought the stragglers hurrying up. Scattered about in the rigid and awkward poses of death, lay the bodies of the unfortunates from Carrizal. The scouts looked here and there, then pieced together from the signs, the story of the battle.

And now the consummate cunning of Victorio revealed itself. The first ambuscade had been cleverly planned and executed. But when did it ever before occur to an Indian leader to use the victims of one victory as bait with which to trap a second party? This is exactly what Victorio had done. The manner in which the Apaches had destroyed the second Carrizal party, as deduced by the scouts, was as follows:

When the rescue expedition from Carrizal, looking for

Don Rodriguez and his companions, arrived at the scene of the battle, there was not an Indian in sight. The Mexicans had every reason to believe the Apaches had been gone for several days. Therefore they relaxed their vigilance and began to gather the bodies of their kinsmen and place them together for burial.

The assumption that Victorio's warriors were gone was tragically wrong. All the time that the Mexicans were carrying the corpses of their friends to a central burying place, fierce eyes were fixed on them from above. Grieving, the Carrizalistas went about their sad work, oblivious of the fact that almost over their heads death awaited only the signal of the leader. Not until the bodies were all collected and the fourteen living Mexicans had gathered around their dead friends did the Apaches fire.

It was a repetition of the first fight. Nor is it likely that it lasted long. The Apaches were too numerous and too well situated. Presently the Indians once more descended into the valley and bent over the dead. Carrizal would never again see the faces of her sons.

Escajeda and Baylor, reconstructing the events which took place in that bloody gorge, had only one thing to do —bury the dead. The bodies were collected and a disquieting thing was learned. The first Carrizal party had numbered fifteen. The second contained fourteen men, a total of twenty-nine in the two parties, which had ridden into the jaws of Victorio's trap. Only twenty-seven corpses were found.[4] What had become of the other two Mexicans? No

---

[4] Singularly enough, although the twenty-seven corpses buried had lain on the ground for nearly two weeks, they were all in an excellent state of preservation, and had not been touched by an animal or a buzzard. The Texans had a strange belief about the bodies of Mexicans. Says one Texas writer of this incident (C. G. Raht, "Romance of Davis Mountains," p. 266): "Neither wild animals nor birds had touched the bodies and it is said to be a strange fact that no wild animal or bird of prey will ever touch the body of a Mexican. If they had been Indians, negroes or whites, the coyotes, buzzards and carrion crows would have eaten them the first day and night."

trace of the missing pair was ever discovered, but everyone knew what had happened to them. Too thorough, too sure was the Apache leader to have permitted them to escape. Somewhere along the trail, these two men, captured alive, suffered out their mortal hours, perhaps hanging head down over a slow fire . . . perhaps staked out, their mouths pried open with sharpened skewers, on some ant hill . . . perhaps twisting and writhing against the poisoned spikes of a tree cactus, lashed by green rawhide bands which, drying in the sun, bound them ever tighter and tighter against the torment . . .

Chapter XVIII

WHAT HAPPENED TO THE MESCALEROS

BACK INTO THE UNITED STATES

AFTER his double *coup* in the Candelaria Mountains, Victorio pressed northward as fast as his horses could carry his people. Early in January he again crossed the border and stood on the soil of New Mexico. His old enemy, Major Morrow, took prompt and strenuous action. Every body of cavalry in the section was set in motion. Victorio found himself in a veritable hornets' nest. Even his matchless skill could not forever keep his people clear of the thronging multitudes of soldiers about him.

Near the head of the Puerco River, on January 9th, he fought a stand-off engagement with Major Morrow and a battalion of the 9th Cavalry. Several of his warriors were hit and on the white side one enlisted man was killed and a scout wounded. Victorio drew off toward the San Mateo Mountains, where Morrow attacked him again on January 17th. It was another inconclusive fight, but a brave young officer, Lieutenant J. Hansell French, was killed and two scouts wounded.

After that Victorio once more disappeared. The troops searched blindly for him through the barren mountains and across sun-smitten flats, but for nearly three months they never were near enough to see the dust cloud raised by his tireless marchers. Back and forth he swung, leaving a smoking wrack behind him. The chief seemed to grow

more savage as the relentless pursuit continued. Some of
the scenes the soldiers stumbled upon as they followed him
endlessly, stirred black rage in their hearts. Women were
found by their charred homes, torn limb from limb. Little
children were discovered, looking as if wolves had worried
them to death. And many men, prospectors, stage drivers,
and cowboys, died horribly in the hills, leaving their
mangled corpses as mute evidence of the bottomless cruelty
of the Apaches into whose hands they had fallen. In that
bloody raid Victorio killed upward of a hundred persons
who are accounted for and enumerated. But there were
dozens of others never heard from, who met their end at
the hands of his desert killers.

Not until April 8th did the soldiers find Victorio. Then
it was the old story—an indecisive fight, with no results to
show for it. Captain Henry Carroll, 9th Cavalry, and seven
enlisted men were wounded during General Hatch's fruitless attempt to drive the Indians out of the strong position
they had taken high up in the San Andreas Mountains.
Three Indians were killed. Victorio drew off toward the
east. Hatch, who took the trail the following day, decided
that he was headed for the Mescalero reservation.

It was too disappointing, too disheartening. Something
had to be done about it.

DISARMING THE MESCALEROS

Those were sad days for the wretched Mescaleros who
remained on the reservation near Fort Stanton and tried
to keep the peace. They were caught between two fires. On
one side were Victorio and their old chief Caballero, incit-
ing them always to the war path, sometimes losing patience
with their pacifistic ways, and doing spiteful deeds against
them. On the other side were the soldiers who never be-

lieved them when they protested their innocence of trouble making, never gave them any rest if they as much as wandered outside of the confines of the agency.

Their one friend was their agent, S. A. Russell, who protected them all he could, advised them, and tried to stand between them and the military. Russell was hampered by the presence among the peaceful Indians of many malcontents who were always stealing supplies and smuggling them to the hostile bands. These supplies appeared frequently when camps of outlying raiding parties were captured, and gave rise to the charges that "The Mescalero Agency . . . largely served as a base of supplies and recruits for the raiding parties of Victorio." [1]

Captain Thomas C. Lebo, on March 6th, 1880, surprised and captured the *rancheria* of some "broncho" Indians at Shakehand Spring, about forty miles south of Penasco, Texas. Lebo's men killed a chief of the band, captured four squaws and one child, and the livestock and supplies of the camp. Much material from the Mescalero Agency was found in this camp, in which, incidentally, a captive Mexican boy, Coyetano Garcia, was rescued and later restored to his parents near del Norte.

Because of this evidence, Generals Pope and Ord, commanding the departments of Missouri and Texas, ordered on March 24th that the Mescaleros remaining on the reservation should be disarmed and dismounted. General Hatch and Colonel Grierson were given the task. Hatch took four hundred men from the 9th Cavalry, sixty infantrymen, and seventy-five Indian scouts. Colonel Grierson had under him two hundred and eighty officers and men of the 10th Cavalry and the 25th Infantry, making a combined force of eight hundred and fifteen officers and men. The two commands were to meet at the agency.

[1] "Record of Engagements With Hostile Indians," p. 94.

In the meantime, a band of peaceful Mescaleros, not knowing of these plans, asked permission of Russell to leave the agency on a hunt. Russell granted the permission. He told the Indians they might camp on the Rio Tularosa, several miles west of the agency limits. This was a common procedure. Years before all the game had been killed off on the reservation and in view of the type of supplies issued by the government to the Mescaleros, the agent thought it no more than fair that they be allowed to eke out their larders with what game they could occasionally kill.

Camping, in accordance with the agent's instructions, near the head of the Tularosa, this band of Indians was "discovered" by Grierson, April 12th, when he appeared through the Sacramento Mountains. The colonel had found many Indian trails on his march. He assumed that these trails were made by "marauding Indians." Just why they should be "marauders" is not clear, unless it was the officer's assumption that every Indian should be placed in that category. Without knowing anything about the band on the Tularosa or bothering himself to ascertain why they were camped there, he prepared at once to attack them.

It was early in the morning. Most of the Mescaleros were still asleep as Grierson surrounded the camp. All was ready for the charge which would be sure to kill many Indians when a messenger came spurring up with a message from Russell. The agent notified Grierson that these Indians were peaceful and were camping there by his special permission. He added that he had just ordered them back to the reservation and they had not yet had time to obey.

There is not much doubt that the Mescaleros in this camp were saved from a dreadful experience by the timely arrival of that courier. Another Camp Grant affair was averted.

Grierson, more or less grudgingly, marched on to the reservation as soon as he saw that the Indians were actually moving. General Hatch had already arrived. The Indians were quiet. Hatch decided he did not need all the troops he had brought. He began to send some of them west, leaving three hundred and fifty or so with Grierson. Russell summoned the chief Nautzilla [2] and told him the purpose of the troops.

The disarming was scheduled to take place on April 16th. Rifle firing was heard south of the agency at about 10 o'clock that morning. The Indians were thrown into a minor panic. Word came in shortly that Lieutenant Charles B. Gatewood had come upon some braves "driving off stock," had killed two of them, and was now bringing the livestock back to the agency. Russell was indignant. It appears that the stock in question had strayed away from the agency and the Indians had been sent by him to bring it back. While they were carrying out this errand, Gatewood had attacked them, with two fatalities resulting. Small wonder that the whole tribe seemed to have a bad case of nerves as Grierson began to disarm them.

It had been agreed between Grierson and Hatch that if more troops were needed than were then at the agency, three signal shots should be fired. Grierson saw that the Mescaleros were sullen and frightened. Some of them even began to slink away. He decided he needed the other troops. The signal shots rang out on the clear air.

Those shots crystallized the panic. In every direction the Indians rushed to escape. The confusion was enhanced by the sudden arrival of Hatch's troops, who tried to halt the Apaches and speedily found themselves fighting. Ten In-

[2] Following the government policy of "making" and "breaking" chiefs, Russell "promoted" Nautzilla to the chieftainship of the Mescaleros when Caballero joined Victorio. Nautzilla was a friend of the agent and Russell counted on him to help in the disarming.

dians were killed. Two hundred and fifty surrendered.[3] But scores got away and made a bee-line for Victorio's camp, where they became among his most vindictive fighters.

THE TEXAS CAMPAIGN

With these reinforcements, Victorio began a southerly retreat. He fought a couple of sharp engagements, but was back in Mexico by early June. There he was temporarily safe. The Mexican government refused to permit United States troops to cross its borders.

A breathing spell was all the Mimbreno wanted. On July 31st Captain Coldwell of the Texas Rangers, on an inspection trip to Ysleta, Texas, began a journey to Fort Davis. Riding in the mail stage coach, of the type called a "jerky" on the frontier, he passed through Quitman Canyon, where he discovered that Indians had cut off the stage coach from the other direction, killing its driver, E. C. Baker, and a passenger, Frank Wyant. In this manner Texas learned that Victorio was back within her borders.

And now began one of the biggest man-hunts in the history of the frontier. An agreement was made between General Ord, commanding the Department of Texas, and General Trevino, commanding the Mexican troops in northern Chihuahua, whereby the two nations were to co-operate in a campaign to run down Victorio. Trevino notified Grierson that about six hundred Mexican soldiers were

[3] "The Indians who surrendered were told that they would be taken care of; that though they must give up their arms . . . they would be properly rewarded if they would submit peacefully. This agreement was not kept. Those who surrendered were placed in a large stock pen, in which horses and cattle had been kept. The refuse from the pens was not even removed and the disconsolate Indians were forced to put up with this indignity. When they would ask concerning the return of horses, guns, etc., and their own release, noncommittal answers would be given." —C. C. Rister, "The Southwestern Frontier," pp. 198-199.

ready to pursue the Indians south of the border, with additional troops coming. Grierson threw every soldier he could get into the campaign. Within the next few weeks, Victorio, whose forces never exceeded one hundred and seventy-five or eighty warriors, had to fight or dodge at least two thousand United States soldiers, and an equal number of Mexican troops, not to mention the hundreds of cowboys, miners and ranchers who hung about him in a cloud.

With only six men Grierson was at the spring of Tanajas de las Palmas, on the day Victorio's invasion was discovered. His young son, out west on a summer vacation from college, was with him "looking for excitement", which he was to find, speedily.

Learning that the Apache camp was within ten miles of him, the colonel sent to Eagle Springs and to Fort Quitman for reinforcements for his small escort, and daringly remained with his half dozen men to watch the movements of the hostile Indians. His order was misunderstood at Fort Quitman where nothing was known of Victorio's proximity. The commanding officer there thought Grierson merely wanted an escort to bring him back to the fort. Lieutenant Leighton Finley was sent with fifteen men— a woefully inadequate force. At once another courier was dispatched by Grierson with peremptory orders for more troops and an explanation of the situation.

Grierson, occupying his exposed position far out in the desert, saw Victorio's advance guard approaching him at about 9 o'clock on the morning of July 31st. His twenty men were in a position as strong as they could find. The Indians observed this and instead of charging, they scattered about the place, ignorant of the fact that a courier had gone for help. Victorio planned to wipe out the whole force, in the Apache manner, with the least possible loss to himself.

Lieutenant Finley was ordered by Grierson to take ten men and prevent this enveloping movement if possible. The carbines began to crackle as the young officer attacked a vastly superior force of the Indians and for more than an hour held them in check. This was probably not so much due to the Apache fear of him, as to the fact that they thought they had all the time in the world and were prepared to carry out their battle plans at leisure.

That hour proved the saving of Grierson. As the men lay among the rocks with the bullets whining overhead, or smacking among the stones and kicking up spiteful jets of sand and dust, blue uniforms appeared over the rise from the direction of Fort Quitman. It was Captain Charles D. Viele, with a troop of cavalry.

The Apache fire slackened. But Viele's troops, coming up, mistook Finley's advance detachment for Indians and opened fire on it. Nobody was hit although the bullets skipped most disconcertingly among the men. To avoid being riddled by his own friends, Finley ordered a retreat to Grierson's main position. The Apaches sprang in hot pursuit as he withdrew, hoping to prevent Viele from joining Grierson. But Viele now saw his mistake. He deployed his men and sent them forward among the rocks so fast that the Indians, in their own immediate danger, forgot all about Finley.

All up and down the field, heated like a blast furnace under the brazen sun of late July, the fight became general. Although there were now about a hundred troopers against him, Victorio pressed them hard. He might have punished them severely, were it not that Captain Nicholas Nolan arrived with another company of cavalry from Fort Quitman.

Outnumbered and half surrounded, Victorio at last retreated. The engagement had lasted four hours. Seven
warriors had been killed and others wounded and carried
back to the rear by the Apaches. The Mimbreno chief's
force was too scanty to permit of such losses. On the white
side, Lieutenant S. R. Calladay was wounded and one enlisted man killed.

Victorio rapidly fell back to the Rio Grande and recrossed into Mexico. But within four days the tireless
raider was across the border into the United States again,
heading with his warriors for the Van Horn Mountains.
Brushing off one detachment of soldiers, he eluded Grierson's main command, which tried to pin him at Bass's
Canyon, and on the evening of August 4th was in the
passes of the Van Horns.

Grierson guessed that Victorio was heading for Rattle-
snake Springs. He made a forced march to that important
point, riding sixty-five miles during the next twenty-four
hours, a terrific march considering the heat. The soldiers
reached the springs well ahead of the Indians. Captain
Viele had two troops in ambush. The Indians arrived at
about 2 o'clock the next morning. They were greeted by
a surprise volley and as the rest of Grierson's force came
up, they were driven from the springs, losing several
warriors.

Undaunted, Victorio fell back toward Bowen's Springs
in the Guadalupe Mountains. But again his arch-foe,
Grierson, anticipated his movements. The chief found Captain William B. Kennedy's force waiting there. In the
brush which followed, two Indians and one soldier were
killed. The Apaches now retreated toward the Sacramento
Mountains. There they came into contact with another

of the swarming detachments, this time under Captain Lebo.

The border was crowded with soldiers as never before. Every way Victorio turned, he met troops. At last, about August 18th, he gave up the attempt to remain in the United States, and once more led his people into Mexico.

Chapter XIX

THE END OF THE HUNTING

IN THE TRES CASTILLOS PEAKS

Hunted like a mad wolf from mountain range to mountain range and from desert tank to alkali spring, Victorio and his faithful followers pushed southward from the Texas border and took refuge in the Tres Castillos Mountains of northern Chihuahua. September and October passed. The chief, now about sixty years old, was tired. But his young men were not. As the month of November opened, a large party of the younger braves went north again, while a second, somewhat smaller band, led by old Nana, Victorio's chief lieutenant, raided through Mexico. The older warriors and all the women and children remained with Victorio in the mountains.

News that the Indians were in the Tres Castillos district quickly reached Colonel Joaquin Terrazas at Chihuahua. He planned immediately a major operation against them. The colonel had spent some time in organizing a body of irregular troops, made up of men from such towns as Ascension, Janos and Casas Grandes, which were called the *Seguridad Publicos*, or, more familiarly, the "S. P.'s". In their duties and semi-military nature, they were patterned after the Texas Rangers. For scouts, Terrazas enlisted a company of Tarahumari Indians from the mountains of that name. These Indians, while lacking the extreme deadly vindictiveness of the Apaches, were little their inferiors in most respects, and in one respect they were the superiors, not only of the Apaches, but probably of every living race of mankind. They were, and still are, peerless foot racers. Their name signifies that and their warriors were able to boast with truth that they could outstrip any horse in a race sufficiently long. It was nothing for them to cover as much as one hundred miles in a day, and they could jog along, kicking a small ball before them, at a speed which carried them forty miles in six or eight hours with the greatest ease.[1]

Terrazas sent a message to Ysleta, Texas, asking Colonel Baylor of the Texas Rangers to cooperate with him, and marched north with his S. P.'s and Tarahumari scouts.

Meantime Grierson's men were on the trail of the young warriors who were raiding into Texas without Victorio as a leader. Captain Theodore A. Baldwin had a short fight with them near Ojo Caliente, Texas. Four of his men were killed, but the action prevented the Apaches' immediate return to the main band which awaited them in Tres Castillos. That delay was fatal. It is hard to believe that Victorio would have remained in one place for the length of time he did, had he not promised his young men to keep a rendezvous with them there. The great chance had come for Terrazas.

The Mexican leader had been joined by several bodies of fighting men from the United States. Colonel Baylor brought twenty of his Rangers. Lieutenant James A. Manney appeared with twenty Negro troopers. And Captain Charles Parker came to Terrazas' camp with sixty-eight Chiricahua Apache scouts. The combined expedition found Victorio's trail and followed it until all doubt that

[1] For further description of this remarkable people, see Hodge, "Handbook of American Indians," pp. 692-693.

it led to the Tres Castillos was gone. Then Terrazas made a surprise announcement.

He blandly requested his American allies to return to their own side of the border, giving as his excuse his belief that Captain Parker's scouts were too wild and too nearly related to Victorio's people for safety. To the Americans it looked simply as if the Mexican, having made sure of his quarry, jealously wished to take all the glory to himself for the victory which had been made possible, in large part, by the scouting of the very Chiricahuas to whom Terrazas objected. There was nothing they could do about it, however, except to return. Reluctantly and thoroughly angry, the American detachments marched north and crossed the border.

THE APACHE WOLF DIES

At one place the Tres Castillos Mountains form a deep basin, which can be entered only through a box canyon. This spot had long been a favorite camping ground for the Indians and thither Terrazas led his command. When he arrived no Apaches were there, and he camped for the night.

Frantic signalling from his pickets posted on the peaks of the mountains overlooking the plain, warned him that something important was afoot. Soon a soldier came running to say that a large dust cloud could be seen coming toward the canyon. Terrazas himself climbed a lookout peak and with his powerful field glasses made out definitely that the dust was raised by a large band of marching Apaches.

Here was unlooked-for good fortune. The Mexican commander hastily deployed his men to places of advantage. All traces of his campfires were concealed. In the

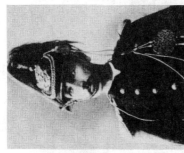

Lieutenant Charles B. Gatewood, who was really responsible for securing the final surrender of Geronimo. Left: John P. Clum, the able agent at San Carlos during the late Seventies.

Bureau of American Ethnology

War Department

Left: Loco, Mimbreno chief, one of the leaders in the battle at Horse Shoe Canyon. Right: Nana, the eighty-year-old chief, who led the most spectacular raid in the history of the Apache wars against the United States.

cliffs around the basin, the soldiers and the fierce Tarahumari scouts lay, with every foot of the interior covered by
their rifles.

For once Victorio was caught napping. The chief had
no idea that troops were in the vicinity. Without fear or
hesitation, he led his band, consisting largely of non-
combatants, through the gullet of the box canyon and
into the inviting valley beyond.

Then, when the Apaches were all inside, the rocks
echoed to the reports of the rifles of Terrazas' men until
the uproar was deafening, the canyon walls grew hanging
curtains of drifting smoke, and the Indians died in a blight
of lead and fire.

As has been said, Victorio's best warriors were away on
a raid. He was greatly outnumbered. But the Apache was
always dangerous, never more so than when he was cornered. Ringed completely around with rifles, and with
the bullets cutting his people down about him, the chief
summoned the survivors to make their going memorable.
The Mexicans paid for their victory.

Darkness fell. Throughout the night the continued
crashing of rifles echoed through the basin and spurts of
fire lit the crags with lurid flashes. At early dawn the few
remaining Apache warriors were still fighting, but their
ammunition was almost all gone. About an hour after
sunup their guns were silent at last. Now the Mexicans
charged forward, brave in the knowledge that their enemies were out of cartridges.

Victorio had been wounded more than once during the
battle, but still he rallied his braves. Creeping forward
with Terrazas' scouts was a Tarahumari Indian named
Mauricio, famed for his uncanny skill with the rifle. Some
time during the battle, he caught a glimpse of Victorio
directing his few defenders. The black eye of the Tara-

humari gleamed down the barrel; for an instant the sight
pricked out the bronze figure of the Apache chief; then
the trigger finger pressed.[2]

And so Victorio died—instantly, in the heat of battle,
as he would have wished. His was a character difficult for
the white mind to comprehend. He was an implacable
enemy and his cruelty was notorious. But his long fight
against the white man, carried on for years in spite of the
heart breaking odds against him, was inspired by something akin to what we call patriotism.[3]

Most of Victorio's band died in the basin of the Tres
Castillos with him. The few who escaped were harried
wildly through the mountains. They were without leaders;
surely Apache resistance was at an end.

[2] So delighted was the Governor of Sonora by Mauricio's feat in killing Victorio,
that he later caused the state to present the Tarahumari with a beautiful nickel-
plated rifle in recognition of the event.

[3] "He (Victorio) outwitted two generals of the American army and one in
command of the Mexican forces. He captured from the Governor of Chihuahua,
in one campaign, over five hundred horses. He and his warriors killed over two
hundred New Mexicans, more than one hundred soldiers and two hundred citizens
of the Mexican Republic. . . . This war was the result of the greed of the settler
and the corrupt policy of the government in the management of the Indian affairs
in the Southwest. If Victorio had been permitted to remain at Ojo Caliente it is
more than likely that the terrible devastation following his removal to San Carlos
would never have occurred."—Ralph Emerson Twitchell, "The Leading Facts
of New Mexican History," Vol. II, p. 440.

VIII.

WARRIORS WITHOUT LEADERS
1880–1883

CHAPTER XX

THE RAID OF OLD NANA

AFTER VICTORIO'S DEATH

VICTORIO was dead. That was a fact of prime importance. You cannot replace, with a mere wave of the hand, a man with the gifts of leadership, courage and fighting qualities possessed by the great Mimbreno. The Apaches south of the Mexican border recognized this fact. After the hue and cry following the Tres Castillos fight died down, such sub-chiefs as were left alive thought hard upon who should take the place left vacant, but without successful conclusion. The Apaches were still unconvinced that the white man was all-powerful, but they looked about in vain for a leader of Victorio's stature.

In the months following they roved in small, scattered bands, rather than the single large body which had followed Victorio in his day. Their raids were individual efforts. There was not the plan and the purpose behind them which was characteristic of every move made by the late chief.

Among the sub-chiefs remaining to the wild tribes in the south was one who, although many years Victorio's senior, had always served in a subordinate capacity—old Nana. Under Mangus Colorado he was a simple warrior. Under Victorio he was a lieutenant only. When the Tres Castillos debacle took place, Nana was about eighty years of age,[1] a short, fat and wrinkled old man, much troubled by rheumatism which practically crippled him. Usually he moved slowly, almost feebly. But on occasion he was capable of displaying tremendous sustained energy—as events were to prove. Superannuated he was and there was reason to suppose that his days of activity as a warrior were over. But a strange, belated glory was to be his. After most men, red or white, would have retired to the comfort of a sheltered fireside, to live in the memories of the past, this unimpressive little octogenarian suddenly flamed across the sky of the desert country to write bloody history.

Nana had been Victorio's friend. Hunched in his blanket, he sat high among the mountains, biding his time and gathering his people. Here and there he found them, one or two at a time, where they lurked, terrified and despairing, like wild beasts who knew that the hunter was upon them. In some way Nana gave back to these people their confidence. Then he set about slowly instilling in them again the old fighting fury. It took more than half a year to do it, but by July, 1881, Nana was ready.

There were only fifteen warriors with the old man as he crossed the international line—all that he could gather of Victorio's old fighting array. But loyalties run deep among the Apaches. On this old Nana counted, and with reason. Within a few days after he entered New Mexico, he had been joined by twenty-five more deep-chested, narrow-eyed, fierce-visaged warriors, Mescaleros all, eager to fight the white man once more.

In wide skirmish order, the forty Apaches drifted

[1] This is the estimate of both Charles F. Lummis ("The Land of Poco Tiempo," p. 183) and Britton Davis ("The Truth About Geronimo," p. 115). Of course Nana, like most Indians, did not know his own correct age. He had a clear memory of the events of Mangus Colorado's time, as he showed in conversations with Lieutenant Davis.

through the country, headed for the Alamo Canyon. They slew the sheep herders and ranchers as they went. Nana was an embittered old man. He cared nothing for policies, least of all for mercy. There was to be none of Victorio's easy way with these people on the present raid.

The Alamo Canyon was reached—just when is not known. Up to this time the troops had only the vaguest information that the Indians were in the country. On July 17th, however, a few of Nana's scouts ambushed the pack train of Lieutenant John F. Guilfoyle's 9th Cavalry command, wounded Chief Packer Burgess and captured three mules after a hot little skirmish. That was the first real indication as to Nana's whereabouts. Guilfoyle hurried a message to General Hatch at Fort Stanton and, with his Negro troopers and a detachment of friendly Apache scouts, swung into pursuit of the Indians.

The trail was plain enough. It led west through the Canyon del Perro, the famous "Dog Canyon", where the Mescaleros had suffered a terrible defeat in 1862, as described in an earlier chapter. Now, however, the Indians had learned a different kind of warfare. There would be no catching of Nana in any such place.

The trail left the Canyon del Perro. Hot on the track, two days later, Guilfoyle's Indian scouts came suddenly upon thirteen Apaches at a small ranch house near the Arena Blanca. They had just finished butchering two Mexican men and a woman. So obsessed were they with the work of slaughter, that they might have been taken easily. But the scouts were over-eager. Their first shots were from such long range that they were ineffective. Worse, the raiders had ample warning and skipped up among the high hills where it was impossible for Guilfoyle's men to overtake them.

Once more the soldiers patiently took up the trail. This

time it led toward the San Andreas Mountains, once a favorite camping ground of the dead Victorio. Was it some sentiment which drew the aged Nana thither, to look once more upon the scenes his old friend had loved? Guilfoyle's scouts, puzzling out the trail on the slopes of the San Andreas peaks, located a *ranchería* there, on July 25th. This time, profiting from the lesson at Arena Blanca, they showed some prudence. Instead of a premature rush, they stalked the place as they would have stalked a herd of deer. At the psychological moment they charged. Dashing through the smoke of their own volley, the troops rounded up fourteen captured horses, gathered together a number of blankets and some provisions. But Nana was gone again.

The soldiers thought they had wounded two of the Apaches in the brief fight, and Guilfoyle so reported. But if such was the case the wounds were not very severe. Apparently unhampered, the hostiles danced ahead, leaving a mocking trail, but nothing more; then turned suddenly south and crossed the Rio Grande below San José. On the way they caught and killed two miners and a Mexican herder.

THE DISCOMFITURE OF MITCHELL

And still the bloody game of tag went on. Next news of the ghastly wanderings of the band came on July 30th, when the bedraggled and blood-spattered bodies of four Mexicans were found in the foothills of the San Mateo Mountains. It was a definite clue and the troops started west again. Two days later came still more conclusive evidence that Nana was really prowling in the San Mateos.

Too impatient to await the arrival of the soldiers, a rancher named Mitchell, who had found an Indian trail, gathered a posse of thirty-six men and pursued the

Apaches. The posse had little organization and like most civilian bodies of the type, its members were probably plentifully braced up with alcoholic courage. Nana did not make much of an effort to disguise his trail and the posse followed it vaingloriously, right up the Red Canyon of the San Mateos. The cowboys were cheerful and nonchalant, but they were ignorant of one circumstance which would have sobered them considerably had they known it. All the time they rode up the canyon, the gimlet eyes of Apache warriors were upon them. Later evidence showed that their entire march must have been paralleled by Nana's wraithlike scouts.

At high noon, August 1st, Mitchell, now well up the canyon, called a halt for dinner. There was not much concern about the Indians. The horses were unsaddled and turned loose to graze. A careless guard lounged near the herd and kept a lacklustre eye upon it, while the rest of the party sat down to eat.

A series of wild yells, the drum-roll of a rifle volley, and with blankets waving, a swooping dash of Apache riders broke out of an adjacent gorge. No western horses were ever able to stand a combination of sights and sounds like that without going into hysterics. This herd bolted down the canyon in a cloud of flying dust and pebbles, leaving the guard staring foolishly after it. Mitchell's men were on foot.

There was a brief, red-hot exchange of rifle shots. The Indians had the range and could see the white men, while the cowpunchers had no idea where the Indians were. One after another, eight of Mitchell's men crumpled to the ground. The posse fought bravely enough. But had Nana wished to do so he could have finished them all. Just now his chief interest was in the horses. In a few minutes he left Mitchell and went off to round up the stampeded herd.

The cowboys counted their casualties. One man was dead. Seven more were badly hit. The Indians were gone. Carrying its wounded, the posse began a crestfallen return on foot to the settlements. Nana had taken thirty-eight first-class saddle horses—every head of stock in the party.

Two days after the Apaches' contemptuous noon-day raid on the Mitchell party, Lieutenant Guilfoyle reached the San Mateos and took up the trail in Red Canyon where the posse had, perforce, abandoned it. He speedily found where Nana had left the gorge—sure evidence, in the form of a Mexican's mangled corpse. Guilfoyle drove his flagging command to the limit of its endurance, and was almost rewarded. On August 3rd he actually caught up with the hostile band—for a minute. But it was only a minute. The Indians were near the Santa Monica Springs. What followed could scarcely be called a fight. A couple of volleys and the Apaches were gone. Guilfoyle again reported the wounding of two of the enemy. And he captured eleven worn-out horses, abandoned by the Indians, together with some blankets. But wily old Nana had slipped away again.

Crippled by rheumatism and bent with old age, the chief had already ridden hundreds of miles with his young men, keeping ahead of the best cavalry in the Southwest, and still he showed no signs of giving out. Cool and crafty as ever, he considered the situation. He knew by now that the entire military establishment of New Mexico was swarming through the mountains and across the deserts to corner him. Nana really had ample reason to feel flattered. General Hatch had put every available soldier in the field. According to army records there were at this time eight troops of cavalry, eight companies of infantry, and two companies of Indian scouts, all hunting for the tiny Apache band. Nana had lost some warriors through wounds and desertions. He had now only about twenty or thirty braves left. But he was undaunted and confident as he prepared to circumvent every plan and resource the soldiers opposed to him.

Without pausing, except to gather up horses wherever possible, he traversed the desert to La Savoya. There, on August 11th, eight days after the brush at Santa Monica Springs, Guilfoyle, still following, came upon the grim signs of Nana's recent presence to which he was by now becoming so accustomed—two Mexicans, their bodies bearing the unmistakable and horrible mutilations of Apache hatred. The troops learned later that two Mexican women had been carried off from this same place.

In spite of his utmost efforts, efforts which well-nigh killed his command, Guilfoyle was falling far behind. What cavalry could follow these raiders? It is a rule of army tactics [2] that twenty-five miles a day is the absolute limit which cavalry can stand in overland marching. Guilfoyle exceeded that every day of his campaign. Some days he did forty miles or more. Yet, Nana, old and crippled, rode away from the troopers as if they had been infantry.

Of course the Indians had a number of advantages. Whenever their horses wore out, they changed them—their remount depots being the nearest ranches or settlements. They carried practically nothing but their arms and ammunition. Their commissary was the country—the mescal, the mesquite bean, and the prickly pear. For meat they occasionally shot a deer, but the usual repast was a horse or mule, slaughtered when it could run no longer, and cut up almost before life was extinct, to be roasted and gorged by the warriors. The Apaches knew

[2] Upton's "Cavalry Tactics," p. 477.

every spot where water could be found, no matter how small and inaccessible. But they did not need water like the white man. With a pebble under the tongue to keep the saliva flowing, one of Nana's raiders could go without water under the blaze of the desert sun two days longer than a white man could survive.

And so Nana left Guilfoyle plodding through the sand, eliminated from further consideration as an antagonist. But another adversary came cutting across at an angle— Captain Charles Parker, who had seen some of the hardest campaigning in the Victorio War. Parker had with him only nineteen 9th Cavalry troopers, but, about twenty-five miles west of Sabinal, on August 12th, he ran squarely into the Apaches. It was foolhardy for the nineteen soldiers to try conclusions with the deadly Apaches who, though reduced in numbers, still outnumbered them. But without hesitation the colored troopers went into action.

There could, of course, be but one outcome to such a contest. Nana's warriors spread out and melted through the underbrush, like the pouring coils of a great serpent. The cavalrymen also took to cover. There was a period of blind shooting. Then, as suddenly as they had appeared, the Apaches were gone. Parker checked his losses. One trooper was dead and three wounded. And one man was missing. There was small doubt that he had been carried off by the Indians. The thought of his fate, somewhere back in those barren hills, when the Apaches had the leisure to devise for him a new way of dying, brought a shiver even to these veteran soldiers.

Parker, of course, was helpless. There was no pursuit —the little command had been too roughly handled in the brief time it had felt Nana's teeth, and, for the time being, nobody wished any further experience of the same kind.

SAFE OVER THE BORDER

Again the Apaches distanced the troops. During this raid they sometimes rode as much as seventy miles a day, with old, rheumatic Nana at their head. They had fought off three separate detachments of pursuers now, but southern New Mexico was swarming with soldiers. Within four days of his fight with Parker, Nana again tasted the mettle of the army.

This time it was Lieutenant Gustavus Valois, with another troop of the ubiquitous 9th Cavalry. Nana knew they were dogging his trail. Not far from Cuchillo Negro, named after the famous Mimbreno chief, the old warrior turned viciously. Always from cover, with never a sign of where they lurked, except for frequent spurts of fluffy rifle smoke, the Indians snaked through the mesquite and cactus. Courageously the troopers fought back. They gave a good account of themselves, but they could not deal with this enemy. They were facing the finest skirmishers in the world.

Lieutenant George R. Burnett, second in command, was wounded twice. Two enlisted men were killed. And a good share of the troop's horses were killed or crippled by the Apache fire. Nana, once he was satisfied that he had left the detachment so it could not follow him, withdrew as quickly as he went into action. Beating off a sally from the flank by Lieutenant F. B. Taylor and another troop of the 9th, the Apache raiders moved rapidly toward the Black Range.

In addition to three or four hundred civilians, General Hatch had approximately a thousand soldiers swarming through the country. Yet Nana with his handful laughed at the efforts to catch him.

Satisfied at last with his raid, the old chief turned back

toward Mexico after his fight with Valois and Taylor. But before he left the United States he stopped to teach the white man a final lesson.

With a detachment of twenty 9th Cavalry troopers, Lieutenant G. W. Smith was toiling on the Indians' trail, near McEver's ranch, on August 18th. George Daly, a rancher, brought a party of cowboys to help the soldiers and see the fun. The combined force far outnumbered Nana's warriors. But the odds failed to worry the old Apache. He chose his ground, and his dusty fighters took to cover. The drifting smoke from their rifles and the staccato rattle of their volley, were the first hint the white men had that they had caught up with their foes.

That Apache fire was wickedly deadly. Daly, leader of the cowboys, was killed. Here and there troopers dropped as the heavy bullets from the Indians' rifles found their marks. Finally the gallant young Lieutenant Smith, in the act of directing his men to a more efficient disposal of their force, crumpled dead in the sagebrush.

That ended the fight. Six men were dead, including both the cowboys' and soldiers' leaders, and others were wounded. Neither the Negro troopers nor the white ranchers cared to go any further into the mattter with Nana. The Apaches drew off and continued their course, unimpeded, to the border. Late in August they reached Old Mexico and rejoined their people in the mountains.

One may search long for a duplicate to this raid. In less than two months, Nana, handicapped by age and physical disabilities, led his handful of braves over a thousand miles of enemy territory, maintaining himself and his followers in the country as they went. He fought eight battles with the Americans, winning them all; killed anywhere from thirty to fifty of his enemy, wounded large numbers more; captured two women and not less than two hundred horses and mules; eluded pursuit by more than a thousand soldiers, not to mention three or four hundred civilians—and did it all with a force which numbered only fifteen warriors at the start and never exceeded forty braves.

Not even Victorio himself ever equalled that record.

Chapter XXI

THE PUNISHMENT OF LOCO

OVER THE BORDER AT DUSK

Chato and Nachite, with their handful of Chiricahuas, squatted in the heights of the Sierra Madre and stared northward across the border. Those pallid mauve shadows of distant ranges they saw over the horizon, were in the United States. Between stretched the dun-gray desert with dark masses of intervening mountains forming opaque blotches on its harsh surface.

The two chiefs presented a vivid contrast. Nachite was the son of the great, dead Cochise. He was said also to be the grandson of the mighty Mangus Colorado, by a daughter of his marriage to a Mexican girl.[1] If this was so he inherited more of the blood of the Mexican beauty than of the Apache bull. He was a tall, loose-jointed, graceful Indian, a dandy in his dress, with a handsome, almost effeminate face, and slender, elegant hands. One thing did he inherit from Mangus Colorado—his magnificent height. Nachite stood six feet, one inch tall in his moccasins. Fonder of drinking and feminine society than of war, he lacked the stubborn force of leadership. Still, he was the hereditary chief of the Chiricahuas, and as such maintained a ranking position in council.

[1] The Mexican girl referred to is the one for whom Mangus is said to have fought his famous double duel. One of her daughters by him was given to Cochise as a wife. This was to cement diplomatic relations between the Mimbrenos and the Chiricahuas.

Chato, on the other hand, was an Apache of Apaches. He was short, barrel chested, with wiry legs and a bull neck. His face was marred by a flat nose, due to his having been kicked by a mule. That was the significance of his name, Chato—Flat Nose. With this disfigurement, his features were a mask of impassivity, and he possessed to the full the right Apache lust for fighting.

Behind the two chiefs sat their lean, dark-visaged warriors, also looking northward. Come nightfall, the danger would begin. It had been months since the Apaches had raided on the American side of the border. All knew of the perils and the success of old Nana's wild ride in the summer of 1881. But this was April, 1882.

It was a bold move the Indians were planning. Somewhere on the other side of the mauve ranges lay the heated flats of the San Carlos reservation. There lived others of their people—Chiricahuas, Mimbrenos and Tontos, chafing in impotence, eating out their hearts like wild animals caged in a zoo, crazy to be free again. Chato and Nachite were going to free them.

The plan was simple but audacious in the extreme. They would strike north at dark, cross the border, and head for the reservation. Once across the line, all knew, every moment would be fraught with peril. United States soldiers patrolled nearly every foot of the border. There were thousands of them, reinforced by hundreds of Apache scouts—trailers and fighters as keen, as tireless, and as deadly as the hostiles themselves. Yet so sure were Chato and Nachite of their own ability, that they considered their coming raid anything but a forlorn hope.

Dusk fell at last. Like lethal spectres the Apaches left the heights, mounted their wiry ponies and began their march. Two days later, on April 20th, every telegraph key in every military post on the border was clicking. The

Chiricahuas had struck—struck so suddenly and so stunningly that the first notice of their presence was the blow itself. A sudden attack at San Carlos, and back toward the border headed the raiders, accompanied by Loco, chief of the reservation Mimbrenos, and several score of the imprisoned Apaches.

Loco was one of the last of the old followers of Mangus Colorado. He was naturally a good-humored man, but he had lost an eye, either through trachoma or some accident, and this gave him an unpleasantly sinister appearance which, those who knew him said, was belied by his true character. He had, for several years, remained peacefully on the reservation, in spite of the almost unsupportable indignities he had to suffer. Even as he rode south with Chato and Nachite, his heart was filled with misgivings. Indeed he would not have come at all had not the raiders threatened him with a rifle and forced him to mount and ride.

Within an hour after the raid at San Carlos troops at all the border posts were ready to move. By dawn next day soldiers and their Indian scouts were on the march everywhere. Arizona was full of them. The fact that many women and children from Loco's band were with them, was a serious handicap to the Apaches. It had been a very dry spring. Most of the streamlets and desert tanks, as well as the springs, were waterless. Cumbered as they were, the Indians must stick to the river courses. Not even Apache women and children could stand the dread *jornada* across the desert without water. They rode along the line of the Gila River which took them over into New Mexico.

Lieutenant Colonel George A. Forsyth,[2] commanding

[2] Forsyth was a frontier hero. He it was who, with fifty white scouts, held off the combined forces of Cheyennes and Sioux in the bloody battle on the Arickaree River, in eastern Colorado, during the fall of 1868. Forsyth knew Indians. His deductions in this case were perfect.

at Fort Cummings, New Mexico, knew the condition of the country and shrewdly guessed the route of the raiders. As soon as word of the attack reached him, he sent a scouting party under Lieutenant C. S. Hall down to the Hatchet Mountains, in the extreme southwest corner of the Territory, and followed at once with six troops—about four hundred men—of the 4th Cavalry.

MCDONALD IS AMBUSHED

Along the eastward border of the Steins Peak Range rode the cavalry. Ranging far off to the side, at the base of the mountains themselves, was Lieutenant D. N. McDonald, with a few Yuma and Mojave scouts and a corporal, trying to "cut" any Indian trails which might lead up into the hills. On the morning of April 23rd, three days after the San Carlos fight, McDonald sent word that he had struck a small trail about twelve hours old, leading toward the Gila. A little later a second message informed Forsyth that another, larger party had joined the first. The colonel was now worried about McDonald. He continued his march but sent two enlisted men back with the messenger. The little party of scouts was at this time about sixteen miles west of the main column. Both bodies were moving in a northwesterly direction.

It was terrifically hot. The dust mounted in stifling clouds, so thick that it was almost impossible to breathe. The hats, uniforms, faces and moustaches of the men were gray with a thick layer of it. Tears from their eyes, caused by the blinding fog, made rivulets of pure mud down their cheeks. Above them a dun cloud mounted in a dense column and hung for minutes after the horses had passed.

A sudden shout at the rear of the column and through the screen of dust the men descried an Indian scout—

one of McDonald's men—lashing his horse across the desert at full speed. In another minute he was with them. By words and signs he told them: McDonald had been ambushed. At least four of his scouts were dead. The lieutenant and his surviving men were besieged, fighting for their lives.

Bugles blared. In perfect order the squadrons wheeled, each in its position, and started off at an angle. "Gallop" sang the bugles. Four hundred horses broke into a run. It was a sixteen-mile gallop across the stifling plain. There was ample reason to fear that the horses could not stand the pace, but with Forsyth grimly leading, stand it they did.

As they neared the mountains, the distant clatter of rifle fire reached their ears. They were in time, then. A few minutes later Forsyth's troopers cheered hoarsely. A man had appeared high up on one of the spurs of the range, waving his carbine. It was McDonald himself. Very soon, breathless but ready for trouble, they reached him and he made his report to Forsyth.

It had been a typical piece of Apache cunning. And it was a bit of carelessness, very rare for these Indians, which prevented the killing of every man in the scouting party. Moving close to the foot of the range that morning, the chief scout, Yuma Bill, pointed out to the lieutenant a wisp of smoke up a gorge. They halted. Were there Indians up there, or was it the dying campfire of some prospector or hunter? McDonald had to find out. Up the defile he cautiously led his men. They found the remains of a camp high up in the gorge—evidently of a considerable number of Indians. No Apaches were there. But the scouts were warned. Save for this discovery, they might have walked later right into Loco's well laid trap.

The march was resumed at the foot of the mountains.

War Department

War Department

Left: Al Sieber (seated in center), chief of scouts in the Department of Arizona, with some of his Apache scouts. The white man in the background is an official from Washington who "dressed up" for this picture. Right: General Adna R. Chaffee, who as a captain, was in command of the troops which defeated the White Mountain Apaches under Nan-tia-tish at the Battle of Chevelon's Fork.

Left: Chato, Chiricahua chief, who chose imprisonment rather than betray
his people. Right: Nachite, the elegant and weak chief of the Chiricahua
Apaches.

It was a plain trail now, leading toward the Gila. Suddenly, with a sharp exclamation, Yuma Bill stopped them. He had caught a glimpse of a movement up ahead. In a moment they all saw—two men on the mountain side. Rifles came forward; but they were lowered in a moment. The men were white prospectors. They had hidden in the underbrush and Loco's Indians by some miracle had passed by without noticing them. Perhaps they were too preoccupied with getting back to Mexico. Not one of them investigated the hiding place. They passed on, gaunt, grim, and deadly, and disappeared.[3]

McDonald sent the prospectors on to Lordsburg and proceeded. Again Yuma Bill stopped and pointed to the rocks above. "Two Injun!" he grunted. Sure enough. A pair of Apache warriors. The scouts dropped out of sight. Cautiously Yuma Bill raised his head above the boulders.

"Watch out, McDonald!" he shrieked. The words were punctuated with a blast of rifle fire which burst almost in their faces. Fourteen or fifteen Apaches lay on the other side of the very rocks behind which the scouts were concealed. Three of McDonald's Indians were killed by that volley. Yuma Bill was badly wounded.

Down the slope galloped the survivors—for life. A bullet sang through the lieutenant's hat and another singed his neck. Yuma Bill did not follow. He sat his horse where he was, gradually buckling forward in his saddle, until he pitched to the ground, dead. The six remaining scouts and the corporal, as well as the officer, owed their lives only to atrocious shooting by the Apaches. Not one was hit as they galloped away.

[3] McDonald said that these two prospectors were the most abjectly terrified men he ever saw. They seemed to think that his Indians were part of the hostile band and it took an almost brutal tongue lashing from the officer to bring them to a realization that they were among friends. Small wonder they were frightened. If ever death passed close to men, it passed close to these two as the Apaches rode by. (See General George A. Forsyth, "Thrilling Days of Army Life," pp. 93-94.)

Extending out from the main range was a high, rocky spur, terminating in a small hill. There McDonald halted. He looked around for a man to ride for help, selected Qua-de-le-the-go (Blood), his youngest scout, and sent him speeding away to find Forsyth.[4] The others began piling rocks in front of them. McDonald knew that he had run into the main body of hostiles. The Indians were so sure of finishing the scouting party that they did not at once advance. First they gathered the bodies of the four dead scouts into a pile and built a bonfire on them.

This was more than McDonald could stand. He crept forward three hundred yards, took meticulous aim under a low-spreading mesquite bush, and brought down one of the Apaches. Still the hostiles delayed their attack. McDonald decided on another retreat. He and his men began to ride down the spurs of the mountain, pursued now by the savages. Forsyth arrived just in time to save them.

THE BATTLE OF HORSE SHOE CANYON

Loco, watching from the heights which his Apaches occupied, must have viewed with considerable distaste the sight on the plateau below him. His warriors occupied the high bluffs on both sides of Horse Shoe Canyon, a deep cleft in the Steins Peak Mountains. As he viewed the advance of the troops, his harsh visage must have scowled and the single eye in it gleamed with ferocity.

It was true that his warriors were of the best. But there were not enough of them to oppose the masses of United States soldiers deploying before them. Old in the game

---

[4] The scouts were fortunate in having the troop race horse with them. This animal "Jumping Jack," a very fast runner, really saved all their lives. Qua-de-le-the-go killed him in the terrific ride to Forsyth, but a slower steed might not have taken the message through in time. As it was the rescuers did not arrive a minute too soon.

of war, Loco and Chato could estimate the numbers of opposing forces as well as anybody. There were four hundred soldiers there, to which the Apaches could oppose only seventy-five braves. And the enemy had all the advantage of ammunition and arms, as well as being unencumbered with non-combatants.

The helpless women and children in his train were what made Loco's problem difficult. Clearly there was no advantage to be gained by fighting the troops. He would much rather have withdrawn as quickly as possible. But he had to cover the retreat of his people.

Dismounted, with carbines in hand, the soldiers were already beginning their climb up the mountain. Well, blood would have to be spilled. Loco, who had gone on the war path unwillingly, prepared to do the best he could, now that battle was thrust upon him.

The deep-cut Horse Shoe Canyon possessed some natural features of which the chief took prompt advantage. To the right were some lofty cliffs. In the middle of the gorge stood a mass of huge rocks, forming a small peak joined to the wall on the right by an escarpment about thirty feet high which formed a causeway over to the central rocks. On these vantage points Loco placed his warriors. Colonel Forsyth later commented thus admiringly upon the dispositions of the Apaches: "The position occupied by the hostiles was a capital one." [5] But just now he was most interested in driving them out.

Two flanking parties, containing two troops of dismounted cavalry each, were formed by Forsyth, with a fifth troop as a horse guard, and the sixth under himself in the center. Major Wirt Davis, commanding the right wing, opened the battle. Carefully Loco watched the advance of the soldiers. His warriors fought warily. As the

[5] Forsyth, "Thrilling Days of Army Life," p. 105.

vastly superior forces of his enemy enveloped his positions, one by one, his braves retreated. Occasionally an Apache crashed down from his perch in the cliffs. But the defense was stubborn. In spite of the tremendous fire superiority the troops maintained throughout the fight, it took hours for the soldiers to dislodge the savages. But step by step Forsyth drove the Indians back. As evening fell the last of the hostile warriors were so far up the canyon that they could not be reached. Then the troops rested.

There were thirteen dead Apaches in that hard-won canyon. And others were wounded. But Loco had succeeded in the one thing which concerned him most. His warriors had held back the white men until the women and children got away. In doing so they had killed three troopers and four scouts, besides wounding eight or ten men. Considering the disparity in numbers, the honors were very much with Loco.

Time was an essential. Leaving Forsyth entangled in the gorge, the Apaches moved swiftly over the range, down on the other side. Across the San Simon Valley they went, toward the Chiricahua peaks. Forsyth extricated his command from the canyon and followed. Next morning he was joined by Captain Gordon and Lieutenant Gatewood, with a troop of cavalry and a company of Indian scouts. If he could only catch up with the hostiles now——

But there was no overtaking them. Carrying their wounded, the Indians crossed the border, killing a number of people in the valley as they went.

COLONEL GARCIA'S VICTORY

For years the Apaches had scoffed at the Mexicans. The Indians lived in the mountains of northern Mexico practically unmolested. But now the Mexicans were to prove themselves as deadly as tarantulas. Colonel Lorenzo Garcia, of the 6th Mexican Infantry, with two hundred and fifty men, was patrolling the border when he heard that the Chiricahuas under Chato and Nachite, had crossed to the north on their raid into Arizona. As brave and skillful a soldier as the Mexican army boasted, Garcia made his plans at once to strike the Indians when they returned. He knew that on their way back the Apaches would be so occupied by the thought of pursuit that they would be unlikely to think of danger ahead.

His scouts, near the western edge of the Janos Plain, brought word to him April 27th that they could see a cloud of dust, made by a large party and travelling fast, coming up the valley from the north. Garcia concluded that it must be the raiding Apaches returning to Mexico.

The trail led up a mountain canyon. Using the Indians' own tactics, he laid an ambush. While he did not know the exact numbers of his enemy, with his two hundred and fifty soldiers he had reason to believe himself numerically superior.

The plan worked out better than he dreamed. Oblivious of danger ahead of them, the Indians came on as they never would have done in the days of Mangus Colorado or Victorio. The women, children and old men were ahead. Far behind hung back the warriors, watching Forsyth's dust cloud, many miles to their rear. The first hint of danger came too late. Like a clap of thunder among the hills the Mexican volley crashed out. The Apache caravan writhed like a shattered snake. It was the non-combatants upon whom the Mexicans had fired. Dropping loot and camp bundles in the trail, the brown figures bolted for the nearest cover. There was something more than loot lying on the trail. A thick cluster of bodies showed where the bullets had cut their swath. As the gray pall of smoke drifted away from in front of Garcia's men, scores of women and children lay stricken.

The Mexicans sprang in pursuit of the fleeing survivors. But now the rocks began to spit fire as the Apache warriors, hurrying up, fought back. There was one death spot in particular. An old Apache, long past his prime, had burrowed into a small depression behind a thick clump of cactus. Venomous as a snake he fought there. Time after time as Garcia's soldiers tried to circle him or rush him, his rifle spat death. Eight Mexican soldiers were killed by him before his ammunition gave out. Then the soldiers killed him.

The fight was still raging. Bullets kept crying like banshees as they struck rocks on the mountain sides and ricocheted. But the advantage was all with the Mexicans. They had four rifles to the Apaches' one. They were in better position. Slowly the Indians retreated down the canyon, until at last they disappeared.

Garcia had lost two officers and nineteen men killed, and three officers and thirteen men wounded, a total of thirty-seven. But the Indians had received a crushing blow. There were seventy-eight dead among the rocks, chiefly women and children. Moreover, there was a huddled group of more than a score of captives, all women and children.[6] It was the most terrible reverse the Apaches had suffered in years.

But the Mexican victory was by no means complete. A disproportionate number of the dead and captured were non-combatants. Most of the warriors—the deadly, vicious

[6] One of these was Loco's daughter. She told the Mexicans her father had been forced to accompany the raiders against his will. This story has been repeated over and over again until the writer believes it was true. Loco may have been forced to go on the war path, but he entered fully into the spirit of the affair once he embarked upon it.

killers—escaped. And among these were Loco, Chato and Nachite. Mexico and the United States were to hear more from them.

Next day Garcia had a delicate duty to perform. Ignoring instructions to the contrary, Forsyth pursued the Indians right across the border into Mexico. Garcia had to stop him.

The two commanders met at a small ravine. The Mexican was courteous but firm. He said his government had ordered him to oppose any invasion of its territory by the Americans. Forsyth was equally meticulous. But he insisted on pursuing the Apaches, who, he said, had murdered many people in Arizona and New Mexico, besides burning homes, stealing livestock and causing great property damage. Then Garcia sprang his surprise.

"If your sole object is the punishment of this band of marauders," he said, "it is already accomplished. My command fought, routed, and scattered them yesterday." [7]

Forsyth had not an argument left. He asked permission to visit the battle field, and Garcia himself took him there. The scattered dead, still lying unburied where they had fallen, were sufficient proof. The American saluted his soldierly acquaintance and with his command started back for the United States.

[7] Forsyth, "Thrilling Days of Army Life," p. 118.

CHAPTER XXII

THE BLUNDER OF NAN-TIA-TISH

TRAGEDY AT CIBICU

AFTER Crook chastised the White Mountain Apaches in 1872, they were exemplary in their conduct for nearly ten years. But in August, 1881, the medicine man Nok-e-da-klinne, by his prophecies and magic working, which convinced the Indians that he was divine, stirred up a deep current of unrest among them.

Nok-e-da-klinne was believed to have the power of bringing the dead to life. He held ceremonial dances to repopulate the country with Apaches and drive out the whites.[1] The situation was reported as "very serious" to General E. A. Carr, commanding at Fort Apache, and late in August he sent a runner to summon Nok-e-da-klinne to a conference. With some of his followers the medicine man came to the fort where General Carr advised them to give up the dances, warning them of serious trouble if they continued to incite the Indians.

But by this time the Apaches were fanatical and when Nok-e-da-klinne returned to his village on Cibicu Creek, about forty miles back in the Indian country, they continued their dances. Up to this time there had been no hos-

---

[1] It is strange how similar this trouble was to the Ghost Dance trouble among the Sioux in 1890, although on a much smaller scale. The same claim, of repopulating the country with Indians and driving out the whites, was made; dances were the chief features of the ceremonies in both cases; and bloodshed was the result of each.

tilities, although the excitement was growing constantly.

Carr considered the condition so serious that on August 30th, after talking with Agent Tiffany, he ordered Captain E. C. Hentig, 6th Cavalry, to proceed to the Cibicu country and arrest the medicine man. Hentig took two troops of cavalry and a company of Indian scouts under Lieutenant Thomas Cruse.

The arrest order was a mistake. Nok-e-da-klinne was an impostor, but he had attained great influence among his people. Some of those who believed in him most profoundly were the very scouts whom Cruse took to make the arrest. Moreover, the act made a martyr out of the medicine man, and some saw in it evidence that the white men feared his powers.

Nok-e-da-klinne was at his home, peacefully preparing to plant corn, when Hentig arrested him. The forty mile journey back to the fort began. There was a queer, strained atmosphere among Cruse's Indian scouts. For days they had been acting strangely, so much so that on August 17th the lieutenant had temporarily disarmed them, and Carr in a telegram on that date to General Irwin McDowell, spoke of the "general belief in their disposition to treachery." The whole command marched about five miles back toward Fort Apache and camped for the night. Almost immediately scores of Apaches from Nok-e-da-klinne's camp appeared on the scene, glowering and threatening.

A tense situation. Hentig felt the electric atmosphere and ordered the scouts to camp at a distance from the soldiers who had charge of Nok-e-da-klinne. Dusk fell. Without a word of warning, Cruse's scouts, who had served faithfully, even heroically, in the Indian campaigns, mutinied.

The overt act came when one of the scouts approached

too close to the soldiers' camp. Hentig shouted an order at him to move away. This Indian, Mosby, had been followed by other scouts. As the captain called out his order, he turned to pick up a rifle.

All in a moment the peaceful valley woke to tumultuous action. Guns crashed. Captain Hentig and Privates Bird, Sullivan, Miller, Levingston, Amick, and Sondergass were killed by that first, sudden volley. Private Foran died later from his wounds. Sergeant McDonnell and Private Betty were wounded. The place was a shambles.

Three of Cruse's scouts, Deadshot, Dandy Jim, and Skitashe, made a daring attempt to release the medicine man from the soldiers' camp during the height of the fighting. But Bugler Ahrens saw them, ran up, and pumped three bullets from his army Colt into Nok-e-da-klinne's head.

Nine men were dead or dying and several had been wounded in the brief minutes of furious shooting. The Indians retreated. Lieutenant W. H. Carter, upon whom the command devolved at Hentig's death, posted sentries and everybody stood to arms during the night. A detail was told off to bury the dead. Sergeant John A. Smith was in command of the squad. While the graves were being dug, Smith observed a movement. Running to where the corpses lay, he saw the horrifying spectacle of the medicine man, Nok-e-da-klinne, the blood and brains oozing from the bullet holes in his head, hitching himself along the ground. The old Indian was blinded, probably shattered mentally by the lead slugs in his brain, but the invincible Apache determination to live drove him to crawl slowly along the ground toward where instinct said safety lay. Smith glanced about. A shot would alarm the command. But an axe lay near. The sergeant seized it, bent over the creeping horror. Once, twice the steel head rose and fell. Smith stepped back. Nok-e-da-klinne crawled no more.[2]

At Fort Apache, meantime, the troops had learned in no uncertain way of the Apaches' resentment. The government telegraph line was cut, and from all about the fort the savages opened fire. Lieutenant Gordon was wounded. There were five or six thousand Indians on the reservation and it was feared they would all join in the revolt. Timely arrival of reinforcements under Major Gorden, from Fort Thomas, saved Carr's troops. The Indians sullenly retreated to their homes. Three freighters whose wagon train had been cut off, two civilians who had left the fort against orders, three soldiers who had been detailed to guard the Black River ferry, a rancher named Fibs, shot in his own shack, and a mail carrier—these were the casualties of the fighting which resulted from the arrest of Nok-e-da-klinne. Eleven soldiers and seven civilians were dead. So far as has been learned, the medicine man himself was the only Indian fatality.

A month after the Cibicu affair, things were complicated at San Carlos when part of the Chiricahuas, refusing to move from Camp Goodwin to Fort Apache, killed Albert Sterling, chief of the Indian police, and tried to kill the sub-agent, Ezra Hoag. Then they cut the throats of all their dogs, that they might not be betrayed by the barking, stabbed their old or ailing horses, to avoid being encumbered by them, and, leaving behind every bit of camp equipment that was bulky or unnecessary, hurriedly and silently fled to the Sierra Madre of Mexico.

[2] As a trophy Smith took from the dead man's neck a medal commemorating the peace established by Colyer. On the obverse side of the medal was President Grant's head and the words: "United States of America. Let us have peace. Liberty and justice." On the reverse was the globe with a number of implements signifying agriculture and the sentiment, "On earth peace, good will to men. 1871." The irony of such phrases on the dead man's breast seems not to have struck anybody at the time.

They fought one skirmish on the way, with two troops of the 6th Cavalry, at Cedar Creek, killed a sergeant and two men and escaped to the mountains where they were a constant menace.

Subsequently a military tribunal dealt sternly with the Cibicu mutineers. Five of the scouts were tried by court-martial. Two were sent to prison on Alcatraz Island. The other three, Dandy Jim, Deadshot and Skitashe, were hanged at Camp Grant, on March 3rd, 1882.

It was thought the trouble was ended. But it was far from that. In April, 1882, little more than a month after the execution of the mutineers, Chato and Nachite returned from Mexico, forced old Loco and his band to accompany them, as described in the preceding chapter, and fought their way back across the border. All these events combined to keep the White Mountain Apaches very much stirred up. Yet they remained peaceful in spite of their execrable treatment by the Indian agents, who seemed to be in league with the malodorous Tucson Ring.[3]

Trouble should have been expected, but when it came it surprised everyone. Without any warning, on July 6th, fifty-four White Mountain Apaches, led by Nan-tia-tish and Ar-she, swept down on the San Carlos Agency. They kidnaped a dozen or more squaws. Then they rode wildly up the San Carlos Valley, killing as they went. A few

[3] The following excerpts from the report of the Federal Grand Jury of Arizona, October 24th, 1882, will give some idea of conditions:

". . . never until present investigations . . . laid bare the infamy . . . could a proper idea be formed of the fraud and villainy which are constantly practiced in open violation of law . . . Fraud, peculation, conspiracy . . . seem to be the rule on this reservation (San Carlos) . . . In collusion with the chief clerk and storekeeper, rations can be issued *ad libitum* for which the government must pay while the proceeds pass into the capacious pockets of the agent. Indians are set to work in coal fields, superintended by white men; all the workmen and superintendents are fed and frequently paid from agency stores and no return of the same is made . . . All surplus supplies are used in the interest of the agent . . . Government contractors . . . get receipts for large amounts of supplies never furnished. In the meantime, the Indians are neglected, half-fed, discontented, and turbulent."

miles from the agency, they ambushed J. L. (Cibicu Charley) Colvig, who had succeeded Albert Sterling as agency police chief. With Colvig died seven of his Indian scouts.

The Apaches now rode north, past the city of Globe, across the Pleasant Valley, and on, leaving behind a trail of blood and smoking ruins. These Indians were the Cibicu White Mountain Apaches, the same who had believed devoutly in Nok-e-da-klinne. Never had they forgiven the arrest and murder of their prophet. As this band rode up the San Carlos and over to the Tonto Basin, it raided every ranch it passed, destroyed property worth many thousands of dollars and killed six ranchers.

With the army's usual promptness, fourteen companies of soldiers, with strong details of Indian scouts, took the field. There was especial anxiety about this outbreak, since the Apaches were headed north and might get into the Navajo Country. But they were found to have gone to the Tonto Basin, where they attacked the Sigsbee Ranch, killing Bob Sigsbee and Louie Houdon.

THE BATTLE OF CHEVELON'S FORK

By the morning of July 17th, ten troops of cavalry were converging on the Indians' trail, with others close behind. Yet they might not have overtaken the marauders, had it not been for a blunder by Nan-tia-tish, leader of the hostile band.

Nan-tia-tish fancied himself a war chief. Thirsty for fame, he conceived a plan of ambushing the leading troop of cavalry, which chanced to be Captain Adna R. Chaffee's white horse troop of the 6th Cavalry. Those white horses were easy to descry on the back trail. The hawk eyed Apaches kept them under surveillance, knew their exact number, and every detail of their movements. So interested were the Indians in Chaffee and his white horses, that they quite overlooked the fact that other soldiers were following behind him. Nan-tia-tish set his trap, basing his plans on his optimistic but sadly mistaken belief that the white horse troop was alone on his trail.

As if a giant axe had split the mountains, a canyon, variously known as Chevelon's Fork of the Canyon Diablo, or the Big Dry Wash, cuts its way through the Mogollons. Only seven hundred yards wide at the top, it drops away fully a thousand feet deep, its sides so steep that they actually overhang in places, with pine trees growing wherever they can find a precarious foothold. At the bottom is a fair-sized mountain stream which appears to be a mere trickle from the heights above.

Here Nan-tia-tish prepared his ambush. Marksmen lay along the side of the canyon in such a way that when the soldiers descended into it, as they must do if they followed the trail which the Indians had purposely left, they would be caught almost helpless. Toward this trap, Chaffee, hot on the track, came riding July 17th, 1882.

On the evening before Captain George L. Converse, with his command, had joined Chaffee. By merest chance Converse's troop was also mounted on white horses. So incompetent was Nan-tia-tish that he did not even notice the increased numbers as the combined force advanced. Victorio or Nana would instantly have seen the change. But the White Mountain leader lacked their calibre. Fatuously confident that he had to deal with only one troop, he proceeded with his plans.

Even with his increased force, Chaffee would have been severely handled had he gone into the canyon as Nan-tia-tish planned. But he had with him Al Sieber, chief of the Arizona scouts, and Lieutenant George H. Morgan, with eight Tonto Apache trailers. The uncanny eyesight of these Indians really unmasked the trap.

As soon as Chaffee was shown the situation, he dismounted his men on the brink of the canyon opposite the position of Nan-tia-tish and waited. He knew, as the Apaches did not, that Colonel Evans was right behind with the main body of the troops. Shortly Evans rode up and Chaffee made his report. The colonel, with generous courtesy, told him to take charge of the fight, as he had found the Indians and deserved the credit. Chaffee was delighted. In the battle which followed, he handled his men like a born general.

At his order Converse's men dismounted and crawled forward to the brink of the canyon, where they opened a heavy fire across the chasm. Lieutenant Frank West took his own troop and that of Chaffee, together with Al Sieber and part of the Tonto scouts, far to the east, looking for a place to cross over the canyon. At the same time Chaffee sent the remaining troops under Captain L. A. Abbott along the canyon wall in the opposite direction. Morgan and the rest of the Tontos accompanied this detachment. The pack train and cavalry horses remained under a guard.

A spitting, snarling rifle duel was already in progress between Converse's troop and the Apaches across the gorge. Early in the engagement a bullet from the hostiles split on a rock and half of it penetrated Converse's eyeball. He suffered intense pain from this wound, but survived.

The Apaches were so busy shooting at Converse's men that they did not observe the two flanking detachments. Far down the canyon West at last discovered a steep pathway by which his men could descend to the bottom and then climb the other side. It was a desperate scramble, real danger every foot of the way. All they could hope was that the situation would remain uncomplicated by their being discovered by the Indians as the troopers hung by their toes and finger nails. Luck was with them. Unchallenged, they reached the top and moved forward in skirmish order through the pine woods.

Abbott's column, meanwhile, had an easier time finding a way across and got into action first. Evans and Chaffee heard the rippling crash of the first volley soon after Abbott departed on his detour. The Apaches had not discovered West's detachment at all. They turned their attention toward Abbott and went swarming through the trees to fight him. While the battle roared in that direction, Sieber and his scouts, closing in from the east, ran right into the herd of Indian ponies. So busy were the Apache horse guards watching in the direction of the battle noise that they did not realize the scouts were upon them until the first point-blank volley wiped them out. The soldiers rounded up the ponies and sent them to the rear.

Let us return now to Abbott. He had run into the Apaches quite unexpectedly. The men climbed down into the canyon and were almost at the top on the other side, when Morgan's scouts warned of a band of hostile Indians coming. The Apaches were headed down the very path up which the soldiers were going. They had no idea, apparently, that the white men were anywhere near. Still fondly supposing that Chaffee was alone, they were slipping down into the canyon with the intention of taking him from the rear. Right into their surprised faces burst the soldiers' first volley. Several Indians were hit. The rest ran for the pines on the crest.

They soon reached their main body which had been fighting the long-range duel with Converse's men across the canyon. Abbott's steady advance continued. The whole band presently began to retreat along the wall of the gorge, slowly toward the east. Suddenly they ran right into the arms of West, Sieber and their men, and were greeted by another murderous blast of fire.

Their line of retreat was cut off but the Indians were not daunted. As the soldiers slipped forward from tree to tree, the Apaches redoubled their fire. Lieutenant Morgan of the scouts was shot through the side. Sergeant Conn and several enlisted men were hit. But Sieber and his scouts had the range now and were dropping one hostile warrior after another. Lieutenant Thomas Cruse led a charge through the woods. Under the cover of some deadly shooting by that same group of scouts, he broke the Apache line.

It was nearly dark. A heavy rain had set in. The Indians scattered in every direction—those who could move. The White Mountain band was almost wiped out. Of fifty-four Indians who started the fight, twenty-one were found dead on the battle field, including the blundering Nan-tia-tish. Five died later from wounds. Few, if any, escaped unscathed. The survivors soon slipped back to the reservation, their stomach for fighting gone.[4]

CROOK RETURNS

Two things of prime importance to the Apaches occurred shortly after the Chevelon's Fork fight. On July 29th, 1882, a treaty was signed between Mexico and the United States, permitting soldiers of each country to cross the borders of the other in pursuit of hostile Indians. No longer was the invisible international line to be a bulwark of safety for fleeing raiding parties.

The second event was the return to Arizona of General

[4] The loss to the troops in this battle was surprisingly light. One scout and one enlisted man were killed, two officers and five enlisted men wounded.

George Crook, who, since 1874, had been in the north fighting the Sioux. Crook took command on September 4th. He found conditions bad. The desert which he had left almost peaceful was at war again. And of the reasons for this, one of his officers, Captain Bourke, wrote as follows:

"But there was a coincidence of sentiment among all people whose opinion was worthy of consultation, that the blame did not rest with the Indians; curious tales were flying about from mouth to mouth, of the gross outrages perpetrated upon men and women who were trying faithfully to abide in peace with the whites . . . No one had ever heard the Apaches' story, and no one seemed to care whether they had a story or not." [5]

Crook set about patiently and skillfully to knit up the ravelled sleeve of affairs. He reorganized the agency police and enforced the rule that the male Indians on the reservations be counted regularly. He went out into the hills, riding his old mule "Apache," to talk with the people who were hiding out there. One warrior, Alchise, who had served loyally as a scout during the Tonto Basin and other campaigns, told Crook:

"When you left . . . we were all content; everything was peace. The officers you had here were all taken away and new ones came in—a different kind. Perhaps we were to blame, perhaps they were, but anyway we hadn't any confidence in them." [6]

Other chiefs such as Cha-lipun, Eskimo-tzin, Santos, Chiquito, and Huan-klishe also interviewed the general. Although he had been gone for years, Nan-tan Lupan still had their confidence. They told him their grievances without reservation. He acted as promptly as possible in their behalf. Trusted officers were placed over them; they

[5] "On the Border With Crook," p. 434.
[6] *Ibid.*, p. 436.

were encouraged to start growing crops again—an activity which had been abandoned completely. On October 5th, he laid down his policy toward the Indians in his General Orders, issued at Fort Whipple:

"The commanding general, after making a thorough and exhaustive examination among the Indians . . . regrets to say that he finds among them a general feeling of distrust and want of confidence in the whites, especially the soldiery; and also that much dissatisfaction, dangerous to the peace of the country, exists among them. Officers and soldiers . . . are reminded that one of the fundamental principles of the military character is justice to all—Indians as well as white men—and that a disregard of this principle is likely to bring about hostilities, and cause the deaths of the very persons they are sent here to protect. In all their dealings with the Indians, officers must be careful not only to observe the strictest fidelity, but to make no promises not in their power to carry out; all grievances arising in their jurisdiction should be redressed, so that an accumulation of them may not cause an outbreak."

Crook's next official action was to expel all squatters and unauthorized miners from the reservations. He announced also that he would oppose further curtailment of the lands of the Indians. He even started an investigation which resulted in a reorganization of the Indian Department and the discharge of some agents and even officials higher up.

His efforts to make the Apaches self-supporting were viewed by the Tucson Ring of government contractors, with the greatest distaste. They knew that, should the Indians ever start to feed themselves, profits to the Ring would immediately be erased. At once began the long-drawn and devious political battle, which was to end only when Crook left the Arizona Territory. But that was not until the Southwest had seen some drama-filled days.

IX.

THE GERONIMO WAR
1883–1886

CHAPTER XXIII

THE SIERRA MADRE CAMPAIGN

GERONIMO

CROOK almost succeeded in pacifying the Apaches. By judicious use of presents, promises and threats, he brought first one band, then another back to the reservations. But a new leader had arisen among the Apaches, destined to be the most famous of them all. His real name was Go-ya-thle (He Who Yawns), but he was known throughout the whole Southwest on both sides of the border as Geronimo.

In the later Apache wars, Geronimo was a potent, menacing figure always. Crook called him "the human tiger." General Nelson A. Miles referred to him with deepest sincerity as "the worst Indian who ever lived." He was cunning, bloodthirsty, and his cruelty was a bottomless pit; and he did more to resist the white man than any of his people since Victorio.

Geronimo's hatred for all people other than Apaches dated from early manhood. He was born high in the headwaters of the Gila River in June, 1829. Writers have called him a Chiricahua Apache, but he himself said that he was born into the tribe of which Mangus Colorado was chief, the Mimbrenos. His grandfather, Maco, was a Mogollon chief, but Geronimo's own father married into the Mimbreno tribe, thus, according to Apache law, becoming a Mimbreno himself.

Geronimo grew up a care-free, pleasure-loving young buck, with no abnormal cruelty or hatred in his heart. His name, He Who Yawns, probably was the indication of a rather indolent, good-natured character. In 1846, when he was seventeen, he was admitted into the council of warriors and married a pretty Apache maiden with the lovely name of Alopé. By her he had three children, and with his widowed mother, they made a happy household.

The Apaches were at peace with Chihuahua in 1858, so Mangus Colorado led his people south that year to trade. Their destination was Casas Grandes, but on the way they camped near the Presidio del Janos. All was peaceful. The Mimbreno warriors went unconcernedly into the town, leaving their women and children in the camp.

At this time General Carasco was military governor of the neighboring Mexican state of Sonora. He was a harsh, strenuous dictator, who impressed into service as soldiers the poor of his state, and forced the rich to supply the money for his campaigns. Carasco learned that a large band of Apaches was at Janos. He had no authority in Chihuahua, but ignoring the boundaries of the two states, he reached Mangus Colorado's camp by forced marches one day while all the warriors were in the town, trading.

There followed scenes of horror which beggar description. The blood-maddened Mexicans weltered in slaughter. Scores of Indian women and children were massacred and ninety were taken prisoner, to be sold later into slavery in southern Mexico. Then Carasco withdrew as quickly as he had come.[1]

The Mimbreno warriors returned from Janos to find

[1] For this act of treachery, Governor Medina of Chihuahua complained to the general government of Mexico, but the administration upheld Carasco. The Mexicans might better have handed him over to the Apaches to wreak their vengeance on him, for the people of Sonora and Chihuahua were destined to pay for decades as a result of his act. Years later Carasco, whose tyranny had grown unbearable, was poisoned by his own people.

their camp sacked, and most of their people butchered or carried away. In the shambles Geronimo discovered his mother, his wife and three children, all dead. The young warrior went nearly insane with grief. Long years after he told in his own simple words his sensations in discovering the terrible tragedy:

". . . without being noticed I silently turned away and stood by the river. How long I stood there I do not know, but when I saw the warriors arranging for council, I took my place.

"That night I did not give my vote for or against any measure; but it was decided that as there were only eighty warriors left, and as we were without arms . . . surrounded by Mexicans . . . we could not hope to fight successfully. So our chief, Mangus Colorado, gave the order to start at once in perfect silence for our homes in Arizona, leaving the dead upon the field.

"I stood still until all had passed, hardly knowing what I would do—I had no weapon, nor did I hardly wish to fight, neither did I contemplate recovering the bodies of my loved ones, for that was forbidden. I did not pray nor did I resolve to do anything in particular, for I had no purpose left. I finally followed the tribe silently, keeping just within hearing distance of the soft noise of the feet . . ." [2]

From that day Geronimo's hand was against the world. He was sent by Mangus Colorado on more than one occasion to stir up other tribes to join the Mimbrenos in war expeditions against the Mexicans. Gifted with eloquence and carrying his well-known wrongs as a grievance, he persuaded both the Chiricahuas and Mogollons, under Cochise and Juh, to join with Mangus Colorado in bloody raids. From 1858 to 1873 there was scarcely a year which did not see Geronimo lead at least two or three war parties into Mexico. On one of these, in 1863, he captured a whole town, the hamlet of Crassanas, forty miles west of

[2] This story was told by Geronimo to S. M. Barrett, at the time superintendent of schools at Lawton, Oklahoma, near Fort Sill. It is quoted by him in his book, "Geronimo's Own Story of His Life," pp. 45-46.

Casas Grandes, and looted it. On another occasion, in the summer of 1865, he led his warriors clear to the Gulf of California. In 1876, Geronimo led an uprising against the white men, and was later arrested by Agent John Clum and taken in chains to Fort Apache. But fortune was with him. Clum resigned, and with nobody to press the charges against him, Geronimo was freed. After two or three flights to the mountains and cautious returns, Geronimo and Juh, on the night of September 30th, 1881, fled once more to Mexico, after killing Albert Sterling, chief of the agency police and whipping a detachment of the 6th Cavalry. The sinister struggle known as the Geronimo War was on.

Geronimo was a combination of many talents. He had the cunning of his race intensified to the highest degree. When he could get them, he took full advantage of the white man's latest weapons. He was courageous, although he gave an impression of cowardice with his skulking tactics. Of his appearance, Charles F. Lummis says:

"He was a compactly built, dark-faced man of one hundred and seventy pounds, and about five feet, eight inches in height. The man who once saw his face will never forget it. Crueller features were never cut. The nose was broad and heavy, the forehead low and wrinkled, the chin full and strong, the eyes like two bits of obsidian with a light behind them. The mouth was a most noticeable feature—a sharp, straight, thin-lipped gash of generous length and without one softening curve." [3]

CHATO'S SECOND RAID

This was the new force with which Crook had to reckon. With Geronimo in the fastnesses south of the border were

[3] "The Land of Poco Tiempo," p. 181.

Captain Crawford's scouts, taken after their return from the expedition into Mexico where their leader was killed. The scouts were commanded by Lieutenant Maus at the time this photograph was made.

Geronimo and his warriors, photographed just before their conference with General George Crook, March 27, 1886. Note the war paint on faces of the warriors. Most of these Indians remained on the warpath with Geronimo after the conference failed.

a number of other redoubtable fighting chiefs. Old Nana was there. So was Juh. And so were Chato, Nachite and Loco.

It was Chato who struck the first blow. With twenty-six men he left the border on March 24th, 1883, accompanied by Mangus, the son of the old giant, and swept through Arizona and New Mexico, seeking chiefly to capture ammunition. Several persons lost their lives in this raid, but it is most memorable because of the murder by Chato's band, of Judge H. C. McComas and his wife, and the abduction of their little son Charley. This tragedy occurred in Thompson's Canyon, near the Gila River, on the morning of March 28th. The McComas family was on its way from Silver City to Leitendorf, a mining camp near Lordsburg. Mrs. McComas, cultured and accomplished, was a sister of Eugene F. Ware, the then popular poet "Ironquill".

The bodies of the judge and his wife were found by Jim Baker, a stage driver. Signs on the trail showed that Judge McComas had leaped from the buckboard, giving the reins to his wife, and had attempted to stand off the Indians while she whipped the horses into a run, trying to escape. The judge was killed where he stood. There were seven bullet holes in his body when he was picked up.

The buckboard travelled less than fifty yards from where the Indians killed the jurist, before one of its horses was shot. Mrs. McComas was clubbed to death and the little boy Charley, just six years old, was carried away by the Indians. For days posses scoured the country, trying to find the child. But he was never again seen alive by any white person. The incident created a national sensation because of the prominence of the persons concerned.

A few days later Chato safely crossed the border into

Mexico again, having won back some of the laurels lost
in the ill-fated expedition which ended in the Garcia fight,
when Loco's band was nearly destroyed in April, 1882.

It was Crook's turn to move. Taking advantage of the
new international treaty, he led a troop of cavalry under
Captain Chaffee and a battalion of one hundred and
ninety-three Indian scouts under Captain Emmett Crawford, 3rd Cavalry, across the boundary line on May 1st.
Somewhere to the south five hundred or more hostile Indians were lurking, the remnants of Victorio's Mimbrenos
under Nana; Loco's band; the Mogollons and Chiricahuas
under Juh, Chato, Nachite and Geronimo, and a few scattered "broncho" Apaches of various tribes.

By May 8th Crook was in the Sierra Madre. The country was so rough that the command lost several pack mules
which rolled over precipices. Everybody was walking and
leading his horse.

Crawford and his Indians surprised a *rancheria* high in
the mountains on May 15th, defeated the hostiles and
captured several prisoners.[4] Eight days later, Nana, Chato
and two hundred and sixty other Indians voluntarily came
to Crook's camp and surrendered, saying they were tired
of war. That made two hundred and eighty-five prisoners,
including forty-eight warriors. Shortly after this Geronimo, Nachite, and Loco also surrendered, and reported
that Juh, with a few of his bitter enders had gone far west

---

[4] After this fight the mystery of what became of Charley McComas was solved.
He was in the *rancheria* when it was attacked. During the fight the little fellow
wandered off into the woods and either starved or was killed. Five Mexican women
and one small child were recaptured from the Indians. It was at first thought the
child was Charley McComas. He was, however, a Mexican boy, the son of Señora
Antonio Hernandez, who was also a prisoner. There should have been no mistake
in this case as the rescued child was only two years old while Charley McComas
was six. The Mexican women were the wives of Mexican soldiers and were captured almost in full view of their husbands, whom they were following on a
march, near El Carmen, on the Mexican frontier. They had been prisoners fourteen days when rescued.

to the Yaqui country to live, hoping thus to escape further pursuit by the troops.[5]

Crook conferred with the chiefs and agreed to return to the United States with the women, children and old men, allowing the warriors time to round up their stock and follow. By this time other Indians were furtively stealing in from the mountains. When the general reached San Carlos, June 23rd, he had with him fifty-two warriors and two hundred and seventy-three women and children. Among the braves were old Nana and Loco, the Mimbreno chiefs.

Crook ordered Lieutenant Britton Davis to wait at the border with a company of scouts, and meet the rest of the hostiles as they came over. Nobody in Arizona believed the Indians would keep faith with the general. There were anxious days as they waited to learn the result of his experiment in making a gentleman's agreement with Apaches.

But Crook knew the Indians. One afternoon Nachite and Zele came riding into Davis' camp with thirty or forty of their band. They were taken to San Carlos.[6] There was another weary wait. Then, six weeks after Nachite's surrender, Geronimo came over the border driving along a large herd of cattle.[7] There was every reason to believe

[5] Juh met a sordid end. In the summer of 1886 he became unromantically drunk, and while attempting to ford a river near Casas Grandes, fell from his horse and was drowned.

[6] On this march a couple of women suddenly dropped out of the line and went off into the bushes. Davis asked one of the scouts where they were going. The Indian laughed. "Bimeby baby," he said. Sure enough, within a few miles the women caught up with the caravan—and the younger was carrying a newborn infant in her arms. What is more, she rode right along on the march and appeared to think nothing of it, to such degree was her body attuned to the hardships of her existence.

[7] A very curious story is told by Davis ("The Truth About Geronimo," pp. 82-83), of how Geronimo's arrival was foretold by a Tonto-Mojave medicine man. After the command had waited for weeks with no sign of the chief, the Indian scouts called on the medicine man to tell how soon he would arrive. There was a day and night of incantation, the burning of *hoddentin*, the sacred pollen, and

the cattle were stolen, but it was necessary to avoid all trouble. Davis started the band, of approximately eighty-five persons, to San Carlos. They were met at Sulphur Springs by a United States marshal and a customs collector, who wished to arrest the whole body of Indians for smuggling cattle across the border without paying duty. It was so stupid that it was almost laughable, but it was serious.

Young Davis did some rapid thinking. A brother officer came along and Davis put the Indians under his charge. That night, while the marshal and the customs collector were snoring at a ranch house near, the Indians were started silently away and by morning were far on the road to San Carlos which they reached safely. The marshal and customs collector found only Davis himself at the Indian camp next morning, waiting solemnly to answer their subpœna. They were furious at first, but the frontier was always ready to laugh, even when the joke was on the person doing the laughing, and the whole thing ended in an uproarious burst of mirth with the marshal congratulating the lieutenant on his resourcefulness.

---

other charms, then he announced that Geronimo was three days away, riding a white mule with a great herd of horses. Five days later Geronimo arrived, with a large herd of stock and *mounted on a white pony.*

Chapter XXIV

ULZANA'S RIDE

BACK ON THE WAR PATH

In their camp on Turkey Creek on the San Carlos reservation, most of the five hundred or more hostile Apaches who had surrendered, lived in peace and apparent content for two years. Lieutenant Britton Davis was their special agent, and he made long strides toward winning back their trust in the white man.

The Indians had brought to the reservation one bad habit which prior to their coming had almost been stamped out among the peaceful Indians already living there. This was the making and drinking of *tiswin*.[1] Crook ordered the manufacture and use of this native Indian intoxicant to cease. There was an immediate flare of rebellion, headed by one Ka-ya-ten-ne, the turbulent young leader of a small band of the wildest Apaches. But Davis, with the troops at his back, arrested Ka-ya-ten-ne and the trouble maker spent eighteen months in Alcatraz Island prison, before Crook obtained his pardon. It was believed that the trouble was over.

In December, 1884, however, a new agent appeared at San Carlos and there was immediate friction between the Indian Department and the army. The Apaches, quickly sensing this change, grew more and more unruly. *Tiswin* drinking, which had practically ceased after the

---

[1] *Tiswin* was a sort of native beer, made out of fermented corn mash. It was fairly intoxicating and had a serious effect on its addicts, making them quarrelsome and irresponsible. Hence the government's efforts to stop its use.

arrest of Ka-ya-ten-ne, reappeared again. The time was ripe for an explosion. Geronimo touched the match to the magazine.

The chief had never been satisfied with conditions on the reservation. As time passed he built up a circle of followers who were ready to do anything he proposed. On May 15th this group of chiefs defied Davis to stop their *tiswin* drinking. Davis telegraphed to Fort Apache for instructions but received none. Two days later, on May 17th, Geronimo, Chihuahua, Nana, Nachite, and Mangus, with thirty-two warriors, eight well-grown boys, and ninety-two women and children, left the reservation.

Davis pursued with his scouts, and had a long-distance fight with part of the band under Chihuahua on May 27th. The Apaches surprised a small camp of soldiers, killed a sergeant and two men, captured all the horses, and burned the wagons and tents. The war was on again in all its bloody earnest. Expeditions under Major Wirt Davis, Captain Emmett Crawford and Captain Dorst traversed the mountains, hunting the hostile Indians. Their lack of success was almost tragic. A woman was killed in an attack on a small *rancheria* near the Bavispe Mountains, June 23rd. Two warriors were ambushed by Davis' scouts and killed in the Hoya Mountains of Mexico, July 29th. Nine days later three braves, a squaw and a child were killed in the Sierra Madre by the same scout detachment. And more than a month later one warrior was shot by the scouts on the Bavispe River. That was the extent of the achievements of the army—six warriors, two women and a child killed in four months of campaigning. Meantime the Apaches had slaughtered scores of white men and Mexicans.[2]

[2] The records show that seventy-three American settlers and soldiers were officially listed as killed during this time. Twelve reservation Indians were also killed and an unknown number of Mexicans.

Among the warriors who went to Mexico with Geronimo was Ulzana, a brother of Chihuahua, and known as a dour fighter. He was not a chief, but he had at one time served with the government scouts against Nana. In that war of 1881, Ulzana learned much about the arts and tactics of raiding from Nana, the old past-master, by following him with the troops and observing his methods and stratagems. And now, in 1885, the former government scout suddenly launched a raid of his own which in many respects threatened to surpass even Nana's exploit.

Early in November, he with ten warriors, slipped across the line and started up into Arizona. He knew that every water hole was guarded, so he deliberately avoided them. The Apaches had developed a technique in handling water which enabled them to laugh at mere stationary guards. A horse, having gone as far at it could stumble, was killed, and the small intestine taken out. Cleaned—very sketchily according to white standards, but satisfactorily to the rudimentary Apache notion of cleanliness—this receptacle was filled with water and thirty or forty feet of it wrapped around the body of a led horse. It contained enough water to last a band of Apaches for days. Carrying his water in this manner, and travelling only over the most difficult parts of the mountains, in the full knowledge that two thousand troops waited to cut them off and exterminate them, Ulzana and his raiders began their perilous invasion of the United States.

Ulzana guessed correctly as to the hue and cry which would be raised as soon as it was learned the Apaches were in Arizona. From every post expeditions set out in pursuit of him. But travelling only at night and spending the days in the rocky ridges, he led his tiny band north to the Gila River. There he and his warriors, pressed too closely, scattered and disappeared completely. A puzzled soldiery marched back to its cantonments. No human wisdom or foresight could predict what Ulzana would do next. The troops could only await his pleasure.

For nearly three weeks nothing was heard from the Apaches. During that time Ulzana was hiding in the mountains of New Mexico, planning his campaign.

THE BLOODY TRAIL

His first stroke was stunning in its unexpectedness. Prowling through the dark, the Apaches descended upon Fort Apache. On the way they caught and killed two settlers, William Waldo and Will Harrison, whom they found November 24th, on Turkey Creek.

Chill and black came the night of November 26th. Suddenly guns began to thud and white-hot flashes lit the gloom around the White Mountain Apache village near the agency. There were wild yells and scurrying figures in the darkness. Then Ulzana's band was gone. It left in its wake the dead bodies of twelve White Mountain Indians and one of its own number, killed during the fight by an axe in the hands of a reservation Apache.

From that hour Ulzana's band, now numbering exactly ten warriors, had a thrilling and bloody career. As the first news of the appearance of the Apaches was flashed by telegraph, troops took the trail from Fort Apache, San Carlos, Fort Thomas, Camp Grant and Fort Bowie. But the Indians were as elusive as so many fleas. On November 29th they left a bold marking of their trail in the dead bodies of W. H. Clark near the sub agency, McAllister at Bear Springs, and Thomas Johnson at Black Rock.

Ulzana now seemed to decide to make for the Mexican border again. He took a straight southerly course, toward the Gila River, arriving near Solomonville on December

2nd, an event he signalized by the killing of two brothers named Wright near that town, and of Dick Mays the next day on the Coronado ranch.

The usual route back into Mexico was the valley which lay between the Dragoon and Whetstone Mountains. But Ulzana had too clear a picture of what was going on. He did not need to be told that the valley was literally alive with soldiers. As a matter of fact, according to Crook's later report, five troops of cavalry were ambushed in that very locality. Laughing at such clumsy planning, Ulzana turned east and travelled up the Gila Valley. He entered New Mexico with the soldiers swarming on his rear. But Ulzana did not fear pursuit. He stopped long enough on December 9th and 10th, to kill four ranchers on the upper Gila. Then once more he disappeared completely, as if into the air. He abandoned his horses and much of the plunder he had picked up. His braves scattered like so many coyotes, and nobody could tell where they would reassemble.

Wildest panic prevailed in Arizona and New Mexico. Efforts were made both by the government and by private citizens, to notify all ranchers, farmers and prospectors of the presence of the Apache death in the country, but it was impossible to do so.[3] Never for one moment did Crook relax his pursuit. Captain Crawford was called back from Mexico, to lead the chase.

Ulzana, in his own good time, made his presence known again on December 19th, when he and his warriors fought a brief battle with a detachment of the 8th Cavalry, killing Dr. Maddox and four men in the Dry Creek Canyon.

[3] "Many of the persons killed were found on roads or trails, at a distance from points of communication. Every possible means was taken to give warning and afford protection, but even had the whole army been employed for the purpose, it would have been impossible to get word to every prospector, farmer and teamster near their (the Apaches') course."—Crook's report, January 11th, 1886.

Troops were rushed to the place at once. It was ascertained that the hostiles were once more headed south. Crawford and Crook guessed that they would pass through the country between the Chiricahua and Peloncillo Ranges. Four troops of the 10th Cavalry and one of the 4th Cavalry were posted in those areas in hope of trapping the ten hostile Apaches as they came down. Behind the Indians came Lieutenant Scott, puzzling out the trail, and pushing Ulzana hard, with a company of Navajo scouts.

Two more white men were killed by the Apaches on November 26th. They were named Snow and Windham, and they were slain near Carlisle, New Mexico. On that same day the raiders crossed over into Arizona and butchered two more men near Galeyville. One of these was Caspar Albert. The other was never identified.

Ulzana showed evident knowledge of the army's plan when he hesitated long before entering the passes between the Chiricahuas and the Peloncillos. Now was the time when Scott should have closed in on him and forced him to go forward into the waiting ambush of soldiers. But Scott's Navajos did not remain staunch. At the critical moment, very fortunately for Ulzana, they refused to go further. That night a heavy snowstorm fell, lasting for three days. There was no further possibility of trailing the Indians. Some time during the next few days Ulzana reached Mexico, by a mule trail over the mountains into Sonora.

Summing up this raid, it would be difficult to believe some of its figures, were they not attested by the military report of General Crook himself, who certainly had no wish to exaggerate the exploits of this band of Indians against him. In four weeks Ulzana and his ten warriors travelled not less than twelve hundred miles through enemy country, maintaining themselves as they went. They killed thirty-eight persons, captured and wore out two hundred and fifty horses and mules, changing mounts at least twenty times during the raid; and, although they were twice dismounted, they eventually got back safely to Mexico. And all this with the loss of only one brave— killed by the White Mountain Apaches near Fort Apache.

Chapter XXV

THE TRAGEDY OF CRAWFORD

ON GERONIMO'S TRAIL

ULZANA's raid proved to Crook that his cavalry was not capable of catching the Apaches. He reorganized his whole fighting system. Two battalions, largely of Indian scouts, were formed to take up the trail and follow it to the end. One of these, commanded by Major Davis, consisted of one hundred and two Indians and a troop of cavalry. This organization was so handicapped by its white contingent that it accomplished little. The other battalion, however, was formed almost exclusively of lean, bronzed, Indian warriors—Mimbreno and White Mountain, with a sprinkling of friendly Chiricahuas. There was much shaking of heads as this body was organized, and free predictions of treachery were made. In spite of that several fine officers volunteered to accompany Captain Crawford, who was to command. Lieutenants Marion P. Maus, W. E. Shipp and S. L. Faison were selected, together with Assistant Surgeon T. B. Davis. Shipp and Maus commanded a company each of approximately fifty Indians and Faison was adjutant of the little force.

They left Fort Bowie November 11th and a few days later crossed into Mexico near Fronteras. It was interesting to the white officers to watch the methods adopted by their Indians in scouting the country. There was no need to give orders. Their system of flankers and advance guards was perfect. When they went into camp, outposts were at once put out, noiselessly and smoothly as if the command was a unit of long experience. Yet most of these Indians had never been on the war path together before. They were following the lessons of a lifetime. It showed Crawford and his lieutenants what might be expected from the hostile Apaches.

For clothing each scout wore only a faded soldier's blouse and a light loin cloth. His hair was bound under the inevitable turban and he scarcely made a sound in his moccasins. The Indians were keen as hounds, tireless and deadly as the wolves they resembled.

Across the Sierra Madre went the expedition and deep into Mexican territory, following a rumor picked up in a Mexican village. There it was found that Geronimo with most of the hostiles had gone far south into Sonora. Crawford called a council of war and decided to leave, under a small guard at the camp, all equipment not absolutely essential, and march on with the bulk of his force. H. W. Daly, chief packer, with most of the packers and six scouts, were detailed to remain with the baggage.

That night the Indians held a medicine dance. Lieutenant Maus afterward described what an impression that ceremony made on him, how the wild and stern mountains seemed to tower above, how the old medicine man, No-wa-zhe-ta, unrolled the sacred buckskin he had carried since he left Fort Bowie, how the dance, with its weird incantations, was followed by each warrior's kneeling before the old man, and pressing his lips to the sacred buckskin, while he received No-wa-zhe-ta's blessing.[1] Next morning, leaving the camp and the weaker members of the party, seventy-nine men, with twelve days' rations on

[1] Maus' very graphic description of this expedition may be found in General Nelson A. Miles' "Personal Recollections," pp. 460-471.

the toughest mules they could find, crossed the Haros River and took up a well-marked trail which they found on the other side.

Moving mostly by night and suffering extreme hardship, the expedition marched toward some extremely rugged mountains, the Espinosa del Diablo or "Devil's Backbone," so called because the broken outline of peaks resembles a series of jagged vertebræ. The topography of the country changed rapidly. Soon they were in almost a tropical land. Palm trees were seen in the river bottoms and once a jaguar, spotted like a leopard, bounded away with a shriek.

Noche, the chief Apache scout, commanding the advance guard, sent a runner back at sunset on January 9th, 1886, warning Crawford that he had located a *rancheria*. That was a cheering message. The stern Indian warriors looked to their rifles and discarded their surplus clothing as they always did when going into a fight. All that night they toiled over the mountain trails, crossing and recrossing a turbulent river that led down the gorge in which the hostile village was supposed to be situated. Captain Crawford was so nearly exhausted that for the last few miles of the march he had to be assisted by an Apache scout on each side.

Just at dawn they heard the braying of burros. Like the geese of Rome, as Maus afterward said, those watch-dogs of the Indian camp saved their masters from surprise.

The still, dark canyon was lit by orange flashes of rifle fire and echoes sprang like thunder-claps from the cliffs. Down the gorge the ghostly figures of Apaches scurried. But the scouts took it with a rush, their flank guardians high on the bluffs, fending the depths below from ambuscade above. One horse was killed by Crawford's men, but the enemy was gone. One by one the scouts returned from the pursuit. The village and its supplies of meat and other food, was destroyed. In the chill dampness of the early morning, the disappointed command gathered around small fires the scouts built, now that necessity of concealment no longer existed.

Within a few minutes an old squaw crept up to this camp. She brought a message from Geronimo and Nachite, saying they wanted to talk. Crawford, surprised and delighted, told her he would see the chiefs next day. The place for the conference was set. It seemed that fortune, who had so far averted her face, was about to smile at last.

CAPTAIN CRAWFORD'S DEATH

But that conference was never to take place. Throughout the campaign, Crawford had been troubled by the hostility of the Mexicans in the districts through which he travelled. Two or three scouts in other expeditions had even been shot by the very persons they were trying to protect from Geronimo's braves.

Early on the morning of January 11th a detachment of Mexican irregulars—the same *Seguridad Públicos* who had brought Victorio to his end—encountered some of Crawford's outposts. They were hunting the same quarry as the American expedition was, and thinking the scouts were hostile Apaches, they fired upon them, wounding three. Crawford and Maus, with Tom Horn, the white chief of scouts, hurried to avert a battle. Out between the lines walked the gallant American captain, holding up his hand and calling "Don't shoot!" Major Corredor, the Mexican commander, seemed equally anxious to stop bloodshed, crying *"No tiran,"* to his men. The Apache scouts lay with their heads peering over the rocks, and the click of their breechblocks sounded clear in the morning mountain air.

At that moment, a single, loud report rang out from off to one side. A group of Tarahumari Indian scouts had crept up unseen from that direction. As the report echoed among the rocks, Captain Crawford fell forward upon his face.

Instantly the whole front of the American line blazed. Crawford was the idol of the Apache scouts and they were filled with a single consuming desire—revenge. Major Corredor fell, shot through the heart. A lieutenant, Juan de la Cruz, was riddled by thirteen bullets. Two more Mexicans were killed. The rest fled.

With Dutchy,[2] one of the scouts, Maus went forward and brought Crawford into the lines. A ragged bullet hole showed in his head and the brains were running down over his face. He was still breathing, but the surgeon said his death was a matter of only a little time.[3]

The command could not stay where it was. The Mexicans outnumbered the Americans two to one. Maus fixed a litter and placed the unconscious captain on it. Another litter carried one of the scouts who had been seriously wounded. Then the retreat began.

The Mexicans drew off after insolently demanding food and other concessions. Maus, who went to pacify them, was held a prisoner for a time, and gave them six mules as indemnity before they would release him.

[2] Dutchy was a Chiricahua with a bloody reputation. At the time he enlisted, he was being sought by civil authorities for the murder of a white man near Fort Thomas. During the march, a marshal from Tombstone, Arizona, who had plenty of nerve, walked into Crawford's camp one day, and in the midst of the scouts served a murder warrant on Dutchy. He had followed their trail for two hundred miles to make the arrest. Crawford convinced him that he could not arrest an enlisted man during a campaign, and the marshal returned without his prisoner. In spite of his reputation, this Indian was one of the best and most faithful of the scouts.

[3] Raht says the man who fired the fatal shot was Mauricio, the Tarahumari who is credited with killing Victorio. ("Romance of the Davis Mountains," p. 271.)

This picture shows the momentous scene when the final council was held between Geronimo and General George Crook in the Canyon de los Embudos, Sonora, March 27, 1886. The following persons can be identified in the picture, left to right: Lieutenant Faison; Captain Roberts; Nachite (top of head can be seen just above hats of Faison and Roberts); Geronimo (facing camera, with turban on head); Coyetano (hidden behind Geronimo); Concepcion; Nana (beside Geronimo); Tom Blair (standing by horse in rear); Noche (sergeant of scouts); Lieutenant Maus; the three interpreters, José Maria Yashez, Antonio Besias, and José Montoya; H. W. Only (above interpreters); Captain Bourke; General Crook; Charley Roberts. Apache warriors in the background are of Geronimo's band, but not identified.

Captain Emmett Crawford, who was treacherously killed by Mexican irregulars, just as he was about to capture Geronimo's band in the Espinosa Diablo Mountains in Sonora.

Judge W. D. McComas and his family, murdered by Chato's raiders between Deming and Silver City, New Mexico. Charley McComas is next to his father.

Only two or three miles were made by the scouts the first day. That night Geronimo himself met Maus outside of his lines and talked with him. Of course the conference was fruitless. The Indian, who had been all ready to surrender, saw the white man in retreat. So he contented himself with outlining his grievances. Maus promised him that General Crook would meet him, to discuss his surrender, in two moons near the San Bernardino Springs. He further agreed that Crook would bring no escort of regular soldiers. After this conference old Nana, now thoroughly tired of war, came to Maus' camp and voluntarily surrendered with eight other Indians, including Geronimo's wife. They accompanied Maus back to the United States, reaching the border February 1st. Captain Crawford died on the march. The expedition had failed just when it seemed sure of success because of a piece of blundering, to call it by its easiest name, or international treachery, to call it by its worst.

THE APACHE DOUBLE CROSS AND CROOK'S RESIGNATION

As soon as Crook learned of Maus' promise to Geronimo, he prepared to attend the conference as agreed. The place designated was the Canyon des Embudos, twenty miles southeast of San Bernardino Springs, near the Arizona line in northeast Sonora. Thither, on March 25th, went Crook with Captains Charles Roberts and John G. Bourke, and Lieutenants Maus, Faison and Shipp, their Indian scouts, several white and Mexican interpreters, and some other Indians, including the chief Alchise and the recently released Ka-ye-ten-ne. They were met by Geronimo, with Chihuahua and Nachite as well as a number of sub-chiefs.

The Apaches were nervous and suspicious. With the

exception of the few who actually took part in the council, they hid themselves in the beautiful ravine, with its lovely stream and cool, shady glades. Geronimo was the chief spokesman.

That was a long talk. As has been said, Crook knew Indians. "Treat them as children in ignorance but not in innocence," were his instructions to his men, and these instructions he followed himself. He sat patiently upon the ground to wait through what he knew would take place —hours upon hours of talk, much of it apparently meaningless. Out of it all he had to sift the few grains of meaning and truth, and from these derive the facts wherewith to drive a bargain with these Indians which should bring them peacefully upon the reservations.

Geronimo began to speak. Indian-like, he devoted much time to a recital of his wrongs, some of which the general knew to be true, and some of which were clearly imaginary. Every once in a while a significant sentence or phrase would drop in the midst of this conversational flood.

"I have several times asked for peace, but trouble has come from agents and interpreters." [4] How well Crook knew the truth of that statement.

"Whenever I meet you I talk good to you and you to me, and peace is soon established; but when you go to the reservation you put agents and interpreters over us who do bad things."

"To prove to you that I am telling the truth, remember I sent you word that I would come from a place far away to speak to you here, and you see us now."

"What I want is peace and good faith."

Thus the chief talked endlessly during the first day,

[4] This and the following quotations are all excerpts from the official transcription of the interpreted speeches, made during the conference at the orders of General Crook.

these sentences being the only statements upon which Crook could lay hold out of his almost interminable speech. They parted in the evening. The next council was two days later, on March 27th. This time there were several to speak for the Apaches. Chihuahua, Nachite and Geronimo all harangued at length. Finally Geronimo abruptly made his decision.

"Two or three words are enough," he said. "I have little to say. I surrender myself to you." Here he shook hands with General Crook. "We are all comrades, all one family, all one band. What others say I say also. I give myself up to you. Do with me what you please. I surrender. Once I moved about like the wind. Now I surrender to you and that is all." Again he shook hands with Crook.

And so the conference ended with a few words by the scouts Alchise and Ka-ya-ten-ne. Geronimo was quite evidently sincere. With a free mind the general prepared to leave for Fort Bowie, the Apaches to follow.

But once more the maleficent influence of the money-grabbing white man spoiled everything. The night before Crook departed, an American bootlegger named Tribolet, who lived on the San Bernardino Springs ranch, sneaked into the Indian camp and began selling liquor to the wild Apaches. Faithful old Alchise and Ka-ya-ten-ne came to the general's tent shortly before daylight of March 28th, with word that the warriors of Geronimo's band were howling drunk. They asked permission to take a squad of their own men and deal with Tribolet. Crook refused permission. One almost wishes he had granted it. The Apaches had a singular flair for dealing unpleasantly with those whom they thought deserving of punishment.

Some of Crook's officers started at once for the Indian camp. By the time they reached the canyon where it stood, the woods and grass were afire, and the Apaches were riding about on their horses and mules, crazed with liquor.

It began to rain, a steady, drizzling downpour. That night Geronimo, Nachite and twenty warriors, thirteen women and six children, stole through the spattering showers and rode again for the fastnesses of the Sierra Madre. They feared the consequences which might follow their drinking Tribolet's liquor. Thus the whole careful plan for ending the war came to nothing. A frontier racketeer had set in motion a new horror which was to cost additional scores of human lives.

Most of the Apaches, including the chief Chihuahua and his brother, the ferocious Ulzana, remained true to their agreement to surrender. Eighty of them accompanied Lieutenant Faison back to the reservation, reaching Fort Bowie on April 2nd.

Meantime an unlooked for complication arose. Crook who knew the people with whom he was dealing, and at the risk of his life had made certain definite agreements with them to surrender, wired the terms of this agreement to General Phil Sheridan, then at Washington.

Sheridan, who knew nothing about Apaches, and whose attitude toward the whole Indian question is summed up by the statement often attributed to him: "The only good Indian is a dead Indian," telegraphed back disapproval of the terms. He directed Crook to receive the Apaches only on unconditional surrender. This was a direct violation of Crook's word to the Indians. The general was not the man to allow his honor to be smirched.

The escape of Geronimo, the hated and dreaded, moreover aroused a storm of criticism in Arizona. The malodorous Tucson Ring which had long chafed under Crook's rule, set about its machinations with renewed energy. The Tucson Ring did not obtain Crook's removal, as it had been plotting for years to do, but there is small doubt that the unpleasantness it made contributed strongly to his decision in what followed.

On April 1st, the man who had done so much to bring order out of chaos in the Southwest, sent a long message to Sheridan, carefully outlining his policy of fairness to both red men and white, describing his plan of campaign and ending with these words:

"I believe that the plan upon which I have conducted operations is the one most likely to prove successful in the end. It may be, however, that I am too much wedded to my own views in this matter, and as I have spent nearly eight years of the hardest work of my life in this department, I respectfully request that I may now be relieved from its command."

The very next day, April 2nd, General Nelson A. Miles, then stationed at Fort Leavenworth, Kansas, was assigned to the command of the Department of Arizona.

CHAPTER XXVI

TREACHERY AT FORT APACHE

MILES' FLYING COLUMN

GENERAL MILES was the most famous and successful Indian
fighter in the United States Army. He was the conqueror
of the Kiowas, the Comanches, the Sioux, the Nez Percés
and other great plains tribes in wars extending over more
than a decade. Now he was suddenly sent south to deal
with the Apaches. The order putting him in command in
Arizona, was a surprise to him and no welcome assignment.
Crook and he were friends and he knew of the efficiency
of the former's administration. But Miles was a soldier.
He had no choice but to obey.

With characteristic energy he applied himself to the
problem of catching Geronimo. There were five thousand
soldiers under his command, and to these he added approximately five hundred Indian scouts. In twenty-five
detachments he sent these troops to combing the entire
desert country.

"Commanding officers are expected to continue a pursuit until capture, or until they are assured a fresh command is on the trail," was the order.

Every water hole in Arizona, no matter how small, was
guarded. Every ranch had its garrison. The Mexican international boundary line meant nothing, since the treaty
with Mexico, and the troops crossed over at will.

But Miles' study of Crook's methods showed that it

would be useless to attempt the subjugation of the Apaches with ordinary soldiers. Therefore he devised a flying column, similar to those of Crook's day, composed of picked desert men and Indian scouts, who were to carry on the final hunt. In command of this column he placed Captain H. W. Lawton, a desert athlete who knew the Indians and the Indian country, and who had a curious strain of bull-dog determination which prevented him from ever knowing when he was beaten.

With this flying column Miles introduced an innovation —the heliograph. This device, the invention of a British army officer, had been used successfully in India. It consisted of a mirror which reflected the sun in flashes of greater or less length for the dots and dashes of the Morse code. Arizona's atmosphere was clear and bright, and experiments showed that messages could be flashed through it for fifty miles or more. The use of the heliograph entailed the establishment of twenty-seven stations on mountain peaks from twenty-five to thirty miles apart. So expert did the heliographers become that once they transmitted a message eight hundred miles over inaccessible mountain peaks, in less than four hours. They handled two thousand, two hundred and sixty-four messages during the months from May 1st to September 30th, 1886.[1]

Thus Miles prepared to hunt down Geronimo and his tiny band. But before he was fully ready the campaign was precipitated by Geronimo himself, with a raid which swept north across the border and into the United States on April 27th.

[1] After Geronimo's surrender, Miles put on a demonstration of the use of the heliograph for his benefit. He asked for some information about the chief's brother, who was held prisoner at a distant fort. The immediacy of the reply stunned Geronimo. He sent word at once to Nachite, who was still hanging out, to "come in and come in quick; there was a power here which he could not understand." Nachite surrendered within a few hours. (See Miles, "Personal Recollections," p. 524.)

Up the Santa Cruz Valley went the Apaches, killing. They captured the Peck ranch, butchered several cowboys, and compelled the rancher, Peck, to witness the torture of his wife until he went temporarily insane. The crazed man was later freed by the superstitious Apaches and so he lived. But they rode away carrying with them the youngest Peck girl, about thirteen years old.

Lawton pursued. The raiders were far ahead and would easily have escaped him had they not run into a band of seventy Mexican irregulars and fought a brief battle with them. One Apache woman was killed. A bullet dropped the horse of the warrior who was carrying the Peck girl. In the confusion she got away, crawling and running through the bushes to safety. The girl was eventually found by rescuers and returned to her father, who recovered his sanity after a few days.

In the meantime the whole Apache band had escaped from the Mexican force, with the single exception of the dismounted warrior who had been carrying the Peck girl. The Mexicans scattered about his hiding place and tried to get him. But the single savage fighter was more than a match for the entire seventy. He killed seven of them and drove the rest back.[2] Then he made his own escape.

On went Geronimo's band. The Indians slaughtered five or six Mexican placer miners at a camp a little farther on, killed seven wood choppers next, and left a trail of blood nearly every mile of their way back toward Mexico.

The veteran Captain Lebo was hunting for them with his troop of the 10th Cavalry, when, on May 5th, Geronimo finally halted in the Pinito Mountains, in northern Sonora, thirty miles south of the border. Lebo attacked him

[2] Captain Lawton, who arrived at the scene of this fight only a few hours after it took place, examined the bodies of these seven Mexicans. Every one of them had been shot through the head, showing the exceptionally deadly marksmanship of which some of the Apaches were capable.

immediately. Smoke plumed out from the rocks above as the soldiers struggled forward across the rugged boulders. The Indians lay in heights which formed a sort of half-moon, occupying almost impossible terrain. Very soon the troops had to fall back.

Out in the open, where the bullets of the Apaches combed the ground, lay the prostrate form of Corporal Scott, so badly wounded that he could not even crawl for cover. His comrades, by keeping up a heavy fire on the Indian position, did their best to protect him, but everybody could see that it was only a question of a few minutes until the wounded man would be killed.

Lying behind some sheltering rocks, Lieutenant Powhatan C. Clarke, fresh from West Point, stood it as long as he could. All at once, without saying what he was going to do, he jumped up and ran toward the wounded trooper. A hail of lead from the Apache rifles literally churned the ground around his feet, but still he kept on. He reached Scott. Lifting him, Clarke turned and staggered back. He was now a target for every rifle in the heights. How he ever reached his own lines is a mystery. But not a single bullet touched him and he deposited the wounded corporal behind a boulder where he was safe from further injuries.

There was no question now in Lebo's mind as to the strength of the Indians and their ability to hold him. As Geronimo drew away, the troops made no effort to follow.

NEVER-ENDING PURSUIT

The Indians rode southward, while behind the pursuit thickened hourly. It was a black situation for them. Five thousand American soldiers, hundreds of Mexican regulars and irregulars, five hundred Indian scouts, and thousands of ranchers and other civilians were in the death hunt. Geronimo and Nachite had only eighteen warriors now. Two of the original twenty had been killed. And they were encumbered by their women and children. But with small evidence of fear or discouragement, they trotted along, alert, lupine, deadly always.

Ten days after Lebo's skirmish, on May 15th, Captain C. A. P. Hatfield stumbled on the hostile camp in the hills between the Santa Cruz and San Pedro Rivers. His charge captured the village and the entire herd of ponies. But it was a short-lived triumph. As he tried to make his way out of the rough country, Geronimo ambushed him in a box canyon, killed two men, wounded two more, and recovered every one of the captured horses, with no loss to his own band.

By now Lawton's flying column had taken the trail in earnest. It was a hand-picked body of men. Every one was a veteran and physically fit. On one occasion they marched twenty-four hours without stopping, for the last eighteen hours without water. Yet even so they were no match for the Indians.

It was the heliograph system which really was the decisive factor. Flashing all day long from mountain top to mountain top, the mirrors kept Lawton and the other commanders continually informed of the progress of the Apaches. Geronimo had not a moment's rest. Ceaselessly he had to keep on the move. As he shook off one pursuing detachment of soldiers or scouts, another would cut his trail. Twist and dodge as he would, he was never free.

But, driven as he was, Geronimo took time to busy himself with the people of the country through which he passed. Apache hate, embittered by the aggravating pursuit, translated itself into slaughter. Lawton picked up as many as ten butchered Mexicans a day during his long chase, and Governor Louis E. Torres of Sonora reported that around five or six hundred of his people were killed during the campaign.[3]

Days dragged into weeks. Doggedly, wearily, Lawton crossed and recrossed the mountains, following the elusive Apache trail. The continual discovery of new instances of Geronimo's grim handiwork in the maimed and disfigured corpses which he left in his wake, set a harder, bitterer look on the faces of white officers and Indian scouts each day as they tramped on and on, to end the prowl of the human tiger.

It was June 6th before Lawton overtook Geronimo. On that day a small detachment of the scouts under Lieutenant R. S. Walsh struck the hostiles. Only the briefest kind of a running fight took place, but the detachment took what satisfaction it could out of the capture of the Apache camp with the food supplies, most of the ammunition, and the herd of ponies. That was a serious blow to Geronimo. He was in sore straits.

Far south into Sonora the bloodhound Lawton followed the Indian trail. The hardships his men underwent were almost unbelievable. One day they would scale an eight or nine thousand foot peak; the next day they would drop down into a desert flat, where the heat was so intolerable that at times the hand could not be placed on the metal work of a gun. Pack trains had to be abandoned because the mules could not keep up in the terrific temperatures. Once the men went for five days without any food except what game they could kill. On another occasion, so terrible was their torture from hours of burning thirst, that some

---

[3] This figure sounds almost incredible, yet it is quoted by General Miles himself. ("Personal Recollections," p. 508.)

of the men opened the veins in their own arms to moisten their lips.[4]

Lawton's persistence was again rewarded on July 13th, when his advance, under Lieutenant R. A. Brown, discovered the hostile village near Tonababu. But the attempted surprise failed as usual and the Indians escaped. Still, something was accomplished. Brown captured most of their remaining horses and supplies.

Once more the endless pursuit dragged on, this time toward the Torres Mountains. Geronimo used every thinkable device to throw Lawton off his trail. In the rough mountain country his people frequently crossed the ranges jumping from rock to rock. Yet Lawton's faithful Indian scouts would pick up the trail and the hunt would continue, the weary, hollow-eyed men, worn to shreds, toiling remorselessly along.

THE FORT APACHE INCIDENT

Throughout all the troubles south of the border the great bulk of the Mimbreno and Chiricahua Indians near Fort Apache remained peaceful. Scores of them, in fact, did more. They enlisted as scouts in Miles' army, and served faithfully, courageously and skillfully in the hazardous and terrifically rigorous campaigns. Among these none had a better record than Chato. When he left the war path, the Flat Nose lived up to every word of his agreement with Crook. He was a first sergeant in the company of scouts commanded by Lieutenant Britton Davis in Crook's campaign against Geronimo, and much of the

[4] Miles, "Personal Recollections," p. 491. This was the second time that men under Miles used their own blood to relieve their thirst. The other instance was when his command was caught without water in the Sweetwater Country of Texas, during the Kiowa-Comanche War of 1874.

success in that operation was due to him. Others also had fine records.

In spite of this, military authorities continued to fear these reservation Indians. Miles called them a "turbulent, desperate, disreputable band." Early in his administration he recommended their removal to some other state, preferably the Indian Territory. But how was he to round up four or five hundred Indians without precipitating another outbreak which would make those which had gone before poor, trivial incidents by comparison?

The solution to this problem was suggested by Lieutenant James Parker. In June, 1886, while talking to Miles at Fort Huachuca, Parker mentioned the system in effect at Fort Apache, where the peaceful Indians were living. Whenever there was news of a raid, he said, the Indians, in order not to become involved in the fighting, went in to the post and were quartered in the quartermaster corral.

Parker suggested that a false report of a raid be spread and when the Apaches came to the corral, they should be surrounded by troops, disarmed, taken to the railroad and shipped east.

Miles stared at him. "Why that would be treachery," he said at last. "I could never do that."

But the thought had been planted.

Word came from the Secretary of War that the general's scheme of removing the Indians from Arizona to some territory in Texas, New Mexico, or Kansas, could not be carried out under the existing laws. Miles' next step was to send a delegation of the leading Indians to Washington, hoping so to impress them with the power of the government that they would return and recommend to their people that they go without resistance wherever they were told.

He placed Chato at the head of this delegation. The Apaches journeyed to Washington and viewed the wonders of the *rancheria* where the Great White Father lived. But for some reason they remained unimpressed. In spite of the pressure brought to bear upon them, the delegates sturdily refused to accede to the demands made upon them. Instead they asked to be taken back to Arizona. As they began their return journey, Captain Dorst, who had accompanied them, wired Miles that the Indians were still defiant. Immediately Miles ordered them held at Fort Leavenworth. Then he notified Dorst to tell the delegates that they must either become "treaty Indians," and work among their people for the wishes of the army, or they should consider themselves prisoners of war.

And so Chato and his companions received still another insight into the strange, incomprehensible villainy of the white man. But they were Apaches and true to their blood. Faced with imprisonment, they refused to betray their people. That was August 20th. Four days later Miles received word from Washington that if he could take into custody the Indians on the reservation, they could be "accommodated" at Fort Marion, Florida.

Miles at once put into operation the very plan suggested by Lieutenant Parker, and denounced by himself as "treachery". Colonel J. F. Wade was in command at Fort Apache. The Chiricahuas and Mimbreno Apaches were told to come in to the agency to be counted, as was the custom when a raid was reported in the section. Unsuspecting, they trooped in.

It was Sunday. Used to seeing the soldiers at the fort go through their inspection on that day, the Indians paid no attention as the regulars marched out and took positions which commanded every point of egress from the place.

Not until too late did the Apaches sense that something

was wrong. Observers at the fort saw the warriors leap to their feet as if at a command, and stand looking about with wild, startled eyes. Then Colonel Wade walked boldly into the crowd, calling to everybody to sit down. The Indians were helpless and they knew it. One by one the grim warriors squatted, until not one remained standing. In the silence of despair they listened as Wade told them that they were to be removed, that they were to part from their desert homes, leave their few pitiful little fields of growing crops, and their friends and familiar scenes, and go away into the unknown as prisoners of the white man, who thus rewarded their peaceful lives and their service to his flag.

A little later they were herded like cattle on trains and, with the women and children wailing and the men staring in stony silence at the panorama of their beloved country whirling behind the flying wheels of their cars, they began the long journey to hot, damp Florida.

Chapter XXVII

THE END OF THE TRAIL

FINAL SURRENDER

But Geronimo and Nachite were still free. And Lawton and the rest of Miles' soldiers were still after them. For three months the hunt had continued. No Indians had been killed, but one soldier died and another was wounded, and many Mexicans gave up their lives under the knives of Apache warriors.

The hostile band was traced south of the Yaqui River, where it captured a Mexican pack train and remounted itself after Brown set it afoot July 13th. Next it was reported near Fronteras.

And now came good news for Miles. Two squaws stole into Fronteras to talk with José Maria, a Mexican whom they knew, as he had once been a captive among them. The man was gone—he was with Lawton as an interpreter for the scouts—but his wife was home and she sent word to the military authorities that the hostiles wanted to give themselves up.

Near Fort Apache lived a Chiricahua named Ka-e-ta, who had deserted the hostiles and voluntarily returned to live peacefully under the white man's authority. Miles decided to send this man with a message to Geronimo. With him went one Martiné, a Chiricahua sub-chief, who had never been on the war path and whose loyalty was unquestioned. Next Miles looked around for a white officer to accompany these two. He chose Lieutenant Charles B. Gatewood, best liked by the Indians of all the officers in Arizona since the death of Crawford.

It was an assignment fraught with desperate danger. Gatewood knew that he was putting his life into the hands of Geronimo and his warriors, but he instantly prepared to go. First he and the two emissaries from the reservation went to Fronteras to pick up the trail of the two squaws. With him was Tom Horn, formerly chief of scouts under Crawford. He also obtained the services of the interpreter José Maria of Fronteras, who had been with the hostile Apaches as a prisoner, and whom the squaws had come to Fronteras to consult. Gatewood learned that the *prefect* of that city had made plans to lure the Apaches to the town, make them drunk, and then massacre them all in the cheerful Mexican manner. The lieutenant was anxious to avert this.

With Horn and José Maria, he and the two Indians began a perilous invasion of the hostile country. They carried before them constantly a piece of flour sacking, tied to a stick, as a flag of truce.

Growing plainer each day, for three days the trail of the squaws led them on. On August 23rd, Martiné and Ka-e-ta, scouting far ahead, discovered Geronimo's camp on the Bavispe River.[1] They approached it boldly. The "broncho" warriors let them in, then closed upon them, breechblocks clicking. But the scouts were unafraid. To Geronimo's very face they delivered Gatewood's message. The chief pondered. At last he gave orders that Ka-e-ta should be held as a hostage, while Martiné returned to the white men with a message that he, Geronimo, would

[1] Geronimo had been watching Gatewood and his men all the way, although they did not know it. He later told the lieutenant that he could not make out what kind of fools comprised such a small party dogging his trail. He did not notice, or did not understand the significance of, the flour-sack flag of truce.

speak with Gatewood alone, unaccompanied by any soldiers. With this message, Martiné reached Gatewood's camp in the canebrakes at sun down.

Lawton's advance guard under Brown had just overtaken Gatewood. But, following the instructions of Geronimo, the lieutenant went to an intermediate meeting place early next morning, accompanied only by Horn, José Maria, and Martiné. Smoke signals were sent up and guns were fired from time to time, to reassure the Indians, who replied in kind.

They met in the river valley. One or two at a time, the Apaches rode up, unsaddled their ponies and allowed them to graze. Geronimo was among the last to arrive. His thin scar of a mouth was thinner than ever as he faced the officer. Pipes were lit and a cloud blown. Then the chief asked what Miles' word was. There was no hesitation in Gatewood's answer, though he knew his words might be his own death warrant.

"Surrender, and you will be sent with your families to Florida, there to await the decision of the President as to your final disposition. Accept these terms or fight it out," he said. [2]

As to the voice of doom the Apaches listened in dead silence. Finally Geronimo passed his hand over his eyes and, as he did so, Gatewood saw it tremble. The iron chief was shaken at last.

But it did not take him long to recover his composure. He asked for time to talk with his warriors, then went into conference with Nachite and others. Presently he was back with a counter-proposition: that they be taken to the reservation and there given the little land they needed, or else they would fight to the death.

[2] These conversations are from Gatewood's own story, as contained in the Arizona Historical Review, Vol. IV., No. 1, pp. 36-38.

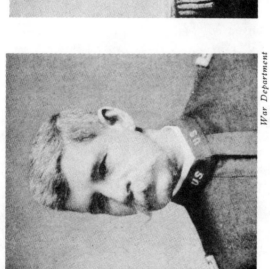

Left: General H. W. Lawton, who as a lieutenant, was Geronimo's nemesis in the final campaign against the hostile Apaches. Right: General Nelson A. Miles as he looked when he took command of the Department of Arizona, in April, 1886.

The children of Geronimo's hostile band, taken in 1886. In the foreground is a little white boy, Santiago McKinn, who was held captive by the Indians for many months. At extreme left is a little Negro boy, also a captive when this band surrendered.

The last of the Apache hostiles, being taken to prison in Florida. Nachite is seated by himself in the center. Geronimo is next on the right, while to the right of Geronimo is his son, Chappo.

The moment was tense. But Nachite, the easy-going, stepped in and smoothed things over. Gatewood now had a chance to tell them of the shipping of their friends and relatives to Florida. That was a stunning piece of news to the Apaches. Again they conferred. When they finished Geronimo returned to Gatewood and said with intense meaning: "We want your advice. *Consider yourself not a white man, but one of us;* remember all that has been said today and tell us what we should do."

"Trust General Miles and surrender to him," was Gatewood's instant reply. Geronimo asked the night to think things over.

Next morning the Apaches had made their decision. They told the lieutenant they would go with him to meet Miles and surrender. That very day, August 25th, the northward trip began.

Almost at once a complication arose. The bloody-minded prefect of Fronteras appeared suddenly with two hundred soldiers. Lawton and his scouts held the Mexicans off while the Apaches, accompanied by Gatewood, fled to the hills. After suitable explanations, the prefect departed, and the Indians were gathered up again and started once more northward.

The end came finally, at a place named as if by inspiration for just such a scene—Skeleton Canyon. There, on September 3rd, Geronimo and Miles met at last—the sole remaining fighting chief of the Apaches, and the representative of the great nation of sixty million people which had finally conquered him. They talked for a time, the fine, handsome, soldierly white man, and the squat, broad-shouldered Indian with the steel-trap mouth. Then Geronimo returned to his village.

Next morning he and his people came in and delivered

themselves into Miles' hands. The Apaches as a tribe had ended their resistance.

PEACE IN THE DESERT

It was a desperate band of savages which Miles had cornered in Skeleton Canyon. So long had they been hunted that they had become almost wild animals. His description of them gives an idea of how they looked:

"The Indians that surrendered with Geronimo have probably never been matched since the days of Robin Hood. Many of the warriors were outlaws from their own tribes, and their boys from twelve to eighteen were the very worst and most vicious of all. They were clad . . . to disguise themselves as much as possible. Masses of grass, bunches of weeds, twigs or small boughs were fastened under their hat bands very profusely, and also upon their shoulders or backs. Their clothing was trimmed in such a way that when lying upon the ground in a bunch of grass or at the head of a ravine, if they remained perfectly quiet, it was as impossible to discover them as if they had been a bird or serpent . . . An unsuspecting rancher or miner going along a road or trail, would pass within a few feet of these concealed Apaches, and the first intimation he would have of their presence would be a bullet through his heart or brain." [3]

Troops met them at Fort Bowie and loaded them on a train; within a short time they had started their long journey east. And here occurred the crowning infamy. Ka-e-ta, who had risked his life and had been held as a hostage by Geronimo while Martiné carried the message to Gatewood; and Martiné himself, whose record of friendliness to the white man was exemplary, were loaded on the same train with the hostile Indians, and sent to Florida with them. Protests availed nothing. Ka-e-ta and Martiné were

[3] Miles, "Personal Recollections," p. 525.

Indians. Like Chato, their services were already forgotten.[4]

Of this cynical act of the government's Captain Bourke wrote:

"Not a single Chiricahua had been killed, captured or wounded throughout the entire campaign—with two exceptions—unless by Chiricahua Apache scouts, who, like Chato, had kept the pledges given to General Crook in the Sierra Madre in 1883. The exceptions were: one killed by the White Mountain Apaches near Fort Apache, and one killed by a white man in northern Mexico. Yet every one of those faithful scouts—especially the two, Ki-e-ta (Ka-e-ta) and Martinez (Martiné) who at imminent personal peril had gone into the Sierra Madre to hunt up Geronimo and induce him to surrender—were transplanted to Florida and there subjected to the same punishment as had been meted out to Geronimo. And with them were sent men like Goth-kli and Toklanni who were not Chiricahuas at all, but had only lately married wives of that band, who had never been on the war path in any capacity save as soldiers of the government and had devoted years to its service. There is no more disgraceful page in the history of our relations with the American Indians than that which conceals the treachery visited upon the Chiricahuas who remained faithful in their allegiance to our people." [5]

Two thousand miles to the east, the Apaches were finally brought to their prison home.[6] Years passed. Interest in

[4] Ka-e-ta and Martiné were actually held as *prisoners of war* for twenty-six years. In 1931 they made demand upon the government for their back pay as scouts, at $2.00 a day for their entire period of imprisonment. The Secretary of War admitted that they had undoubtedly rendered service of great value to the nation, but said that there were no funds available to pay them for it.

[5] Bourke, "On the Border With Crook," p. 485.

[6] One member of Geronimo's band escaped on the way to Florida. Miles thus describes the incident: "Just after they passed St. Louis, one Indian contrived to make his escape from the train despite all precautions which had been taken. True to his wolfish nature he succeeded in avoiding settlements and people who would be likely to arrest him, and though it took him a year to work his way back to the San Carlos reservation, he finally succeeded in doing it. Like a hyena he occasionally, at long intervals, stole down upon the Indian camp at San Carlos, captured an Indian woman, carried her back up into the mountains, kept her for several months, then cruelly murdered her and returned to repeat the same crime. This

their case was aroused through the nation as a result of the efforts of Herbert Welsh, secretary of the Indian Rights' Association. His investigations showed that although Miles' definite promise was that the surrendering Indians should be sent with their families to Florida, they had been separated and kept at hard labor without them for three years. Under pressure from interested persons all over the United States, the Apaches were removed to Alabama. Some seven hundred of them had been taken to Florida in 1886. When they were transferred to Alabama, they were very much reduced in numbers. Later they were moved again, this time to Fort Sill, Oklahoma. At that time only three hundred and eight of them were left alive. Finally, in 1907, through the efforts of Dr. Henry Roe Cloud, a full-blooded Winnebago, then a student at Yale University, and now superintendent of Haskell Indian Institute, the remnants of the tribe, then numbering only two hundred and fifty, were permitted to return to New Mexico, where they settled on the Mescalero reservation.

.   .   .   .

There is peace in the desert today. Not, however, because the Apache has in one whit abated his fiery spirit. Old Chato died just a few months ago, August 16th, 1934, at the age of ninety. His passing was at the Mescalero

---

he did several times, and his movements were as secret and stealthy as those of a reptile. One Indian girl whom he had captured made her escape and told of his habits and cruelty. This man was afterwards reported killed."—Miles, "Personal Recollections," p. 529.

Surely nobody but an Apache could have equalled the feat of this unnamed Indian warrior. He escaped from the prison train in a thickly settled part of the country. He had to find food and a hiding place each day. He crossed Illinois, Missouri, Oklahoma, Texas and New Mexico. It took him more than a year to make the trip. Yet in that entire period not a single human eye was ever laid on him. Without weapons, without a map, with only his unerring homing instinct guiding him, he journeyed straight to the desert and reached there some time in the fall of 1887. If history records the fellow to this exploit it has so far escaped the writer's attention.

Agency hospital. And about his grave still lingers the aura of hate.

South of the international boundary line, outbreaks continue to occur occasionally. As recently as April 10th, 1930, Apaches from the Sierra Madre raided a settlement and killed three persons only a few miles from Nacori Chico, in northern Sonora.[7]

But on the United States side of the border, the Indians keep a sullen, dogged peace. If the white man was too strong for them in the days of Geronimo, what would now be their fate, in the day of the machine gun and the airplane?

What men must do, they do.

[7] The following news dispatch published in the press of the United States April 23rd, 1930, tells the story of the most recent Apache outbreak:

"Tucson, Ariz., April 22 (INS)—Riding out of their wilderness hideout, high in the Sierra Madre Mountains, a band of wild Apache Indians scalped three persons, April 10, in a settlement near Nacori Chico, Sonora, Mexico, it was reported today by V. M. White, a mining engineer.

"The three victims were Mexicans who opened fire on the marauders while the latter were looting the village.

"Armed parties immediately set out to trail the painted savages and attempt to engage them in battle before they reached their impregnable and historic cliffs.

"The Apaches are believed to have been led, White said, by Geronimo III, the grandson of the Geronimo who was chased by the U. S. Army for three years during the '80's in Arizona."

BIBLIOGRAPHY

Arizona Historical Review, 1928–1934.

Arizona Legislative Assembly, "Memorial and Affidavits Showing Outrages perpetrated by the Apache Indians, in the Territory of Arizona,
for the years 1869 and 1870," San Francisco, 1871.

Bancroft, Hubert Howe, "History of Arizona and New Mexico," San
Francisco, 1889.

Barrett, S. M., "Geronimo's Own Story of His Life," New York, 1906.

Bartlett, J. R., "Personal Narrative of Explorations," New York, 1854.

Bourke, Captain John G., "An Apache Campaign in the Sierra Madre,"
New York, 1886.

Bourke, Captain John G., "On the Border With Crook," New York,
1891.

Brady, Cyrus Townsend, "Northwestern Fights and Fighters," Garden
City, 1910.

Browne, J. Ross, "Adventures in the Apache Country," New York,
1874.

Cochise County, Arizona, "Resolution Adopted at Meeting of Residents of Cochise County, Regarding Outbreak of Indians from San
Carlos Reservation," Washington, D. C., 1885.

Colyer, Vincent, "Peace With the Apaches," report to the Board of
Indian Commissioners, Washington, D. C., 1872.

Cook, James H., "Fifty Years on the Old Frontier," New Haven,
1923.

Cooke, General P. St. George, "The Conquest of New Mexico and
California," New York, 1878.

Cremony, Captain John C., "Life Among the Apaches," San Francisco, 1868.

Davis, Lieutenant Britton, "The Truth About Geronimo," New
Haven, 1929.

Dodge, Colonel Richard I., "Our Wild Indians," Hartford, 1885.

Dunn, J. P., "Massacres of the Mountains," New York, 1886.

Forsyth, Colonel G. A., "Thrilling Days of Army Life," New York, 1900.

Frazier, Robert, "The Apaches of the White Mountain Reservation," Philadelphia, 1885.

Hafen, LeRoy R., and Ghent, W. J., "Broken Hand," Denver, 1931.

Hodge, Frederick W., "Handbook of American Indians," Bulletin 30, Bureau of American Ethnology, Washington, D. C., 1912.

Howard, General O. O., "My Life and Experiences Among Our Hostile Indians," Hartford, 1907.

Hyde, George E., "Rangers and Regulars," pamphlet, Denver, 1933.

Indian Affairs Office, Annual Reports, 1876–1886.

Inman, Major Henry, "The Old Santa Fé Trail," New York, 1896.

Irwin, General B. J. D., "The Apache Pass Fight," Infantry Journal, April, 1928.

Jackson, Helen Hunt, "A Century of Dishonor," Cambridge, 1885.

Kansas Magazine, New Series, 1886–1888, Kansas City, Kansas.

Lockwood, Frank C., "Pioneer Days in Arizona," New York, 1932.

Lummis, Charles F., "Land of Poco Tiempo," New York, 1893.

Mazzanovitch, Anton, "Trailing Geronimo," Los Angeles, 1926.

Manypenny, George, "Our Indian Wards," Cincinnati, 1880.

Marcy, R. B., "Thirty Years of Army Life on the Border," New York, 1866.

Miles, General Nelson A., "Personal Recollections," Chicago, 1896.

New Mexico Historical Society Records.

Powers, Stephen, "The Modocs," Overland Monthly, Vol. X.

Proceedings of the Military Commission on the Modoc Indians, Executive Documents, 1873–1874.

Raht, Carlisle Graham, "Romance of Davis Mountains and Big Bend Country," El Paso, 1919.

Read, Benjamin M., "Illustrated History of New Mexico," Santa Fé, 1912.

Rister, C. C., "The Southwestern Frontier," Cleveland, 1928.

Ruxton, George Frederick, "Adventures in Mexico and in the Rocky Mountains," New York, 1848.

Stone, Charles Pomeroy, "Notes on the State of Sonora," Washington, 1861.

Twitchell, Ralph Emerson, "Leading Facts in New Mexican History," Cedar Rapids, 1912.

War Department, Annual Reports of the Secretary of War, 1846–1886.

War Department, "Record of Engagements With Hostile Indians," Official Compilation, 1868–1882.

War of the Rebellion; a Compilation of the Official Records of the Union and Confederate Armies, Washington, 1880–1891.

Welsh, Herbert, "The Apache Prisoners in Fort Marion, St. Augustine, Florida," report to the Indian Rights Association, Philadelphia, 1887.

White, Owen P., "Scalping the Indians," Collier's Magazine, March 3, 1934.

INDEX

Note: Surnames were unknown among Indians until within the last few years. Even when a white name was adopted by an Indian he used it as one title, not dividing it and using part at one time and part at another. A white man named John Smith is "John" to his close acquaintances and "Smith" or "Mr. Smith" to those with whom he is on a more formal footing. An Indian named John Smith would have been John Smith to everybody. Hence Indian names are all listed according to the alphabetical order of their first names, even when white names had been adopted. Thus, Mangus Colorado is to be found in the "M's," Captain Jack in the "C's," Juan José among the "J's" and so on.